Lecture Notes in Computer Science 10391

Commenced Publication in 1973
Founding and Former Series Editors:
Gerhard Goos, Juris Hartmanis, and Jan van Leeuwen

Carl Gutwin · Sergio F. Ochoa
Julita Vassileva · Tomoo Inoue (Eds.)

Collaboration and Technology

23rd International Conference, CRIWG 2017
Saskatoon, SK, Canada, August 9–11, 2017
Proceedings

 Springer

Editors
Carl Gutwin
Computer Science
University of Saskatchewan
Saskatoon, SK
Canada

Sergio F. Ochoa (iD)
Computer Science
Universidad de Chile
Santiago
Chile

Julita Vassileva (iD)
University of Saskatchewan
Saskatoon, SK
Canada

Tomoo Inoue (iD)
Library, Information and Media Science
University of Tsukuba
Tsukuba
Japan

ISSN 0302-9743   ISSN 1611-3349   (electronic)
Lecture Notes in Computer Science
ISBN 978-3-319-63873-7   ISBN 978-3-319-63874-4   (eBook)
DOI 10.1007/978-3-319-63874-4

Library of Congress Control Number: 2017946696

LNCS Sublibrary: SL3 – Information Systems and Applications, incl. Internet/Web, and HCI

Printed on acid-free paper

This Springer imprint is published by Springer Nature
The registered company is Springer International Publishing AG
The registered company address is: Gewerbestrasse 11, 6330 Cham, Switzerland

Preface

This volume contains the papers presented at the 23rd International Conference on Collaboration Technologies, CRIWG 2017. The conference was held during August 9–11, 2017, in Saskatoon, Canada. The conference is supported and governed by the Collaborative Research International Working Group (CRIWG), an open community of collaboration technology researchers. Since 1995, conferences supported by CRIWG have focused on collaboration technology design, development, and evaluation. The background research is influenced by a number of disciplines, such as computer science, management science, information systems, engineering, psychology, cognitive sciences, and social sciences.

The 33 submitted papers were carefully reviewed through a double-blind review process involving three reviewers appointed by the program chairs. In all, 14 submissions were selected as full papers and five were selected as work in progress. Thus, this volume presents the most relevant and insightful research papers carefully chosen among the contributions accepted for presentation and discussion at the conference.

The papers published in the proceedings of this year's and past CRIWG conferences reflect the trends in collaborative computing research and its evolution. There has been a growing interest in collaborative learning, collaboration through social media, participation in online communities, and techniques and approaches for collaboration technology design. This year there was strong participation from Canada and Chile, each having five papers, and then Germany with three papers, Japan and Brazil with two papers each, and Norway and USA with one paper.

As editors, we would like to thank everybody who contributed to the content and production of this book, namely, all the authors and presenters, whose contributions made CRIWG 2017 a success, as well as the Steering Committee, the members of the Program Committee, and the reviewers. Last but not least, we would like to acknowledge the effort of the organizers of the conference, without whom this conference would not have run so effectively. Our thanks also go to Springer, the publisher of the CRIWG proceedings, for their continuous support.

August 2017

Carl Gutwin
Sergio F. Ochoa
Julita Vassileva
Tomoo Inoue

Organization

Program Committee

Leila Alem	Thoughtworks, Australia
Nikolaos Avouris	University of Patras, HCI Group, Greece
Nelson Baloian	University of Chile, Chile
Lars Bollen	University of Twente, The Netherlands
Marcos Borges	Federal University of Rio de Janeiro, Brazil
Ivica Boticki	FER UNIZG, Croatia
Luis Carriço	University of Lisbon, Portugal
Raymundo Cornejo	CONACYT-UACH, Mexico
Alexandra Cristea	University of Warwick, UK
Gert-Jan de Vreede	University of South Florida, USA
Yanis Dimitriadis	University of Valladolid, Spain
Alicia Díaz	Lifia, UNLP, Argentina
Orlando Erazo	State Technical University of Quevedo, Ecuador
Jesus Favela	CICESE, Mexico
Mikhail Fominykh	Independent researcher
Benjamín Fonseca	UTAD/INESC TEC, Portugal
Kimberly García	Siemens, USA
Marco A. Gerosa	Northern Arizona University, USA/ University of São Paulo, Brazil
Luis A. Guerrero	University of Costa Rica, Costa Rica
Francisco J. Gutierrez	University of Chile, Chile
Carl Gutwin	University of Saskatchewan, Canada
Valeria Herskovic	Catholic University of Chile, Chile
Ramón Hervas	University of Castilla-La Mancha, Spain
Ulrich Hoppe	University of Duisburg-Essen, Germany
Gwo-Jen Hwang	National Taiwan University of Science and Technology, Taiwan
Tomoo Inoue	University of Tsukuba, Japan
Seiji Isotani	University of Sao Paulo, Brazil
Ralf Klamma	RWTH Aachen University, Germany
Tun Lu	Fudan University, China
Stephan Lukosch	Delft University of Technology, The Netherlands
Wolfram Luther	University of Duisburg-Essen, Germany
Alexandra Martínez-Monés	University of Valladolid, Spain
Sonia Mendoza	CINVESTAV-IPN, Mexico
Roc Meseguer	Universitat Politècnica de Catalunya, Spain
Alberto Morán	Autonomous University of Baja California, Mexico
Hideyuki Nakanishi	Osaka University, Japan

Contents

X   Contents

Spatial Continuity and Robot-Embodied Pointing Behavior in Videoconferencing

Yuya Onishi[✉], Kazuaki Tanaka[✉], and Hideyuki Nakanishi[✉]

Department of Adaptive Machine Systems, Osaka University,
2-1 Yamadaoka, Suita, Osaka 565-0871, Japan
{yuya.onishi,tanaka,nakanishi}@ams.eng.osaka-u.ac.jp

Abstract. There are several ways in which a conversation partner points to a remote place in videoconferencing: (1) displaying the partner's pointing gesture, that is, ordinary videoconferencing, (2) displaying the partner's arm on a tabletop display, (3) projecting a laser dot and it is synchronized with the laser pointer held by the partner, and (4) embodying the partner's pointing behavior by a robotic pointer or a robotic arm. In this study, we implemented these methods on the videoconferencing system and compared the effect on social telepresence (i.e. the sense that a participant feels as if he/she meets with the conversation partner in the same place). We found that the fourth method, which embodied the remote partner's pointing behavior, enhanced social telepresence.

Keywords: Videoconferencing · Social telepresence · Pointing behaviors · Video-mediated communication

1 Introduction

There are several merits to embody a remote partner's body to a video conference: showing it physically, making physical contact, and enhancing social telepresence. Social telepresence is the illusion where the partners who are actually in geographically separated places feel as if they were meeting face-to-face with each other [5]. In previous studies, a robot hand created for handshaking was combined with a video conference. This study suggested that adding the function of body contact could enhance social telepresence [19]. In addition, a robot arm, which the remote partner's arm seemed to pop out from the display, enhanced social telepresence [20]. However, there is the possibility that the robot hand, which seems to pop out from the remote partner's video, improves the feeling of being in close proximity to each other. Therefore, social telepresence may be enhanced by showing continuity between remote space and local space. The purpose of this study is to clarify the influence of a design that embodies continuity of these two spaces on social telepresence.

As a way to show how effective it is to embody a part of the body, we focused on the face-to-face interaction of pointing behavior. There have been many efforts pursuing a seamless remote communication experience [1–4, 6–8, 16–18, 21, 23–25]. Ishii et al. used ClearBoard, a calibrated projection of a remote partner overlaid on a drawing glass, to create an illusion that the partners from remote places are working on the two sides of the same

C. Gutwin et al. (Eds.): CRIWG 2017, LNCS 10391, pp. 1–14, 2017.
DOI: 10.1007/978-3-319-63874-4_1

glass [10]. In addition, using a table to display the remote partner's behavior has been suggested [11, 12, 15, 22, 28, 29]. Pauchet et al. shared the space using a video with a horizontal display, which the display remote partner's arm [22]. Tang et al. added contact traces to VideoArms, an augmentation that participants described as useful [29]. A quantitative approach to evaluating abstract components added to realistic embodiments adopted by Yamashita et al. who replayed entire gestures using a form of motion blur to reduce the time needed for conversational grounding [30]. However, it is difficult to point to remote objects and is impossible to touch them. For example, there is a problem that the directions to which a remote instructor points are unclear.

There are also researches focusing on supporting remote assistance tasks by projecting the annotation on the surface of physical objects. GhostHands tried to fill the gap by overlaying on the view of worker's field and the virtual hands of an expert modelled in real-time with the Augmented Reality technologies [9]. In addition, the teleoperated robot was embodied with the behavior of a remote partner, and it can move local space and communicate with a remote partner. GestureMan [13] uses a teleoperated robot to move in space and point to the physical objects with a laser beam. WACL uses a wearable camera, which is placed on a shoulder and points to the objects with a laser beam [26]. These systems lack the remote partner's image and facial expression, and they reduce social telepresence [27].

In another study, a robot hand created for handshaking was combined with a video conference. This study suggested that adding the function of body contact could enhance social telepresence [19]. InFORM, a dynamic shape display, can physically show a remote partner's arm [14]. In these experiments, the robot hand was embodied with the remote partner's body.

Therefore, we can consider several ways to point to a remote space in the video conference. These include a face-to-face interaction that is specialized in a pointing behavior with a video conference as illustrated in Fig. 1, which shows five conditions.

- **Video condition:** The condition using only a vertical display, which is a conventional video conference.
- **Combined video condition:** The condition using a combination of the horizontal display and vertical display. The horizontal display is placed on the table and it displays the remote partner's arm.
- **Laser pointer condition:** The condition using a combination of a laser pointer and vertical display. The partner grips the laser pointer device, and the laser beam is projected in the local space.
- **Pointing rod condition:** The condition using a combination of an instruction rod and vertical display. The partner in the video seems to grasp a pointing rod, which is placed in local space.
- **Robot arm condition:** The condition using a combination of a robot arm and vertical display. The robot arm, which the remote partner's arm, seems to pop out from the display.

In this paper, we compared these pointing behaviors to verify the influence on social telepresence.

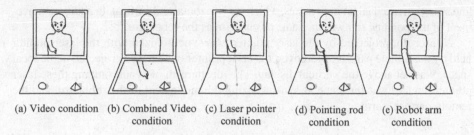

(a) Video condition   (b) Combined Video condition   (c) Laser pointer condition   (d) Pointing rod condition   (e) Robot arm condition

Fig. 1. Situations of pointing gestures in videoconference.

2 Design of Remote Pointing

We developed the robot arm, which was combined with a video conference system. The remote partner can point to a remote site with the robot arm (Fig. 2). Our robot arm moves synchronously with the remote partner. A robot arm moves and rotates on a display, on which the remote partner's image is displayed synchronously with a motion of a remote partner's arm. It shows a nearly life-size picture of the remote partner's upper body and has a horizontal axis linear motion mechanism under the display. A robot arm is connected to the linear motion mechanism through an acrylic board, and a connective point of the robot arm possesses a rotary system. By the rotary mechanism and the linear motion mechanism of the robot arm, a robot arm performs translation and rotation of an indication side of the display in synchronization with the movement of the remote partner's arm in the picture. At that time, the length of the robot arm from the screen changes. In other words, an extendable mechanism regulates the length of the robot arm. This mechanism lets you expand and contract the arm by pulling a wire in a rewind device and lets the edge of the acrylic board go along the wire to be inconspicuous.

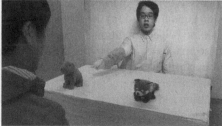

Fig. 2. Snapshots of our system.

Movement of the remote partner's arm is acquired by motion tracking. Because the picture of the former arm is unnecessary, the picture of the former arm removed from the boundary surface of the display by image composition, such as a chrome frame composition. The picture of the part, which was removed, is composed it with a picture of scenery prepared beforehand. The instructions to perform this device were only in the right and left directions, but the instructions at the top and bottom directions could be completed by the linear motion mechanism in two axes, which are horizontal and vertical. In addition, movement of the pointing rod was the same mechanism as the robot arm.

A laser dot projected by the laser pointer was synchronized with the laser pointer held by the remote partner. Moreover, the laser pointer, which was projected in the local space, was set above the vertical display. The mechanism of synchronizing these laser pointer devices was the same as synchronizing the movement of the robot arm and the remote partner's arm.

3   Experiment

We considered that the physical embodiment would enhance social telepresence than video when it moved dynamically. It was also conceivable that the interpersonal distance was influenced by the distance between a participant and a fingertip of the remote partner. Therefore, we made the following three hypothesis.

Hypothesis 1: Showing the remote partner's physical behavior enhances social telepresence.

Hypothesis 2: The participant feels the remote partner points to participant's room, by showing as embodiment of the remote partner's instructions.

Hypothesis 3: The participant feels the distance closer between the experimenter who is in the video and the participant, by showing as embodiment of the remote partner's instructions.

To verify these hypotheses, we compared pointing behaviors, which are shown in Fig. 2. The comparison of the conditions for remote pointing could be within-subjects, since all the conditions included the pointing behaviors. However, there was a possibility that impressions could be confused for participants, if participants experience all conditions in one experiment. Therefore, we divided to three experiments and evaluated it progressively. In experiment 1, we compared (a) the video condition, (b) the combined video condition and (e) the robot arm condition. In experiment 2, we compared (b) the combined video condition, (c) the laser pointer condition and (e) the robot arm condition. These conditions showed that the remote space and the local space are continuous, and this experiment was a comparison of video, light and embodiment of the remote person. In experiment 3, we compared (b) the combined video condition, (d) the pointing rod condition and (e) the robot arm condition. In this experiment, the pointing rod condition and the robot arm condition presented the pointing method of the experimenter as embodied, and verified the difference of the embodiment.

Forty-one subjects participated in our experiments. We separate three groups. A subject participates only one experiment. Eighteen subjects participate in Experiment 1, twelve subjects participate in Experiment 2, and eleven subjects participate in Experiment 3.

3.1   Setup

Figure 3 depicts the structure of the rooms used for the experiments. As shown in Fig. 3(a), the robotic device, which is the robotic arm of robotic pointer, is attached to the display. To facilitate the illusion, the color of the clothes of the presenter and the robot hand was the same. The experimenter seated and all the participants thought that he was seating. We used a wide screen display to show a nearly life-size picture of the remote partner's upper body. As shown in Fig. 3(b), we set the field of view of the webcam to 77 vertical degrees. The height of the base on which the participant stood was adjusted to make the participant's eyes level with the experimenter's eyes. We prepared the same performance webcam for each horizontal display and vertical display. In addition, we adjusted the position of webcams to show the arm that was connected. The experimenter could see the participant's room, participant's face and robot arm from the camera, which is set the top of the display. At the pointing rod condition and the robot arm condition we set the robotic device on the display. At the laser pointer condition, the experimenter holds the laser pointer in experimenter's space. Moreover, the laser pointer device, which set above the display in the participant's space, synchronized with the laser pointer held by the experimenter. After the experiment, we conducted a questionnaire and interview after the experiment.

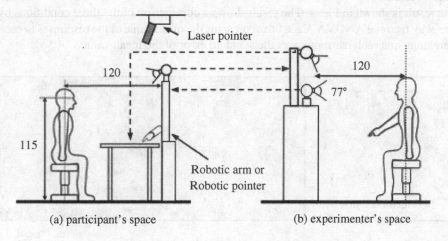

Fig. 3. Experimental setups (length unit: centimeters)

3.2 Experiment 1

We compared the video condition, the combined video condition and the robot arm condition in experiment 1. We compared three conditions by the within-subjects experiment. In all conditions, we placed two stuffed animals, which were pointed to by the remote partner. In addition, we had a simple conversation and question about them. The experimenter pointed to different objects between conversations. We conducted a questionnaire and interview after the experiment.

3.2.1 Participants

The participants were undergraduate students whose ages ranged from eighteen to twenty-four years. There were eighteen participants, consisting of nine females and nine males. We implemented a counter balance so as not to influence the order of conditions.

3.2.2 Questionnaires

We conducted a questionnaire after the experiment. Questions are follow:

Question 1:   I felt as if I were close to the partner in the same room.
Question 2:   I felt as if the partner points to the object in my space.
Question 3:   How long did you feel the distance between partner and you?

Each question corresponds to hypothesis. The statements were rated on a 7-point Likert scale where 1 = strongly disagree, 4 = neutral, and 7 = strongly agree. In addition, at the third question was answered with numerical values (length unit: centimeters).

3.2.3 Results

The result is shown in Fig. 4. The result shows a comparison of the three conditions by one-way factorial ANOVA. Each box represents the mean value of the responses to each statement, and each bar represents the standard error of the mean value.

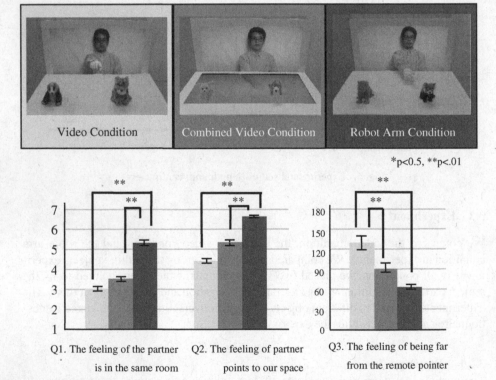

Fig. 4.   Results of experiment 1 (N = 18).

We found a significant difference in the feeling of being close to the partner in the same room ($F(2, 17) = 12.698, p < .01$). Multiple comparisons showed that this feeling was significantly stronger in the robot arm condition than the video condition ($p < .01$) and the combined video condition ($p < .01$). We also found a significant difference in the feeling of being pointed to the object in participant's space by the experimenter ($F(2, 17) = 14.061, p < .01$). Multiple comparisons showed that this feeling was significantly stronger the robot arm condition than the video condition ($p < .01$) and combined video condition ($p < .01$). According to the comments, the participants felt that it was really like a remote partner being in the same room in the robot arm condition. In addition, some participants felt pointing action was done under the table in the combined condition. Moreover, these results support the hypothesis 1 and the hypothesis 2. We also found a significant difference in the feeling of distance ($F(2, 17) = 8.465, p < .01$). Multiple comparisons showed that this feeling was significantly stronger in video condition than the combined video condition ($p < .01$) and the robot arm video condition ($p < .01$). This means participant feels farther in the video condition than other conditions. However, we did not find a significant difference between the combined video condition and the embodied video condition. According to the comments, the feeling of distance was influenced by the distance from a fingertip. Therefore, hypothesis 3 is rejected from this result.

3.3 Experiment 2

We compared the laser condition and other conditions in experiment 2. In experiment 1, the score of the video condition was lower than other conditions. Therefore, we excluded the video condition and compared the laser condition, combined video condition and robot arm condition. In all conditions, we placed two stuffed animals, which were pointed to by the remote partner. In addition, we had a simple conversation and question about them. The experimenter pointed to different objects between conversations. We conducted a questionnaire and interview after the experiment.

3.3.1 Participants
The participants were undergraduate students whose ages ranged from eighteen to twenty-four years. There were twelve participants, consisting of five females and seven males. We implemented a counter balance so as not to influence the order of conditions.

3.3.2 Questionnaires
We conducted a questionnaire after experiment. We were afraid that individual differences might cause undesirable differences in the perceived quality of the presentation, which might affect the degrees of social telepresence. We added three questions as shown in follow:

Question 1: The video was sufficiently clear.
Question 2: The audio was sufficiently clear.
Question 3: The presentation was intelligible.

Moreover, each question, which shows in follow, corresponds to hypothesis.

Question 4: I felt as if I were facing the partner in the same room.
Question 5: I felt as if the partner points to the object in my space.
Question 6: How long did you feel the distance between partner and you?

The statements were rated on a 7-point Likert scale where 1 = strongly disagree, 4 = neutral, and 7 = strongly agree. In addition, at the sixth question was answered with numerical values (length unit: centimeters).

3.3.3   Results

The result is shown in Fig. 5. The result shows a comparison of the three conditions by one-way factorial ANOVA. Each box represents the mean value of the responses to each statement, and each bar represents the standard error of the mean value.

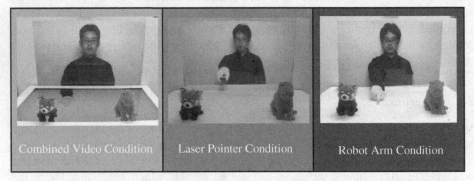

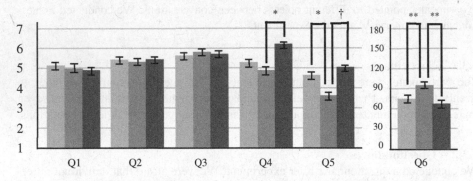

Fig. 5. Results of experiment 2 (N = 12).

There was no significant difference in the perceived clearness of the live video and the audio, and in the perceived intelligibility of the presentation, so the audio-visual quality and the quality of the presentation seemed not to affect the results.

We found a significant difference in the feeling of being close to the partner in the same room ($F(2, 11) = 3.38$, $p < .1$). Multiple comparisons showed that this feeling was significantly stronger in the combined video condition than the laser pointer condition ($p < .1$) and in the robot arm condition than the laser pointer condition ($p < .05$). We also found a significant difference in the feeling of being pointed to the object in participant's space by experimenter ($F(2, 11) = 5.111, p < .1$). Multiple comparisons showed that this feeling was significantly stronger the robot arm condition than the laser pointer condition ($p < .01$). However, we cannot find a significant difference between the combined video condition and the robot arm condition. Moreover, these results support the hypothesis 1 and the hypothesis 2. We also found a significant difference in the feeling of distance ($F(2, 11) = 14.97, p < .01$). Multiple comparisons showed that this feeling was significantly stronger in the laser pointer condition than the combined video condition ($p < .01$) and the robot arm condition ($p < .01$). This means participant feel farther in the video condition than other conditions. However, we did not find a significant difference between the combined video condition and the robot arm condition. According to the comments, participant answered that we use a laser pointer to point to an object at a distance place. Therefore, hypothesis 3 is rejected from this result.

3.4 Experiment 3

We compared the combined video condition, the pointing rod condition and the robot arm condition in experiment 3. The pointing rod condition and the robot arm condition presented the pointing method of the experimenter as embodied, and verified the difference of the embodiment. We compared three conditions by the within-subjects experiment. In all conditions, we placed three stuffed animals, which were pointed to by the remote partner. In addition, we had a simple conversation and question about them. The experimenter pointed to different objects between conversations.

3.4.1 Participants

The participants were undergraduate students whose ages ranged from eighteen to twenty-four years. There were eleven participants, consisting of six females and five males. We implemented a counter balance so as not to influence the order of conditions.

3.4.2 Questionnaires

We conducted a questionnaire after experiment. We were afraid that individual differences might cause undesirable differences in the perceived quality of the presentation, which might affect the degrees of social telepresence. We asked three questions as shown in follow:

Question 1: The video was sufficiently clear.
Question 2: The audio was sufficiently clear.
Question 3: The presentation was intelligible.

Each question, which shows in follow, corresponds to hypothesis. However, since it could be verified in the previous experiments, the question of the feeling of sense that the partner was pointing to an object in the participant's space, was excluded in Experiment 3.

Question 4: I felt as if I were facing the partner in the same room.
Question 5: How long did you feel the distance between partner and you?

The statements were rated on a 7-point Likert scale where 1 = strongly disagree, 4 = neutral, and 7 = strongly agree. In addition, at the question 7 was answered with numerical values (length unit: centimeters).

3.4.3   Results

The result is shown in Fig. 6. The fill color of the box corresponds the color of the picture, which shows the condition. Each box represents the mean value of the responses to each statement, and each bar represents the standard error of the mean value. The result shows a comparison of the three conditions by one-way factorial ANOVA.

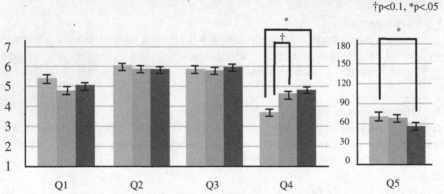

Fig. 6. Results of experiment 3 (N = 11).

There was no significant difference in the perceived clearness of the live video and the audio, and in the perceived intelligibility of the presentation, so the audio-visual quality and the quality of the presentation seemed not to affect the results.

We found a significant difference in the feeling of being close to the partner in the same room ($F(2, 10) = 11.59$, $p < .01$). Multiple comparisons showed that this feeling was significantly stronger in the pointing rod condition than the combined video condition ($p < .1$) and in the robot arm condition than the combined video condition ($p < .05$). We also found a significant difference in the feeling of distance ($F(2, 10) = 14.97$, $p < .01$). Multiple comparisons showed that this feeling was significantly stronger in the laser pointer condition than combined video condition ($p < .01$) and embodied video condition ($p < .01$). This means participant feel farther in video condition than other conditions. There was no significant difference in each question between the combined video condition and the robot arm condition.

4   Discussion

4.1   Effect of Embodying Video

In this paper, we compared five pointing methods, which are the video condition, the combined video condition, the laser pointer condition, the pointing rod condition and the robot arm condition. In addition, we divided to three experiments and evaluated them progressively.

In experiment 1, we compared the video condition, the combined video condition and the robot arm condition. As the result, we found that the score of the robot arm condition is higher than other conditions. According to the questionnaire, participants felt that a display looked like a window and the remote partner pointed to a stuffed animal from there, in video condition. In addition, the score of the video condition is lower than the combined video condition. We consider that the video condition has the boundary surface of the vertical display and separates the remote space from the local space. Moreover, it was caused by giving the participant the impression. Since the task was done smoothly, participants were not feel a sense of discomfort that the partner's arm was a robot arm.

In experiment 2, we compared the combined video condition, the laser pointer condition and the robot arm condition. These conditions showed that the remote space and the local space are continuous and there were comparisons of video, light and embodiment. As the result, we found that the laser pointer condition scored lower than other conditions. According to the interview, no participants noticed the pointing mechanism under all conditions, and there was no reduction in the score by them. Although the method of projecting a laser dot can be pointed beyond the space, we consider that the connection of the remote space and local space seems to be discrete.

In experiment 3, we compared the combined video condition, the pointing rod condition and the robot arm condition. The pointing rod condition and the robot arm condition were embodying the remote partner's pointing behavior. As the result, we found that there was a tendency to enhance social telepresence regardless of the method of embodiment, when showing the embodiment continuity between remote space and local space. According to the questionnaires, some participants felt the robot arm condition was closer than the pointing rod condition. However, when the pointing behaviors were embodied, many subjects felt that social telepresence was equivalent on both the pointing rod and the robot arm. Through the experiments, we found that the pointing rod condition and the robot arm, which had two properties: showing spatial continuity and embodying the remote partner's pointing behavior, enhanced social telepresence.

4.2   The Feeling of Being Pointed to the Object in Local Space

When we asked about the feeling of sense that the partner was pointing to an object in the participant's space in experiment 1, the result showed that the score of the robot arm condition scored higher than other conditions. We considered that the video condition has the boundary surface of the vertical display and separates the remote space from the local space. According to the questionnaire, participant felt that the pointing behavior was done under the table in the combined video condition. In addition, we did not get these comments in the robot arm condition.

In experiment 2, the robot arm condition scores higher than the other two conditions. According to the interview, participants answered that the laser condition was instructed by light, and they received an impression given from a distant position. Through the experiments, the feeling of sense about the partner was pointing to an object in the participant's space was improved by showing the pointing behavior as if it was popping out from the remote partner's video.

4.3   The Feeling of Being Far from the Remote Pointer

When asked about the feeling of being far from the remote partner in experiment 1, the result showed that the video condition scored higher than other conditions. This means that participants felt farther in the video condition than other conditions. We did not give any information to the participant about the length of device and the size of the table during the experiment. We placed the display where the distance between the participant and the vertical display was 120 cm. This means the vertical display was placed between the video condition and the combined video condition. As the result, the participant felt that the partner was seated behind the display when the partner was shown only a vertical display. Moreover, the participant felt closer when the arm of the partners was showed prior to the vertical display. In addition, the result showed that the laser pointer condition scored higher than other conditions in experiment 2. We found that the sense of distance was influenced by showing the arm in front of a vertical display. In experiment 3, the arm and pointing rod of the partner was shown prior to the vertical display. Although we found the significant difference between combined video condition and robot arm condition, there was not much difference in the score as compared with other experiments. We considered the feeling of distance was influenced by the distance from the tip of pointing behavior.

5   Conclusion

In this study, we verified the influence of a design, which embodies continuity of two spaces between remote space and local space, on social telepresence. In previous study, a robot arm, which the remote partner's arm seemed to pop out from the display, enhanced social telepresence [20]. We compared five pointing behaviors to a remote place in videoconferencing: (1) displaying the partner's pointing behavior, that is, ordinary videoconferencing, (2) displaying the partner's arm on a tabletop display, (3) projecting a laser dot and it is synchronized with the laser pointer held by the partner, and (4) embodying the partner's pointing behavior by a robotic pointer and (5) embodying the partner's pointing behavior by a robotic arm. We found that the fourth and fifth methods, which had two properties: showing spatial continuity and embodying the remote partner's pointing behavior, enhanced social telepresence. In addition, we found that the sense of distance was influenced by showing the arm in front of the display.

In this research, we focused on the pointing behavior. However, there is a possibility that embodying remote partner has an effect in not only the pointing behavior but also the remote assistance task. Moreover, we verified only the effect of social telepresence in this research. Verification of the relationship between enhancing social telepresence and effective of the remote assistance task is a future work.

Acknowledgment. This work was supported by JSPS KAKENHI Grant Numbers JP26280076, JP15K12081, KDDI Foundation, Telecommunication Advancement Foundation, Foundation for the Fusion of Science and Technology, Tateishi Science and technology Foundation and JST CREST.

References

1. Alem, L., Li, J.: A study of gestures in a video-mediated collaborative assembly task. Adv. Hum.-Comput. Interact. **2011**, 1–7 (2011)
2. Bainbridge, W.A., Hart, J.W., Kim, E.S., Scassellati, B.: The benefits of interactions with physically present robots over video-displayed agents. Int. J. Soc. Robot. **3**(1), 41–52 (2011)
3. Bondareva, Y., Bouwhuis, D.: Determinants of social presence in videoconferencing. In: Proceedings of AVI 2004, pp. 1–9 (2004)
4. Chidambaram, V., Chiang, Y.H., Mutlu, B.: Designing persuasive robots: how robots might persuade people using vocal and nonverbal cues. In: Proceedings of International Conference on Human-Robot Interaction (HRI 2012), pp. 293–300 (2012)
5. De Greef, P., Ijsselsteijn, W.: Social presence in a home tele-application. Cyberpsychol. Behav. Soc. Netw. 307–315 (2001)
6. Finn, K.E., Sellen, A.J., Wilbur, S.B.: Video-Mediated Communication. In: Proceedings of CSCW 1999, pp. 299–301. Lawrence Erlbaum Associates (1997)
7. Fussell, R.S., Setlock, D.L., Yang, J., Ou, J., Mauer, E., Kramer, I.D.A.: Gestures over video streams to support remote collaboration on physical tasks. In: Proceedings of HCI 2004, pp. 273–309 (2004)
8. Genest, A., Gutwin, C.: Evaluating the effectiveness of height visualizations for improving gestural communication at distributed tabletops. In: Proceedings of CSCW 2012, pp. 519–528 (2012)
9. Giuseppe, S., Fridolin, W., Peter, S.: The GhostHands UX: telementoring with hands-on augmented reality instruction. In: Proceedings of IE2015, pp. 236–243 (2015)
10. Ishii, H., Kobayashi, M.: ClearBoard: a seamless medium for shared drawing and conversation with eye contact. In: Proceedings of CHI 1992, pp. 525–532 (1992)

11. Izadi, S., Agarwal, A., Criminisi, A., Winn, J., Blake, A., Fitzgibbon, A.: C-Slate: a multi-touch and object recognition system for remote collaboration using horizontal surfaces. In: Proceedings of Tabletop 2007, pp. 3–10 (2007)
12. Kirk, D., Rodden, T., Fraser, S.D.: Turn it this way: grounding collaborative action with remote gestures. In: Proceedings of CHI 2007, pp. 1039–1047 (2007)
13. Kuzuoka, H., Oyama, S., Yamazaki, K., Suzuki, K., Mitsuishi, M.: GestureMan: a mobile robot that embodies a remote instructor's actions. In: Proceedings of CSCW 2000, pp. 155–162 (2000)
14. Leithinger, D., Follmer, S., Olwal, A., Ishii, H.: Physical telepresence: shape capture and display for embodied, computer-mediated remote collaboration. In: Proceedings of UIST 2014, pp. 461–470 (2014)
15. Luff, P., Heath, C., Kuzuoka, H., Yamazaki, K., Yamashita, J.: Handling documents and discriminating objects in hybrid spaces. In: Proceedings of CHI 2006, pp. 561–570 (2006)
16. Nakanishi, H., Murakami, Y., Nogami, D., Ishiguro, H.: Minimum movement matters: impact of robot-mounted cameras on social telepresence. In: Proceedings of CSCW 2008, pp. 303–312 (2008)
17. Nakanishi, H., Murakami, Y., Kato, K.: Movable cameras enhance social telepresence in media spaces. In: Proceedings of CHI 2009, pp. 433–442 (2009)
18. Nakanishi, H., Kato, K., Ishiguro, H.: Zoom cameras and movable displays enhance social telepresence. In: Proceedings of CHI 2011, pp. 63–72 (2011)
19. Nakanishi, H., Tanaka, K., Wada, Y.: Remote handshaking: touch enhances video-mediated social telepresence. In: Proceedings of CHI 2014, pp. 2143–2152 (2014)
20. Onishi, Y., Tanaka, K., Nakanishi, H.: Embodiment of video-mediated communication enhances social telepresence. In: Proceedings of HAI 2016, pp. 171–178 (2016)
21. Ou, J., Chen, X., Fussell, S., Yang, J.: DOVE: drawing over video environment. In: Proceedings of Multimedia 2003, pp. 100–101 (2003)
22. Pauchet, A., Coldefy, F., Lefebvre, S., Louis, S., Perron, L., Bouguet, A., Collobert, M., Guerin, J., Corvaisier, D.: TableTops: worthwhile experiences of collocated and remote collaboration. In: Proceedings of TABLETOP 2007, pp. 27–34 (2007)
23. Prussog, A., Muhlbach, L., Bocker, M.: Telepresence in videocommunications. In: Proceedings of Annual Meeting of Human Factors and Ergonomics Society, pp. 25–38 (1994)
24. Riether, N., Hegel, F., Wrede, B., Horstmann, G.: Social facilitation with social robots? In: Proceedings of HRI 2012, pp. 41–47 (2012)
25. Sakamoto, D., Kanda, T., Ono, T., Ishiguro, H., Hagita, N.: Android as a telecommunication medium with a human-like presence. In: Proceedings of HRI 2007, pp. 193–200 (2007)
26. Sakata, N., Kurata, T., Kato, T., Kourogi, M., Kuzuoka, H.: WACL: Supporting telecommunications using wearable active camera with laser pointer. In: Proceedings of Wearable Computers 2003, pp. 53–56 (2003)
27. Tanaka, T., Nakanishi, H., Ishiguro, H.: Comparing video, avatar, and robot mediated communication: pros and cons of embodiment. In: Proceedings of CollabTech 2014, pp. 96–110 (2014)
28. Tang, J., Minneman, S.: VideoWhiteboard: video shadows to support remote collaboration. In: Proceedings of CHI 1991, pp. 315–322 (1991)
29. Tang, A., Pahud, M., Inkpen, K., Benko, H., Tang, C.J., Buxton, B.: Three's company: understanding communication channels in three-way distributed collaboration. In: Proceedings of CSCW 2010, pp. 338–348 (2010)
30. Yamashita, N., Kaji, K., Kuzuoka, H., Hirata, K.: Improving visibility of remote gestures in distributed tabletop collaboration. In: Proceedings of CSCW 2011, pp. 95–104 (2011)

Sharing Composite Web Applications
with Multiple Coupling Levels

Gregor Blichmann$^{(\boxtimes)}$, Christopher Lienemann, and Klaus Meissner

Technische Universität Dresden, Dresden, Germany
{gregor.blichmann,christopher.lienemann,klaus.meissner}@tu-dresden.de

Abstract. Developing and utilizing situational long-tail Web applications for scenarios with multiple persons interacting gains increasing importance. Thereby, adjusting the style of coupling during runtime is necessary to support changing situational requirements and long-tail collaborative situations. Main problems comprise the lack of universal coupling levels which are characterized in a sufficient and understandable granularity, missing analyses for potential synchronization points in the context of black-box-based Web applications, and an adequate user interface (UI) support for managing and reviewing individual coupling levels for multiple users simultaneously. To this end, we present a novel concept for managing different levels of coupling within composite Web applications. The seven proposed sharing modes support Web users with no programming skills by a default configuration of couplings, permissions and sharing objects. A wizard-like interaction concept enables these users to create and manage personal sharing definitions during runtime while considering various levels of coupling for each collaborative partner. A first user study provides preliminary evidence about the acceptance of the sharing modes and the interaction features for the target group.

Keywords: Mashup · End-user development · Collaborative work · Permission management · Coupling levels

1 Introduction

Approaches for universal composition like CRUISe [1] or mashart [2] allow for a platform-independent modeling of composite Web applications (CWAs) and a uniform description of components spanning all application layers. Imagine a setting with multiple users collaborating in an online session by utilizing a platform for CWAs. Each user has an individual set of components as part of a shared application instance and can modify this by adding or removing, e.g., *mashup components*, even at runtime. Collaboration is achieved by defining shared components, which activates a partial application state synchronization. Thus, the roles *inviter* and *invitee* emerge, which both are in the target group of Web users with no programming skills. They perform situation-driven development of applications for niche purposes, also known as the "long tail".

© Springer International Publishing AG 2017
C. Gutwin et al. (Eds.): CRIWG 2017, LNCS 10391, pp. 15–31, 2017.
DOI: 10.1007/978-3-319-63874-4_2

1.1 Motivation

Using groupware synchronously in a distributed group implies a certain coupling level. Several works (e.g. [3,4]) rated a flexible coupling support as essential for supporting multiple application purposes and changing tasks during runtime. Coupling levels can vary significantly. Tight coupling, as used in screen and desktop sharing applications like TeamViewer[1], proposes identical screens to all participants and synchronizes changes in a strict What You See Is What I See (WYSIWIS) manner. Loose coupling, for example used in Google Docs[2] or Zoho Docs[3], enables users to view different parts of a shared text and individually rework different paragraphs. Multiple coupling levels in parallel can be desired in various collaborative use cases and therefore require sophisticated support for awareness as well as coordination. Traditional, collaborative Web applications are monolithic and suffer from a predefined, restricted functional scope as well as a mostly fixed level of coupling. In this paper, we present a platform for the situational development of collaborative, composite applications for arbitrary collaborative use cases. Users with no programming skills can search, integrate and share any application part in the form of components according to their current context during runtime. The platform supports distributed mixed-focus collaboration [5], in which distributed users permanently switch between working individually and together.

This causes a major research challenge for this work. Since participants' requirements and tasks are strongly varying during runtime, suitable couplings can not be predicted or hard-coded. Users have to understand effects of the current coupling level for all parts of their application and be able to change the level depending on the current work context on their own [3]. Although approaches like [3,4] are present, no generic classification of possible coupling levels for arbitrary application and collaboration purposes exists. In the context of CWA, which synchronizes black-box components by their public interface, analyzing coupling possibilities is another challenge of this work. Suitable awareness in the context of mixed-focus collaboration is already well studied for professional users (e.g. [5]). However, our target group includes daily Web users without programming skills. For them, necessary configurations have to be automated and technical details to be hidden. Managing multiple coupling levels for different group members by the runtime environment is also a challenge tackled by this paper.

Since the presented challenges for introducing multiple levels of coupling for collaborative CWAs are not covered by any work yet, this paper presents three contributions: First, a deep analysis of different possible levels is introduced. This mainly considers the synchronization of situational, collaborative CWAs assembled by black-box components of various vendors. On top, non-programmers, as our primary target group, will be empowered to change coupling levels during runtime supported by a set of preconfigured sharing modes. An adequate UI support simplifies selection and understanding of different levels for them. Finally,

---

[1] https://www.teamviewer.com.

[2] https://docs.google.com.

[3] https://www.zoho.eu/docs/.

a prototype and a user study prove the user acceptance and sustainability of the concepts. The practical significance of the described problems and contributions is clarified in the following reference scenario.

1.2   Reference Scenario

The following travel planning scenario illustrates the main research challenges of this paper. Bob wants to collaboratively organize his next round trip with his friends Charlie and Alice, both currently on a business trip. Since they did not agree on a destination, Bob initiates a new mashup including three map components. Each map visualizes one of his favorite places in Spain, Italy, and Canada. To discuss his proposals, Bob shares the application by using the tightly coupled presentation mode with Charlie and Alice. Thereby, all collaborative partners will see the viewport of Bob. This includes the synchronization of his basic application layout and its changes as well as the synchronization of all his scroll and zoom activities. Charlie and Alice can only consume Bob's changes and use the integrated video chat to bring in their ideas.

After they selected Canada, Bob removes the other maps and adjusts the sharing configuration for Charlie and Alice to a tightly coupled collaboration mode. Thereby, all users can change the components' content, for example by adding markers or change the visual appearance, for example by changing the map type. Due to this coupling level, both kinds of changes of all users are synchronized with all members of the group.

Some discussions later, the map contains a set of markers representing the desired places of the planned round trip. To agree on the date of the trip, Bob adds a calendar component to the application and shares it with the other both. He selects a coupling level, which synchronizes only the calendar's data elements, like created appointments. All UI specific configurations, like the currently visible week, can be adjusted individually by each group member. Using this level of coupling, each of the three friends can scan for available dates separately and as soon as one of them creates or adjusts the appointment representing their trip, it is visible for everybody.

Finally, Alice integrates a notepad component. She adds all necessary tasks to be achieved before starting the tour, like booking flights or reserving hostels. Afterward, she shares the component with the other both and uses a coupling level, which enables them to choose from a set of alternative notepad components. After accepting the invitation, Bob and Charlie can work with an individual notepad while the platform synchronizes the underlying list of tasks by facilitating the semantic annotations.

The remainder of this paper is structured as follows: Sect. 2 briefly introduces a runtime environment for collaborative, composite Web mashups. Next, Sect. 3 discusses possible coupling levels and sharing modes and presents their integration into the process for sharing composition fragments during runtime. In Sect. 4, visual interaction tools and awareness features are discussed with regards to fit the proposed concepts to the target user group. Section 5 describes the underlying prototype, the methodology and the results of a user study. Related work is discussed in Sect. 6. Finally, Sect. 7 concludes this paper by discussing the achievements of the proposed results.

2   Collaborative Usage of Composite Web Applications

Traditional monolithic groupware systems lack interoperability and customizability. To overcome these limitations, our concept adheres to the universal composition approach introduced by [1]. So-called compositeWeb application (CWA) combine arbitrary components from all application layers, including data, logic, and UI. By utilizing recommendation techniques and visually hiding the underlying application complexity, users with no programming skills are empowered to build and customize desired app functionalities during runtime iteratively. Different third-party vendors develop the application's components, which encapsulate arbitrary Web resources like data feeds, Web services or UI widgets as black-boxes. To establish an orchestrated data flow between components, all of them implement a public interface comprising operations, events, and properties. Properties represent a part of the component's inner state utilizing semantically typed key-value pairs. State changes, indicated by events, can be used to invoke operations by parameterized messages. Such interfaces as well as the component's overall functionality may be annotated with semantic *capabilities* to facilitate user-driven composition and data type mediation. Therefore, concepts of third-party ontologies are used to increase interoperability of different components. As a basic functionality for awareness features, interface elements, such as properties, may be assigned to a set of UI representations by an additional annotation. These *view bindings* make use of Cascading Style Sheets (CSS) selectors to address corresponding visual component elements, such as a label, a diagram or an input field, flexibly. A composition model represents all application-specific elements, like the included components, their communication channels, layout, and screen flow.

On top of that, the work of [6] enables users of the target group to define and evaluate custom sharing definitions by just managing visual triples of *who*, *what* and *how*. These triples can be used to share arbitrary applications, single components or even parts of them with different collaboration partners for simultaneous use during runtime.

3   Levels of Coupling for Composite Web Applications

To present coupling levels for CWAs, the terms shared session, sharing definition, coupling, and synchronization have to be clarified within the scope of this work. A shared session defines a set of sharing definitions. A sharing definition potentially includes arbitrary triples with not less than one user, one composition fragment, and one permission each. A user can define multiple sharing definitions during runtime by using the sharing view of the platform. As soon as an invitee accepts a proposed sharing, its components are coupled and will be synchronized each time a state change appears according to the corresponding level of coupling and permission.

In the following, Subsect. 3.1 discusses potential coupling levels in the context of composite mashup applications. Furthermore, Subsect. 3.2 introduces seven sharing modes and Subsect. 3.3 aligns them with the existing sharing process.

3.1 Access Options and Coupling Levels of Composite Web Applications

In contrast to traditional, monolithic groupware, CWAs contain black-box components which exchange data using semantically annotated interfaces. Therefore, it is necessary to analyze potentially suitable coupling levels and the possible access options within suchlike applications. As indicated in Fig. 1, access options for defining different levels of coupling originate from three abstraction layers. The *platform* layer comprises all runtime environment and device specific features, which are independent of an application instance. This includes, e.g., the current *viewport* present to the user, the set of received *recommendations* for additional components or application reconfigurations, or the *list of users* currently online. The *composition* represents all application-specific characteristics specified by the composition model. This includes *screen flow*, *layout*, the *set of components*, their data flow (*communication*), and its *adaptivity* behavior. The *component* layer, due to the black-box paradigm, contains all component-specific elements in form of component interface parts like properties, operations, and events. Since properties can represent arbitrary parts of a component's inner state, it is necessary to analyze their semantics in more detail. Practically, properties can represent basic *configurations* necessary to instantiate the component, like name, size, the URL of the backend or used APIs. Properties can also represent states necessary for the correct *visual rendering* of the component, like the currently selected map type in Google Maps or the chosen theme in a text editor. Finally, properties can represent parts of the underlying *data* model, which can be both represented directly or indirectly on the UI.

As indicated by the highlighted fields in Fig. 1, our work uses seven of the analyzed elements to differentiate six primary coupling levels presented on the right. To support non-programmers best, the number of levels should be kept at a minimum. To consider the most significant cases of typical collaborative scenarios only, synchronizing options like recommendations or the adaptivity behavior are intentionally excluded. Coupling levels are organized as a hierarchy from top to bottom. Tighter, upper levels subsume more loose, lower ones. Likewise, arbitrary level combinations are not intended. The assumption, that a hierarchy fosters simplicity and clarity of the concept for daily Web users with no programming skills was proven by our user study (cf. Sect. 5). The definition of tightness rest on the number of access options coupled, which is used as the primary order criterion. The tightest level is denoted with *screen flow + viewport*. At this level, all parts of a CWA are synchronized including transitions between screens or scroll and zoom events at the viewport. The layout is the same for all users, which can cause problems in case of different screen sizes or resolutions.

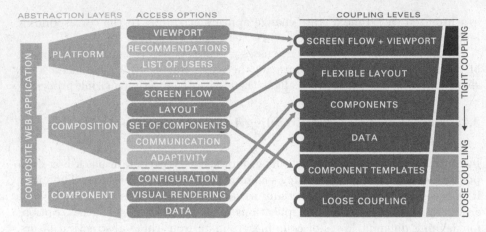

Fig. 1. Derivation of possible coupling levels for composite web applications

The *flexible layout* only synchronizes layout information about the components order, relative size of the viewport, and position within the grid system. In contrast to the tighter level, users will receive an optimal user experience for devices with different screen sizes or resolutions while still be able to work tightly coupled. The level *components* allow for an individual layout configuration of each participant. While components' order and size as well as screen flow and scroll events are not synchronized, each component of the application, including its configuration, visual rendering, and data model are synchronized. To support cases, where participants need individually configured component UIs, like for example individual scroll positions in a text editor or different map types on a map, the level *data* can be used. Within each component, only the properties representing the data model are synchronized. To support use cases, which are more based on coordination than collaboration, the last two levels can be used. *Component templates* only couple the initial set of components shared by the owner as templates for initializing the applications of all participants. Afterward, all group members work individually with the same set of components and can synchronize only single data elements like the current list of hotels or a set of locations. *Loose coupling* indicates a level, where every collaboration partner can individually choose components to work with. Again, the only synchronized connection between each user can be represented by a single data element, which represents the task to be accomplished.

3.2 Sharing Modes

Since the differentiation of the presented coupling levels is hard for end users with no programming experiences, we additionally introduce seven sharing modes. These sharing modes provide an end-user-oriented abstraction layer by subsuming coupling levels with suitable sharing objects and permissions. Thereby, each mode represents a typical collaboration scenario by a suitable identifier, easy to understand for non-programmers. The following seven modes can be distinguished:

Tight presentation mode represents the most restrictive mode by adopting the level of *screen flow and viewport*. It enables an inviter to present content without interruption. This mode automatically shares the entire application with the permission only to view state changes (see first sharing of Bob within the reference scenario).

Free presentation mode utilizes the level of *flexible layout* to support participants with different devices and screens while enabling the inviter to present content tightly coupled. The entire application is shared under view permission by default.

Tight collaboration mode represents the combination of the coupling level *components* with the permission to edit the content of the shared parts. This enables a collaborative usage of the entire application or single selected components. Thereby, all shared components have identical and synchronized visual appearances.

Free collaboration mode similarly is based on the permission to edit but uses the coupling level *data*. This implies that users can work synchronously on data with an individually configured visual appearance of the shared components.

Tight individual mode targets asynchronous scenarios where collaborative partners use a fixed set of components, which is not synchronized. This mode grounds on the level *set of components*. By selecting the permission *edit* for single component properties, for example, the inviter can force participants to independently search for hotels and exclusively synchronize their result list with the inviter.

Free individual mode in contrast to the previous mode, participants can choose alternative components from a set of given components. This can be used to define a clear workspace for the invitees, but consider their personal preferences, for example by using Bing as map provider instead of Google.

Coordination mode represents the level of *loose coupling*. Within this mode, invitees are completely free in their choice of the right components for the assigned task of the inviter. By assigning edit permissions to single properties, the inviter can create a set of tasks in form of desired data elements to be filled by his collaborative participants. The platform recommends suitable components for the invitees.

Even if some modes includes predefined, not changeable sharing objects, it is possible to customize single component properties. For each mode, the inviter can define individual data elements to be private or only viewable instead of editable. How this can be done, is explained in the next subsection.

3.3   Coupling-Aware Sharing Process

Figure 2 presents the process for creating sharing definitions for CWAs, which extends the initially introduced process of [6]. The extended process comprises three steps to invite new users or extend existing collaborative sessions. In *step 1*, one of the seven sharing modes introduced in the previous section has to be selected. Selecting the sharing mode, and therefore the desired coupling level has do be done first because it implies restrictions for the set of selectable objects and permissions. *Step 2* includes the definition of the sharing triple. As a subject, arbitrary combinations of groups and single users can be defined ①. For each subject, tuples of object and permission can be attached ②. Thereby, users can select objects and permissions which are allowed for the current sharing mode. In general, possible objects can be arbitrary composition fragments (entire application or single components), composition features, or composition data ③. Permissions at this step can be *edit* or *view*. With the second step, multiple triples of subject, object, and permission can be defined ④. The final *step 3*, optionally allow for fine-grained customization of permissions for single fragments in form of composition features or data ⑤. This includes, for example, the selection of confidential data to be hidden as private for other participants. Thereby, the concepts presented in [7] are being applied. Independent of the current sharing mode, single fragments of the selected sharing object can be selected to customize their specific permission. Users can assign view or edit permissions to single fragments. This can be used especially in the case of coordination, where participants use, for example, the *free individual mode*. Because this implies no general synchronization, single fragments can be specified as to be synchronized for exchanging, e.g., the result of a hotel search. If the object equals the entire application, then single components, features or data elements can be selected. If single components were selected initially, only features and data can be chosen here. Within each sharing definition, steps 2 and 3 can be iteratively repeated ⑥. Finally, the creation of a new sharing definition is finished by sending the invitation to join a new or extend an existing collaborative session to the users specified as subject. Afterward, anytime during the collaborative session, users can start creating or adopting other sharing definitions ⑦.

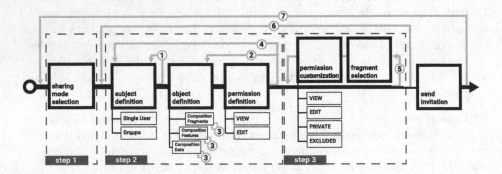

Fig. 2. Process of creating a sharing definition

4   User Interface and Awareness

The defined sharing process comes with integrated visual tooling support, which is based on the UI concept presented in [6]. This section describes the extensions made to consider different coupling levels during sharing and the awareness features in live view to review applied settings.

4.1   Defining New Sharings During Runtime

Step 1, 2, and 3 of Fig. 2 form the basis for a wizard-like interface concept. Figure 3 includes four screenshots which exemplify their practical execution.

As indicated in (A), the process of creating a sharing definition starts by opening a modal dialog. After a short introduction text, as defined in the sharing process, users have to select their desired sharing mode first. To ease the understanding of the seven sharing modes introduced in Subsect. 3.2 for non-programmers, an additional level of abstraction was introduced. By following typical practical, collaborative activities, users first have to select the intended purpose of their collaborative session in form of *present* some information, *work together* with others, or *assign tasks*. This lowers the initial set of possible choices to three instead of seven and therefore, reduce the users' cognitive load. Screen (A) highlights the case, when a user hovers the *work together* option. After selecting this purpose, (B) indicates, that only suitable sharing modes are visualized. In this case, the user first hovers, later selects the *free collaboration mode. Present* covers *tight* and *free presentation mode. Tight* and *Free Individual Mode* as well as *Coordination Mode* are represented by *assign tasks*. Within each mode, a short description as well as a bullet list of synchronized elements are displayed, to ease their differentiation for non-programmers. The *user guide* on the right permanently displays additional information depending on the current step and its current configuration.

After finishing step 1, as indicated in (C) of Fig. 3, users are asked to configure their basic sharing definition by visually composing a triple of *who, what*, and *how*. According to the selected sharing mode, *what* and *how* may be preselected and can not be changed (cf. Subsect. 3.2). In any case, the user has to specify a set of users or groups which should receive an invitation for sharing. Here, Alice was selected as subject for the triple. Details about the definition of triples were already presented and evaluated by [6] and therefore, are not in scope of this paper.

Within the final step (D), users can customize permissions or hide private data. This step is optionally and can be skipped by directly clicking at the *share* button, which was activated by opening this step. The *preview* button can be used, to review the current settings before sharing them by using an impression view introduced by [7]. Step 3 further extends the results of [7], which introduced an UI for visually selecting data elements and component features to be hidden as private within a collaborative session. The screen lists all data elements shared, grouped by the components they are originating from. This applies for the components' features too. Because the user has chosen the

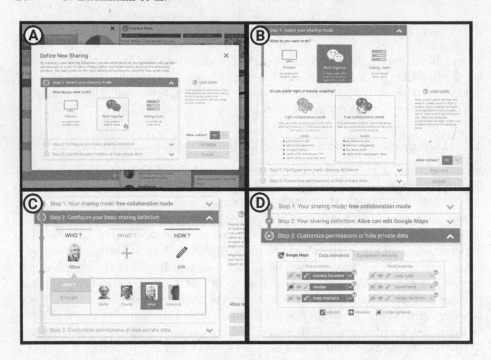

Fig. 3. UI support for new sharing definitions with multiple coupling levels

free collaboration mode in this example, all component properties configuring the visual appearance are skipped from synchronizing and therefore visually grayed out. For this sharing mode, all data elements are marked as synchronized per default indicated by their blue color. In addition, each element receives the basic permission specified in step 2, in this case *edit*. The user can now change the permission of each data element to either *viewable*, *editable*, or *private*. The last implies, that the element is handled as private following the concept of [7].

In case one of the three coordination modes were selected (purpose *assign tasks*), no data element or component feature gets synchronized and therefore is marked as active within this panel. Thereby, single elements can be activated, to indicate, that the list of hotels or the current location should be synchronized as a result of the assigned task. The whole process is assisted by a green status indicator at the left. It displays a green check mark for each successfully processed step. In addition, each step includes small circles indicating the number of actions necessary within.

After finishing a sharing definition, the platform notifies the selected participants and changes to the application's live view. After an invitee joins, the platform ensures the correct synchronization of corresponding application events, like scrolling or adding components, and component state changes, like a changed data property, depending on the conceptual specifications of the selected sharing mode (c.f. Sect. 3).

4.2   Live View Awareness and Adaptation

After creating some sharing definitions for different collaborative partners, it is necessary to constantly be aware of all granted permissions and coupling levels. As indicated in Fig. 4, for each shared component of an application, a small pop over menu can be opened by clicking on the icon that indicates the number of collaborating users for this component. The dialog is divided into an overview at the right side Ⓔ and a detail view for one selected participant at the left Ⓕ.

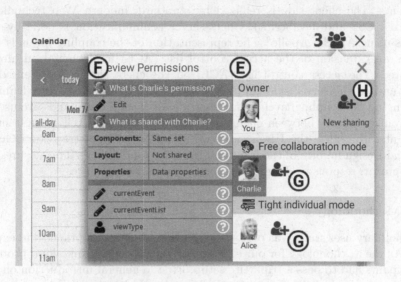

Fig. 4. Awareness for current sharing definitions

The overview visually separates all participants by their assigned sharing mode. By clicking at the plus icon Ⓖ, a new sharing definition with the same sharing mode can be created. Therefore, the sharing dialog of Fig. 3 opens by initially showing step 2 Ⓒ. To start a new sharing definition with a different sharing mode, the *new sharing* icon at the upper right can be used Ⓗ. The current screen shows the perspective for Bob, the owner of the component, who has invited Charlie and Alice. If Alice or Charlie would open this view, they only can check their own sharing mode and the name of the owner.

The detail view initially shows the active sharing mode and insights on the permissions for each data element for the current user. As soon as one user present at the overview gets hovered, the detail view changes and visualizes the permissions for them.

5   Evaluation

The concept of different coupling levels for collaboratively used, composite Web applications is evaluated with regard to its practicability by a reference implementation within the Composition of Rich User Interface Services for Everybody

(CRUISE) runtime environment (Subsect. 5.1). To prove the user acceptance, a user study was conducted (Subsects. 5.2 and 5.3).

5.1 Implementation

The CRUISE platform hosts mashup applications to enable their collaborative usage and reconfiguration during runtime. Therefore, a server-side coordination layer is implemented as a singleton using Enterprise Java Beans (EJBs) for all clients. The client side is realized by standard, modern Web technologies (HTML5, CSS and JavaScript). Client-server communication is done by Web sockets using Apache Apollo[4] The representation of the coupling levels is realized as an extension of the access control list (ACL) implementation already presented. The access control list (ACL) on the client side is represented via JSON and on the server side via Java. After creating a new sharing definition or changing the coupling level during runtime, dedicated commands are used to synchronize updates between client and server to keep the ACL consistent for all clients. To realize the UI support, we mainly used Bootstrap[5] and Google Material Design in form of the front-end framework propeller[6]. This ensures fast development, responsive design, and consistent user experience.

5.2 Methodology

A preliminary user study was performed to evaluate user acceptance and experience. As the methodology for our experiment, we used the think-aloud protocol. Participants had to pass a tripartite setup. First, a general introduction on how to create, use, and modify composite Web mashups with the EUD-mashup platform of CRUISE as well as on the reference scenario presented in Subsect. 1.2 was given. Second, participants were asked to complete four tasks with increasing complexity by using an interactive click prototype, that was created with the tool *invision*[7]:

- Share the calendar component and select an appropriate coupling level which allows others to choose an individual calendar formatting style.
- Share the map component to present your marked locations, consider individual screen resolutions, and ensure, that invitees can only change the map markers.
- Review and explain the present awareness information, in case of a not valid and a not meaningful sharing definition (created by the moderator).
- Log in as an invitee. Explain the sharing awareness features by exemplifying configured coupling levels and permission restrictions.

---

[4] https://activemq.apache.org/apollo/.
[5] http://getbootstrap.com/.
[6] http://propeller.in/.
[7] https://www.invisionapp.com/.

A moderator noted comments. Finally, the participants were asked to fill in the System Usability Scale (SUS) questionnaire to get a comparable, standardized result.

As presented in Table 1, the study was conducted with the help of six male and three female participants including ages from 21 to 48 years (29 on average). All daily use the Web. Seven had no or basic programming skills. They fit the target group best. Professions were widely spread, including physics, economy, engineering, accounting, earth science, and architecture.

5.3   Results

The overall feedback from all participants was very positive. Selecting the appropriate sharing modes was in general no problem for the participants. Since the initial version of the UI showed all seven sharing modes in parallel, three users reported being overwhelmed. As a consequence, we introduced the purpose selection of step one (see ① in Fig. 3). Understanding the purpose of each sharing mode was easy for almost everybody due to the used icons and short descriptions. However, five participants reported, that they had to read the description of all modes to be sure about their selection at the initial test. In the original version, five users directly tried to click on the share button after selecting the sharing mode. To emphasize the necessary inputs in step two even more, the progress bar on the left side and some additional animation for the transition to step two were introduced.

Within step two, as proven in previous tests, users confirmed the simplicity of creating a sharing triple again. Similarly, the preselection of a permission originating from the selected sharing mode was clear for all participants. Six users had problems to understood that the whole application was preselected as the object. We added a visual and textual hint on that.

Within step three, six participants criticized the icon for private and not synchronized data elements, which we adjusted afterward. Visual hints for incorrect or missing definitions, tested by task three, were understood by everybody. The awareness features were intuitively opened and interpreted correctly by seven participants. Two had problems to identify that the icon at the components top bar can be clicked. Overall, the visual separation within the awareness view was rated as very positive. The only big misunderstanding within this view originated when users clicked on the provided help icons. The initial version presented a textual description of the sharing mode. Since users expected a live preview of the given permissions, the impression view, which was introduced in [7] is reused here.

In general, users were very interested in the idea of the overall platform and confirmed that they could imagine to use it for their daily activities. Once again, we observed, that self-descriptiveness is a crucial requirement for Web systems today. Participants only rarely read hints and use help icons. They prefer the paradigm *exploration before reading*. All participants filled in the SUS questionnaire and created an average score of 81.67, which indicates a good value for the general usability of the evaluated concepts. Individual results are listed in Table 1.

Table 1. Characteristics and SUS ratings of study participants

Age	Sex	Profession	Programming skills	Web usage	SUS rating
21	♂	Business informatics student	Advanced	Daily	92.5
24	♀	Business student	Beginner	Daily	95
26	♂	Business engineering student	Beginner	Daily	85
23	♂	Mechanical engineering student	Advanced	Daily	80
23	♂	Physics student	Beginner	Daily	75
48	♂	Food economics	None	Daily	77.5
48	♀	Accounting	None	Daily	72.5
25	♀	Landscape architecture student	None	Daily	80
24	♂	Earth sciences student	Beginner	Daily	77.5

6   Related Work

Today, only few a platforms allow for collaborative usage of EUD mashup applications. Approaches like PEUDOM [8], MultiMasher [9], or the vision of Tschudnowsky et al. [10] more or less enables users, to define different permissions for components of their composite application for synchronized usage. Nevertheless, none of the existing solutions discusses the provision or change of coupling levels at all. Sharing is based on a fixed, implicit degree of coupling whereby users never can review details about it.

Cooperative learning environments like [11] or [12] allow sharing parts of their workspaces with a set of users while keeping other parts as private. In difference to mashup platforms, they focus files or texts as content only and do not support interactive content. Although visual permission management metaphors exist, defining different coupling levels for various work scenarios is not part of these solutions.

Dewan and Choudhary [3] analyzed different, flexible coupling modes. Thereby, Boolean attributes indicate for each data property of an application whether value, format, or view coupling is desired. It is not possible to differentiate the coupling mode for different users. Also, users have to decide on their own about the meaningfulness of a configuration, which excludes end users without programming skills.

Gutwin and Greenberg [5] coined the phrase mixed-focus collaboration and discussed necessary awareness in these situations. They analyzed workspace navigation, interaction with artifacts, and view representation, which served as the foundation for this work. However, the analysis is very generic in the scope of this work. No runtime support for sharing parts of an application with arbitrary coupling levels is provided. Pinelle and Gutwin [13] separated loosely and tight coupling by interdependence, differentiation, and integration. Although the presented *Mohoc* framework required the mechanisms to change between these levels, more fine-grained level definitions and the adoption for non-programmers and their need for runtime changes were not covered.

The Component Groupware of ter Hofte [14] provides means for addressing different coupling levels. Similar to our classification, they define a hierarchy of four status levels which result in four coupling levels. Concerning the research challenges of this work, this classification was used as a foundation, but is too broad and offers no runtime support for our target group. Inter alia, the work was extended by [15] by providing components exchangeable during runtime. Within a similar approach, the usage of the proposed components enables to switch the coupling level during runtime between interface, user, collaboration, and resource. However, also here detailed concepts for supporting users to evaluate and configure the right coupling level are missing.

Tandler [4] provided an environment for ubiquitous computing which considered coupling levels based on data, application, user interface, environment, and interaction model. As before, the results have to be detailed to work for composite Web applications and provides no runtime support for finding and reviewing required coupling levels.

Overall, none of the approaches enables non-programmers to define or adjust multiple coupling levels for their shared composite Web applications. Despite, many classifications and aspects of elements relevant for coupling exist, none sufficiently covers the particular challenges of CWA and none provides runtime support for non-programmers.

7   Conclusion and Future Work

By facilitating the mashup paradigm and universal composition, situational Web applications were proven to be intuitive and easy to use for collaborative scenarios. Even users with no programming skills are empowered to do user-driven development by the provided features for individual application tailoring during runtime. However, the analysis of related work showed significant deficiencies when considering different coupling levels for collaborative Web applications based on black-box components. This includes missing classifications and useful abstraction layers for coupling levels as well as UI support to enable the target group of users to share applications on their own.

This paper has three contributions. It presents an analysis and classification for elements in composite Web applications relevant for coupling. Besides, the clustering of theses elements combined with preselected permissions and sharing objects results in seven common sharing modes, which can be used by non-programmers to fulfill individual collaboration needs efficiently. To this end, any user is enabled to manage multiple coupling levels based on an integrated tooling during the initial specification of new sharing definitions as well as the review and awareness of these during runtime. The suitability of this approach for users with no programming skills is approved by a user study including nine participants from different professions. The major part was based on a think-aloud test. Its results yielded very positive feedback and an average SUS score of 81.67, which we found to be a good outcome. The feedback from the user study is already considered within the improved concept discussed in this paper.

Future work includes the adjustment of the existing workspace awareness approach. Currently, users can integrate proper awareness information as widgets on their own. It is not possible yet, to filter the set of available widgets, e.g., based on rules like presented in [5]. The goal is an excellent alignment of coupling level and selected awareness widgets. Nevertheless, we believe, that the proposed work is an essential factor for the acceptance of Web-based collaborative platforms in real life scenarios. Due to their generic nature, it is essential to support arbitrary application and collaboration scenarios by the coupling levels needed from daily Web users to fulfill their tasks successfully.

Acknowledgments. The work of Gregor Blichmann is funded by the European Regional Development Fund and the Free State of Saxony.

References

1. Pietschmann, S.: A model-driven development process and runtime platform for adaptive composite web applications. Technology **2**(4), 277–288 (2009)
2. Daniel, F., Casati, F., Benatallah, B., Shan, M.-C.: Hosted universal composition: models, languages and infrastructure in mashArt. In: Laender, A.H.F., Castano, S., Dayal, U., Casati, F., Oliveira, J.P.M. (eds.) ER 2009. LNCS, vol. 5829, pp. 428–443. Springer, Heidelberg (2009). doi:10.1007/978-3-642-04840-1_32
3. Dewan, P., Choudhard, R.: Flexible user interface coupling in a collaborative system. In: Proceedings of the SIGCHI Conference on Human Factors in Computing Systems, CHI 1991, New Orleans, Louisiana, USA, pp. 41–48. ACM (1991). doi:10.1145/108844.108851. ISBN: 0-89791-383-3
4. Tandler, P.: Synchronous collaboration in ubiquitous computing environments: conceptual model and software infrastructure for roomware components. Ph.D. thesis. Darmstadt University of Technology, Germany (2004)
5. Gutwin, C., Greenberg, S.: Design for individuals, design for groups: tradeoffs between power and workspace awareness. In: Proceedings of the 1998 ACM Conference on Computer Supported Cooperative Work, CSCW 1998, Seattle, Washington, USA, pp. 207–216. ACM (1998). doi:10.1145/289444.289495. ISBN: 1-58113-009-0
6. Blichmann, G., et al.: Triple-based sharing of context-aware composite web applications for non-programmers. In: Proceedings of the 12th International Conference on Web Information Systems and Technologies, WEBIST 2016, Rome, Italy, 23–25 April 2016, vol. 2, pp. 17–26. SciTePress (2016). doi:10.5220/0005862800170026. ISBN: 978-989-758-186-1
7. Blichmann, G., et al.: Private data in collaborative web mashups. In: Proceedings of the 13th International Conference on Web Information Systems and Technologies, WEBIST 2017, Porto, Portugal, 25–27 April 2017 (2017, in press)
8. Picozzi, M.: End-user development of mashups: models, composition paradigms and tools. Ph.D. thesis. Politecnico di Milano, March 2014
9. Husmann, M., Nebeling, M., Norrie, M.C.: MultiMasher: a visual tool for multi-device mashups. In: Sheng, Q.Z., Kjeldskov, J. (eds.) ICWE 2013. LNCS, vol. 8295, pp. 27–38. Springer, Cham (2013). doi:10.1007/978-3-319-04244-2_4

10. Tschudnowsky, A., et al.: Towards real-time collaboration in user interface mashups. In: ICE-B 2014 - Proceedings of the 11th International Conference on e-Business, Vienna, Austria, 28–30 August 2014, pp. 193–200. SciTePress (2014). doi:10.5220/0005049001930200. ISBN: 978-989-758-043-7
11. Schümmer, T., Haake, J.M., Haake, A.: A metaphor and user interface for managing access permissions in shared workspace systems. In: Hemmje, M., Niederée, C., Risse, T. (eds.) From Integrated Publication and Information Systems to Information and Knowledge Environments. LNCS, vol. 3379, pp. 251–260. Springer, Heidelberg (2005). doi:10.1007/978-3-540-31842-2_25
12. Bogdanov, E.: Widgets and spaces: personal & contextual portability and plasticity with opensocial. Ph.D. thesis. Ecole Polytechnique Federale de Lausanne (EPFL), August 2013
13. Pinelle, D., Gutwin, C.: A groupware design framework for loosely coupled workgroups. In: Gellersen, H., Schmidt, K., Beaudouin-Lafon, M., Mackay, W. (eds.) ECSCW 2005. Springer, Dordrecht (2005). doi:10.1007/1-4020-4023-7_4. ISBN: 1-4020-4022-9
14. Henri ter Hofte, G.: Working apart together -foundations for component groupware. Ph.D. thesis. Telematica Instituut, Enschede, the Netherlands (1998). ISBN: 90-75176-14-7
15. Farias, C.R.G., Gonçalves, C.E., Rosatelli, M.C., Pires, L.F., Sinderen, M.: An architectural model for component groupware. In: Fukś, H., Lukosch, S., Salgado, A.C. (eds.) CRIWG 2005. LNCS, vol. 3706, pp. 105–120. Springer, Heidelberg (2005). doi:10.1007/11560296_8

Factors Affecting the Willingness to Share Knowledge in the Communities of Practice

Vivek Agrawal$^{(\boxtimes)}$ and Einar Arthur Snekkenes

Department of Information Security and Communication Technology,
Norwegian University of Science and Technology,
Teknologivegen 22, Gjøvik, Norway
{vivek.agrawal,einar.snekkenes}@ntnu.no

Abstract. The purpose of this study is to investigate various factors that can affect the willingness of the IT professionals in Norway to share their knowledge in the open communities of practice. The study is conducted through an online survey among the IT professionals working in Norway. The findings of the study present various factors that increase or decrease the willingness to share knowledge on open communities of practice. These factors are further explained with the help of the descriptive theories. The findings of this study are useful to get the initial insight into the determinants that influence the willingness to share knowledge on the communities of practice.

Keywords: Communities of practice · Information sharing · Knowledge · Motivation · Trust

1 Introduction

The IT professionals working in different organizations in Norway often face many of the same problems and design similar solutions. The IT professionals also collect and apply the same knowledge to design their solutions. However, it is inefficient if they do it so largely on their own [7]. Therefore, proper sharing and reuse of knowledge among the IT professionals can improve the quality of their work [20]. We believe that open communities of practice (CoP) [23] can help achieving the IT professionals in Norway to an optimal level of knowledge sharing. Therefore, we explore the significance of communities of practice for the IT professionals in Norway in this study. There is a lack of studies on the willingness of the IT professionals in Norway to sharing knowledge on open communities of practice. To conduct the study, the prospective members from the industry and academia in Norway are invited to participate in an online survey to state their preference regarding the sharing of knowledge on CoP. We collected the response of the participants for the duration of six weeks. Our study provides insight into the factors that can increase or decrease one's willingness to share knowledge in communities of practice. We believe that these insights are essential to improve the current state of knowledge sharing. We are particularly interested in answering the following research question in this study:

© Springer International Publishing AG 2017
C. Gutwin et al. (Eds.): CRIWG 2017, LNCS 10391, pp. 32–39, 2017.
DOI: 10.1007/978-3-319-63874-4_3

What are the factors that influence the willingness of the professionals working in Norway to share their knowledge in the open communities of practice?

CoP is a common way to engage professionals in sharing knowledge, discuss issues, and learn from others' experience to resolve several challenges in many organizations. CoP often focus on sharing best practices and creating new knowledge to advance a domain of professional practice. However, the community members often tend to hide the information or not share with others if they perceive that the knowledge they possess is valuable and important [3]. Therefore, it is imperative to determine the factors that act as a motivation or barrier for the IT professionals to share knowledge with others in a community-based information sharing arena. This study contributes to our understanding of the motivation and barriers that IT professionals in Norway face in sharing knowledge on the *open* CoP. CoP that exist as a *closed internal* or *joint venture* are not considered as a part of this study. We are more interested to learn about the preferences of the members towards the CoP where the membership is not dependent on the member's affiliation. In this study, knowledge refers to all professional information i.e. income, affiliation, ability to learn a concept, critical thinking, problem-solving ability.

2   Related Work

The term 'communities of practice' is a relatively new term in the area of knowing and learning, but the phenomenon it refers to has a very old existence [23]. According to Wenger [22], *"Communities of practice are groups of people who share a concern or a passion for something they do and learn how to do it better as they interact regularly."* Knowledge sharing is a process that exploits existing knowledge by identifying, transferring and applying to solve tasks better, faster and cheaper [12]. Knowledge sharing is essential for the innovation in organization and the individual. Cabrera et al. [5] presented several difficulties that an organization faces in encouraging its employees to share knowledge with co-employees and presented several knowledge-sharing dilemmas. Ardichvili et al. [3] conducted a qualitative study to investigate the motivation and barriers to employee participation in online communities of practice at Caterpillar Inc. This study revealed that the members of the community are skeptical towards knowledge sharing because of the fear of criticism or misleading others. There are several studies [9,15] that explored the role of trust with the context of professional online communities. Gagné [8] presented a model of knowledge-sharing motivation based on a combination of the theory of planned behavior (TPB) and self-determination theory (SDT). He argues that more positive attitudes toward knowledge sharing can be achieved out of interest or personal meaning. The influence of culture on the knowledge sharing strategies in online CoP is studied in [4].

3   Research Method

In this study, the determinants, which increase and decrease the willingness to share knowledge on CoP, are drawn by the response stated by the respondents. An online survey-based technique is designed to collect the preference of the professionals working in IT-industry in Norway.

A free open source software survey tool, LimeSurvey, was chosen to create an online quantitative questionnaire survey. The survey was hosted on our project domain. The survey comprised of 39 questions[1] in total that assessed various aspects of information sharing and previous experiences with CoPs. The survey was distributed online through several media from 28.11.2016 to 10.01.2017. The online survey was available in both English and Norwegian. Seven-point Likert-type scales ranging from '1' (Not at all) to '7' (Extremely) were used throughout the questionnaire. The idea of using a Likert-type scale to conduct this survey is derived from the work of [18], and the range of scale (1–7) is selected based on the argument given in [1].

A total of 52 respondents (43 males, 8 females, 1 undisclosed) volunteered to complete all the sections of the online survey. The majority of the respondents were between the ages of 25–34 years (34.6%). The majority (about 76.9%) of the participants are affiliated with a university and industry. However, the survey does not include student as a potential participant as we are interested in getting the opinion of the professionals for this study.

We used IBM SPSS Statistics 24 (licensed) to analyze the survey response. We used median or mode to compare the response, and assign a weight for the survey questions that involve answers on the numerical rating scale (1 = Not at all, 7 = Extremely). The mathematical model in our survey design assumes that the interval between values is not interpretable (i.e. the distance between 1–2 is not the same as the distance between 6–7). Therefore, calculating mean or standard deviation of the given data is not a suitable approach to building any conclusion.

4   Research Findings

In this section, the result of survey response is presented to get an insight into the research questions.

4.1   Participation in CoP

Out of 52 respondents, 28 respondents have already participated in CoP. The other 22 members stated that they want to join a CoP. The remaining two respondents neither participated nor they want to participate in any CoP. Among the 28 respondents who have participated in a CoP previously, 43% have participated in the online CoP (web portal, online forum), whereas only 11% have taken part in the offline CoP in the form of face to face discussion.

---

[1] Survey link: https://www.unrizk.org/survey/index.php/346746?lang=en.

Table 1. Participation of respondents on different types of CoP

Nature of the community	Percent
Both online and offline	43
Offline	11
Online	43
Other	4

Table 1 gives the information that there are a few respondents who have participated in both online and offline form in the community.

The respondents, who stated that they have participated (n = 28) in a community of practice before, were asked to state the domain of the community.

Table 2. Domains of the community where the respondents participated

Domain of the CoP	Percent
Information security	33
Other	26
Software engineering	14
IT management	12
Web development	6
Safety	3
Online marketing	3
Journalism	3

Table 2 displays that most of the respondents (33%) have participated in Information security community, 15% of the respondents have participated in software engineering community. The respondents have also mentioned the communities that were not given in the questionnaire options. For instance, knowledge formation in the organization, building rules and regulation of the organization.

4.2   Factors Increase Willingness to Share Knowledge

Respondents were asked to rate different factors that increase their willingness to share knowledge with others on the scale of 1–7 (Likert scale). Figure 1a displays the graph representing the distribution of median of various factors. Respondents stated that having trust with the receiver of the information, and meeting the person face to face are the most important factors that increase their willingness to share knowledge. The presence of a privacy policy that includes the detail about how the shared knowledge can be treated and used is also important for the participants. The respondents also stated that an incentive (Useful knowledge, money, fame, reward) is necessary to encourage them to share knowledge. Having an incentive system gives them a better perspective of high return on investment, where the investment is an apparent effort, time, and giving out knowledge. According to our study, anonymity and the presence of online platform do not contribute much toward increasing the willingness to share knowledge.

4.3   Barriers to Share Information

Figure 1b shows the median distribution of different factors that act as a barrier to sharing knowledge in the community. The higher the value on the median scale the stronger the given factor serves as a barrier to sharing knowledge. The biggest barrier that was stated by the respondent is the breach of confidentiality. The participants of the community may share something that is very useful for the receivers, but at the same time can contain some sensitive information. The leakage of the confidential/sensitive information can harm the individual. The second biggest barrier is the concern of privacy breach by participating in the knowledge sharing task in the community. A few respondents indicated that they do not share information if they feel that they will lose the competitive advantage by sharing it. The concern of receiving irrelevant information from the others also lower down the willingness to share something useful with others. The presence of limited IT resources is also a major barrier for a few respondents. The respondents have indicated the effect of culture as a barrier as very low.

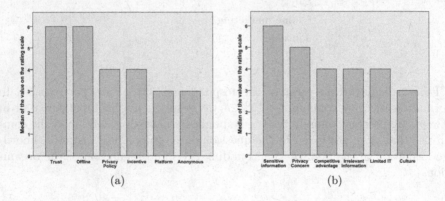

Fig. 1. (a) Factors increase the willingness to share professional information (b) barriers to share professional information

5   Discussion

The main objective of the present study was to identify and understand the determinants of knowledge sharing task on communities of practice. The survey results indicate the influence of social exchange theory (SET); people are concerned about the absence of any benefits to share knowledge. People tend to share the knowledge they possess with others when they feel that they will also receive quality information from others. However, the tendency to share knowledge decreases when it is perceived that they are receiving irrelevant or not so useful information from other members. In this study, respondents indicated that from their experience, the communities did not score well in providing meaningful incentives to the members. Therefore, it is important for a CoP to design the incentive schemes to enhance knowledge sharing practice in the community.

In our study, we considered the *competence* and *integrity* aspects of trust to understand the preference of the respondents towards knowledge sharing tasks in CoP [19]. The benevolence-based trust considers the self-motivation through a sense of moral obligation to become a part of a community. Therefore, the individual that receives the knowledge in the community does not play a major role in influencing benevolence-trust of the person willing to share the knowledge. However, we are more interested in understanding the role of the trust established based on the action of the person receiving the knowledge, and not just on the basis of self-motivation.

We can also see the effect of social presence theory (SPT) [17] in the setting of learning in communities of practice. The presence of other participants in CoP is important because it enables direct or indirect contact with others. The effect of SPT in the knowledge sharing behavior of the members of the virtual community and computer-mediated communication is explored by [10]. In this study, we can see that survey participant indicated that they prefer to communicate with trusted party, whether face-to-face (offline) or by any other means. The perception of the high degree of social presence and having direct or indirect human contact contribute to the building of trust.

Knowledge is highly personal to an individual or a team [6]. There are several ways that people understand the meaning of privacy. In this study, we define privacy as *"control over the flow of one's personal information, including the transfer and exchange of that information"* [16]. People who perceive higher threats to privacy are less willing to disclose information about themselves as they have the fear to lose control on the information on the electronic platform [11]. In contrast, when the privacy policies are communicated and enforced, people perceive lower privacy risks, and they are willing to share more information [21]. The result of data analysis in this study affirms that the privacy concerns can act as the major barrier to sharing knowledge, and the presence of privacy policy increase the willingness to share knowledge with the members of the community.

In our study, respondents were asked to state the influence of security on their knowledge sharing willingness in a CoP. The respondents in our study indicated that the lack of security, leakage of sensitive information act as the most severe barrier to their knowledge sharing willingness on CoP. However, our findings contradict the success of StackOverflow, a community of over 4 million programmers asking questions and providing answers in the field of Information Technology. In 2016, StackOverflow exposed the email addresses and phone numbers of the members of the community at inappropriate places due to a bug in their system [13] yet they succeed to pull experts from all across the globe to the community. Researchers argued that reputation [2] and emotion [14] play a major role in encouraging people to use StackOverflow.

6 Research Limitations and Future Work

We used an online self-administered survey to collect response from the prospective members of UnRizkNow. Therefore, the questionnaire could be interpreted by the respondents according to their understanding in the given area, and it could influence their response. Furthermore, we collected the data from the participants who volunteered for it. It signifies that the response is collected from the people who had enough time and interest to complete the survey. The result might have differed if we had selected the participants randomly. However, the recruitment process that we used in this study could not provide the provision to select the sample randomly. The study also inherits the limitation on the honesty of free-willed respondents. This is the main reason that we always considered the response stated by the respondents as 'stated preference'. The 'revealed preference' can be collected only through empirical study i.e. by direct or indirect observation. Future research could endeavor to carry out this research approach.

Acknowledgment. This study is a part of UnRizkNow project, which is partially funded by CCIS. Adam Szekeres provided his useful input to formulate the questionnaire. Martin Stokkenes and Gaute Wangen helped us to translate the online questionnaire to Norwegian Language. NorSIS supported our research work by distributing the survey to the people in industry in Norway.

References

1. Alwin, D.F., Krosnick, J.A.: The measurement of values in surveys: a comparison of ratings and rankings. Pub. Opin. Q. **49**(4), 535–552 (1985)
2. Anderson, A., Huttenlocher, D., Kleinberg, J., Leskovec, J.: Discovering value from community activity on focused question answering sites: a case study of stack overflow. In: Proceedings of the 18th ACM SIGKDD International Conference on Knowledge Discovery and Data Mining, KDD 2012, pp. 850–858. ACM, New York (2012)
3. Ardichvili, A., Page, V., Wentling, T.: Motivation and barriers to participation in virtual knowledge-sharing communities of practice. J. Knowl. Manag. **7**(1), 64–77 (2003)
4. Ardichvili, A., Maurer, M., Li, W., Wentling, T., Stuedemann, R.: Cultural influences on knowledge sharing through online communities of practice. J. Knowl. Manag. **10**(1), 94–107 (2006)
5. Cabrera, A., Cabrera, E.F.: Knowledge-sharing dilemmas. Organ. Stud. **23**(5), 687–710 (2002)
6. Davenport, T.H., Prusak, L., Prusak, L.: Working Knowledge: How Organizations Manage What They Know. Harvard Business School Press, Boston (1997)
7. Fenz, S., Parkin, S., Moorsel, A.V.: A community knowledge base for it security. IT Prof. **13**(3), 24–30 (2011)

8. Gagné, M.: A model of knowledge-sharing motivation. Hum. Resour. Manag. **48**(4), 571 (2009)
9. Gefen, D., Karahanna, E., Straub, D.W.: Trust and tam in online shopping: an integrated model. MIS Q. Manag. Inf. Syst. **27**(1), 51–90 (2003). Cited by 2452
10. Gunawardena, C.N.: Social presence theory and implications for interaction and collaborative learning in computer conferences. Int. J. Educ. Telecommun. **1**(2), 147–166 (1995)
11. Gupta, A., Dhami, A.: Measuring the impact of security, trust and privacy in information sharing: a study on social networking sites. J. Direct Data Digit. Market. Pract. **17**(1), 43–53 (2015)
12. Christensen, P.H.: Knowledge sharing: moving away from the obsession with best practices. J. Knowl. Manag. **11**(1), 36–47 (2007)
13. NaXa: Sensitive info disclosure (2016). https://meta.stackoverflow.com/questions/338573/sensitive-info-disclosure. Accessed 15 Mar 2017
14. Novielli, N., Calefato, F., Lanubile, F.: Towards discovering the role of emotions in stack overflow. In: Proceedings of the 6th International Workshop on Social Software Engineering, SSE 2014, pp. 33–36. ACM, New York (2014)
15. Ratnasingam, P.: Trust in inter-organizational exchanges: a case study in business to business electronic commerce. Decis. Support Syst. **39**(3), 525–544 (2005). Cited by 87
16. Shin, D.-H.: The effects of trust, security and privacy in social networking: a security-based approach to understand the pattern of adoption. Interact. Comput. **22**(5), 428–438 (2010)
17. Short, J., Williams, E., Christie, B.: The Social Psychology of Telecommunications. Wiley, Chichester (1976)
18. Tamjidyamcholo, A., Baba, M.S.B., Shuib, N.L.M., Rohani, V.A.: Evaluation model for knowledge sharing in information security professional virtual community. Comput. Secur. **43**, 19–34 (2014)
19. Usoro, A., Sharratt, M.W., Tsui, E., Shekhar, S.: Trust as an antecedent to knowledge sharing in virtual communities of practice. Knowl. Manag. Res. Pract. **5**(3), 199–212 (2007)
20. Von Krogh, G.: Care in knowledge creation. Calif. Manag. Rev. **40**(3), 133–153 (1998)
21. Weber, R.H.: Internet of Things - need for a new legal environment? Comput. Law Secur. Rev. **25**(6), 522–527 (2009)
22. Wenger, E.: Communities of Practice: Learning, Meaning, and Identity. Cambridge University Press, Cambridge (1998)
23. Wenger, E., McDermott, R., Snyder, W.: Cultivating Communities of Practice: A Guide to Managing Knowledge. Harvard Business School Press, Boston (2002)

U-Learning: A Collaborative Experience in the Urban Context

Josilene Almeida Brito[1,2(✉)], Bruno de Sousa Monteiro[4(✉)], Alex Sandro Gomes[2(✉)],
Ricardo José Rocha Amorim[3(✉)], Luma da Rocha Seixas[2(✉)],
and Ivanildo José de Melo Filho[2,5(✉)]

[1] IF-SERTÃO – Federal Institute of Sertão Pernambucano, Floresta, Brazil
josilene.brito@ifsertao-pe.edu.br
[2] UFPE – Federal University of Pernambuco, Informatics Center, Recife, Brazil
{asg,lrs3}@cin.ufpe.br
[3] UNEB – University of State of Bahia, Education Department, Senhor do Bomfim, Brazil
amorim.ricardo@gmail.com
[4] UFERSA – Federal Rural University of the Semiarid Region, Mossoró, Brazil
brunomonteiro@ufersa.edu.br
[5] IFPE – Federal Institute of Pernambuco – Belo Jardim Campus, Belo Jardim, Brazil
ivanildo.melo@belojardim.ifpe.edu.br

Abstract. Mobile and ubiquitous technologies provide new learning experiences anytime, anywhere. In this type of learning mode, there are mechanisms that combine real scenarios with ubiquitous technologies, favoring a greater and meaningful exchange between individuals and groups through collaboration. In this sense, this study introduces an experience in the urban context supported by an u-learning environment in professional education. We used a ubiquitous learning platform called Youubi to lead an experiment at a public vocational school in Brazil. The theory of meaningful learning was used to support the interpret knowledge construction phenomena presents in the ubiquitous learning situation. It was proposed learning situations that allowed the exchange of meanings, based on the teachers' planning based on the urbanization theme of the cities. The method was based on a hybrid-qualitative and quantitative analysis of ubiquitous learning in urban context. The results indicated that the features of the U-learning environment promoted collaboration around the didactic content outside the classroom in a dynamic way, allowing collaboration and knowledge sharing among those involved, mainly strengthening existing meanings and the perception of problems in life related to the proposed content.

Keywords: U-Learning · Significant learning · Learning strategies · Collaboration · Urban context · Youubi

1 Introduction

The popularization of immersive computing technologies in people's daily lives has changed communication practices and, consequently, expanding the possibilities of performing activities that allow students to relate acquired knowledge to real-world

© Springer International Publishing AG 2017
C. Gutwin et al. (Eds.): CRIWG 2017, LNCS 10391, pp. 40–48, 2017.
DOI: 10.1007/978-3-319-63874-4_4

problems. It is known that situations combining real learning resources with immersive and ubiquitous technologies can promote a better learning [1]. According to [2], u-learning is a paradigm that takes place in a ubiquitous computing environment, it allows teaching to happen "anywhere, anytime and right". While [3] reinforces that ubiquitous computing in the educational process augments the capacity to perceive both the situation and the states of the students to provide them adequate assistance. The u-learning paradigm is related with a context-awareness, this allows to recommend learning materials to students to meet their circumstantial needs in learning activities and everyday situations. In general, pedagogical experiences with ubiquitous technologies have been gradually applied in learning environments. For [4], a u-learning environment integrates computing, communication and devices with sensors incorporated into daily´s life in order to make learning even more immersive.

Several studies have demonstrated a growing interest in the development of u-learning [5–8]. Therefore, it is important to design tools to promote a greater interaction between the knowledge acquired in formal and informal learning situations. According to [4] with regard to these educational modalities, one of the most fragile points identified by different researchers is about the didactic-pedagogical questions in these environments. The author, states that it is not enough to have access to new and advanced technologies, it is necessary, above all, to know how to use them to provide learning. Consequently, inappropriate applications of u-learning may also lead with inefficient and ineffective learning practices. Thus, it is necessary to evaluate how an information system inserted in the learning processes can influence to reach the goals on meaningful learning.

The adoption of practices based on the Meaningful Learning Theory [9] has the purpose of designing learning situations that incorporate the connections between the knowledge absorbed in the classroom and the prior knowledge of concepts associated with the real environment. Thus, for students to learn significantly, they must be intentionally engaged in combining prior knowledge with acquired new knowledge [10]. Therefore, in view of these possibilities and challenges, the present work describes a ubiquitous meaningful learning approach based on practices using didactic learning situations in individual form or in a group using learning challenges supported by ubiquitous learning environment called Youubi [11]. In this direction, a experiment was conducted to investigate the following question: (1) Practices guided by ubiquitous learning activities in the form of learning challenges, modeled on the theory of meaningful learning, promote collaboration between groups to achieve meaningful learning?

2 Ubiquitous Learning Environment Youubi

According to [11], the Youubi system is composed of a client-server architecture. The Youubi API, implemented over a webservice, provides 63 post methods and 69 get methods. These services allow developers to build client-applications with requirements of: social networking, content authoring, gamification, and recommendations based on user context. This last feature allows any content or group to be recommended to any other user, not just the friends' stuff. In addition, anyone can be recommended, not just friends-of-friends.

Youubi considers as context the following variables: static profile information (name, age, course, profession and gender), privacy preferences, user geographical coordinates, user movement speed, device state (battery, screen, connection and operating system), list of friends, list of contents that was interacted, list of hash-tags and subjects of interest.

To better understand future possible scenarios with Youubi, it is important to understand its elementary entities. They refer to entities of the data model that represent users (Person) and other objects (Post, Event, Question, Place, Group, and Mission) that can be created and manipulated by users. All these entities have geolocation attributes and can be represented by a QR code. This association allows them to point to a real places. Besides these attributes, there are other more common ones, such as, title, description, URL and image.

Person: is the central entity of the data model and represents each user. It has simple attributes and relationship attributes to represent its static and dynamic context. There are three types of roles for the Person entity: admin, moderator, and simple user. It is also important to note that a user can view the profile and send asynchronous private messages to another user.

Post: represents a simple content that can be created, commented, rated, checked-in and shared in a group by users.

Event: represents an event in time that can be created, commented, rated, checked-in, and shared in a group by the user. Its adoption is based on self-regulation strategies and self-direct learning [12].

Place: represents a geographic place that can be created, commented, rated, checked-in, and shared in a group by users.

Question: represents a question that can be created, commented, rated, checked-in, shared in a group, and answered by the user. It allows the development of ludic practices based on the principles of active learning [13] and gamification strategies [14].

Group: organizes a group of people who create and share information, such as messages, posts, events, places, and questions. A group can be created, rated, checked-in, and requested (to join) by the user. In addition, there are two types of group: closed (author can allow new members) and open (anyone can be a member). This entity allows practices based on social interactionist theory [15] and situated cognition.

Mission: represents a trail of contents related to certain action. For example, in a single mission it would be possible to check-in, rate or comment on places and contents, as well as answer questions. In other words, a mission encapsulates a set of element-action.

The entire set of user interactions is computed by the server-side. This feature allows it to provide gamification services, such as: ranking (for all elementary entities), achievement medals, user experience points and relevance points (popularity and quality) for contents.

In addition, due to the entry of all interactions, moderators can consult details about "realized interactions" by users and data about "suffered interactions" by the objects of all elementary entities of the system. This type of feature is important for scenarios where the teacher can easily monitor students' actions and interests and act more accurately.

For this experiment, a client-application for smartphones and tablets was implemented. It was developed for Android operational system and consumes the services of the Youubi API and uses the elementary entities described above (except Mission because it was a feature developed after the experiment).

This application allows coordinate learning scenarios in which teachers and students interact in ubiquitous learning situations throughout the urban space. Some examples of Android Youubi screens are shown in Fig. 1.

| a) Questions recommended | b) Map | c) Ranking |

Fig. 1. Screen examples from Youubi Android.

3   Method

To evaluate the effectiveness of the proposed approach and evaluate how the proposed practices can fostering meaningful learning. It was planned and applied an experimental approach using quantitative and qualitative measures, participant data generation analysis from the capture of many aspects of the behavior in the ubiquitous learning situations supported by the Youubi applications. In the following section are described: context and participants, procedures and data collection and analysis.

3.1   Context and Participants

The context of the study was the urban area of the city of Petrolina, Northeast of Brazil. The institution was the federal public school involved in this research. The educational environments were technical vocational courses. A total of eighteen students from a technical vocational Computer Science course and twenty students from a technical vocational Chemistry course. The average age of the students was nineteen years old.

The activities were conduct by a teacher of Geography, both of class were conducted independently, for this, two groups: Computer Science and Chemistry followed the same didactic situations and discussed topics related to urbanization with focus "Hydrography and Biome".

3.2 Procedures

This proposed approach model is experimental and it consists of three phases. According the theory of meaningful learning, the first one corresponded the application of a pre-test in order to identify the previous knowledge of the students. The second phase involved the execution of the experiment using the Youubi environment. Finally, in a third phase, the post-test document was applied. The learners were initially instructed on basic knowledge about "Hydrography and Biome". Then they answered the pre-test survey to analyze the prior knowledge regarding the subject in matter. This prior data collection happened before any interaction with the Youubi applications. Just after performing this initial pre-test, both groups received initial training on Youubi client functionalities and the didactical u-learning situations were designed considering this scenario.

The students were invited to solve some challenges previously elaborated by their teachers. They could answer quizzes, search for objects and classmates nearby, read QR code tags related to some content and interact with which other thought the application. After that, they were invited to create and share their own contents using the application. Among the activities, the learners had to accomplish some missions such as: take pictures that illustrate urban problems and post it using the environment, create their own challenges to defy classmates and new learning objects using the Youubi functionalities related to the topics used to discuss in their formal learning experiences. Those activities were designed to stimulate students to observe and gather information about their urban context, build new meanings and share with their classmates. Even using Youubi at home and around the city, they had to use it at school with teachers' guidance.

3.3 Data Collection

The measuring instruments and techniques in this study were: (1) Pretest survey to capture students' prior knowledge; (2) User interaction logs generated at Youubi server-side; (3) Meaningful learning questionnaire proposed [16] and (4) Posttest survey. The pre-test was composed of five open questions developed to evaluate the prior knowledge about the "Urbanization Process" and "Relationship between urban space and rural space for the development of a country". The students' learning activities were assessed according to the pre-test and post-test questionnaires. For this, the teacher used the following criteria in the answers reported by the students: CC (completely constructed, or 100%), CP (partially constructed, or 70%), EC (constructed wrong, or 50%), and NC (not constructed, 0%).

At the end of all activities, the user's interactions logs were collected from the Youubi server database.

Lastly we analyzed the answers from the questionnaire investigating the dimensions of significant learning [16]: active (Q1, Q2, Q3), cooperative (Q4, Q5, Q6), authentic (Q7, Q8, Q9), constructive (Q10, Q11, Q12) and customized (Q13, Q14, Q15), using Likert scale (5 = Strongly Agree, 4 = Agree, 3 = Neutral, 2 = Disagree, 1 = Strongly Disagree). Cluster analysis was adopted, using the hierarchical clustering algorithm, with the objective of grouping and classifying apprentices by groups.

4 Results

4.1 Evaluating the Didactic Strategy of Ubiquitous Learning

From 28 learners who answered the pretest survey, 20 of them declared had not yet constructed previous knowledge on "Urban space in the contemporary world", content from Geography syllabus. Only 7 learners declared had mistakenly constructed knowledge about it. Others 1 ones declared had partially constructed. It was verifying a low level of previous knowledge construction among the majority learners. The users' interactions data were collected in the Youubi server.

Posting, responding and creating are actions to construct comment and involves a greater cognitive load. Posting was very frequent among the group (n = 513). Even more frequently are reasoning in responding (n = 918). Creating new learning challenges are less frequently (n = 83). The performance indicators are another important and motivating element that can be consulted and monitored in real time by users of the environment, they are organized in the form of ranking. The environment was adequate to verify performance indicators. Learners and teachers can monitor the interactivity episodes and have immediate access to performance results anywhere, anytime through the real-time environment-generated ranking.

4.2 Comparison of Profiles According to the Frequency of the Dimensions of Meaningful Learning

We analyzed the answers from the questionnaire investigating the dimensions of significant learning [16]: active (Q1, Q2, Q3), cooperative (Q4, Q5, Q6), authentic (Q7, Q8, Q9), constructive (Q10, Q11, Q12) and customized (Q13, Q14, Q15). Cluster analysis was adopted, using the hierarchical clustering algorithm, with the objective of grouping and classifying apprentices by groups (Table 1).

Table 1. Average of the proficiency indicators of the apprentices for the four (4) identified groups. Source: Own author.

	Active			Cooperative			Authentic			Constructive			Customized		
	Q1	Q2	Q3	Q4	Q5	Q6	Q7	Q8	Q9	Q10	Q11	Q12	Q13	Q14	Q15
G I	3	3,25	3	3	3,5	3,25	3,25	3,25	3	2,5	2,75	2	3	3,25	3,5
G II	4,57	4,71	4,86	4,71	5,00	5,00	5,00	4,71	5,00	4,86	4,86	4,57	5,00	4,29	4,14
G III	4,00	4,09	4,00	4,18	4,36	4,55	4,09	4,09	4,18	4,45	3,82	3,82	3,55	4,09	4,00
G IV	4,00	4,00	3,67	4,67	4,50	4,50	4,17	3,83	4,00	4,17	4,33	3,83	3,50	2,83	3,00

Of the four groups formed, the apprentices belonging to **group II** obtained higher averages in the five dimensions analyzed. In this group, the most evident dimensions were **cooperative** and **authentic**. Then, group III, with a larger group of apprentices, also obtained higher averages the cooperative and authentic dimensions, and with a lower average the customized dimension. However, group IV, with approximate means to group III, obtained higher averages in the cooperative and constructive dimensions, with the smaller the customized dimension.

Finally, the group I that obtained lower averages in its groupings for the five dimensions. The dimension, with the highest average for the group, was the **cooperative** and **personalized** dimension and the dimension that obtained the lowest mean was **constructive**.

The learners pointed out the sharing of discussions with colleagues and the exchange of knowledge in learning activities, as well as the authenticity in observing and learning with authentic materials related to the environment. We can conclude that the learning strategies used in the experiment allowed an authentic, more collaborative and constructive learning for the groups of learners involved in the experiment.

4.3   Evolutionary Learning Outcomes for Apprentices Between the Pretest and Posttest

Posttest According to Significant Learning Theory, to assess the level of student learning, it is necessary to identify prior knowledge about the new content. The graph in Fig. 2 shows the evolution in the apprehension process of the involved students who migrated from the categorization of non-constructed CC to build CP and constructed CC.

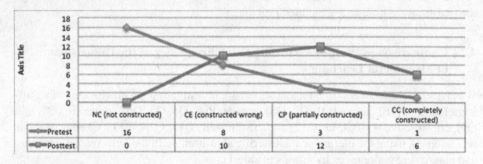

Fig. 2.   Comparing the previous knowledge of apprentices about urbanization with the posttest.

Thus, in context-sensitive learning, students learn through the experiences of interpreting new information and relate it to what they already know. For example, students interact with information in the vicinity of the classroom, related to the subject studied in the classroom.

5   Conclusions

In this paper, we analyzed the practice of ubiquitous learning activities in the form of learning challenges, modeled on the theory of meaningful learning, through the Youubi learning environment, in a technical training course. To evaluate it, we proposed ubiquitous learning strategies using learning challenges, geolocation features, and QR code tags. Experimental results show that these learning strategies can significantly improve collaborative learning.

The learners pointed out the sharing of discussions with colleagues and the exchange of knowledge in learning activities, as well as the authenticity in observing and learning with authentic materials related to the environment.

As well as the ubiquitous learning environment Youubi fostered practices guided by learning activities with more flexibility of time and space to seek knowledge, allowing a greater motivation and exchange of students' knowledge in their learning process, they use flexibility Time and space and immersive technologies, to seek knowledge under the most diverse digital forms available in their environments.

It was possible to have evidence of a behavioral profile of the learners when performing learning activities in a ubiquitous learning environment, where they perceived a profile with predominant characteristics of active, collaborative, cooperative and intentional.

References

1. Ogata, H., Yano, Y.: Context-aware support for computer-supported ubiquitous learning. In: Proceedings of the 2nd IEEE International Workshop on Wireless and Mobile Technologies in Education, pp. 27–34. IEEE (2004)
2. Yahya, S., Arniza, A.E., Jalil, K.A.: The definition and characteristics of ubiquitous learning: a discussion. Int. J. Educ. Dev. Inf. Commun. Technol. (IJEDICT) 6(1), 117–127 (2010)
3. Huang, Y.M., Lin, Y.T., Cheng, S.C.: Effectiveness of a mobile plant learning system in a science curriculum in Taiwanese elementary education. Comput. Educ. 54(1), 47–58 (2010)
4. Saccol, A.: M-learning e u-learning: novas perspectivas das aprendizagens móvel e ubíqua. Pearson Prentice Hall, São Paulo (2011). Saccol, A., Schlemmer, E., Barbosa, J. ISBN 978-85-7605-377-4
5. Hwang, G.-J., Chu, H.-C., Lin, Y.-S., Tsai, C.-C.: A knowledge acquisition approach to developing mindtools for organizing and sharing differentiating knowledge in a ubiquitous learning environment. Comput. Educ. 57(1), 1368–1377 (2011)
6. Wu, W.H., Wu, Y.C.J., Chen, C.Y., Kao, H.Y., Lin, C.H., Huang, S.H.: Review of trends from mobile learning studies: a meta-analysis. Comput. Educ. 59(2), 817–827 (2012)
7. Johnson, L., Adams, S., Cummins, M.: The NMC Horizon Report: 2012 Higher Education edn. The New Media Consortium, Austin (2013). http://www.nmc.org/nmc-horizon/. Accessed 28 Nov 2016
8. Martin, S., et al.: State of the art of frameworks and middleware for facilitating mobile and ubiquitous learning development. J. Syst. Softw. 84(11), 1883–1891 (2011)
9. Ausubel, D.P.: The psychology of meaningful verbal learning. Calif. Med. 99(6), 434 (1963)
10. Cadorin, L.: Meaningful learning in healthcare professionals: integrative review and concept analysis. In: The European Conference on Education, Brighton, UK (2013)
11. Monteiro, B.S.: Ambiente de aprendizado ubíquo youubi: design e avaliação, p. 2014. Tese de doutorado. UFPE, Recife (2015)
12. El-Bishouty, M.M., Ogata, H., Ayala, G., Yano, Y.: Context-aware support for self-directed ubiquitous-learning. Int. J. Mob. Learn. Organ. 4(3), 317–331 (2010)
13. Prince, M.: Does active learning work? A review of the research. J. Eng. Educ. 93(3), 223–231 (2004)
14. Rocha Seixas, L., Gomes, A.S., de Melo Filho, I.J.: Effectiveness of gamification in the engagement of students. Comput. Hum. Behav. 58, 48–63 (2016)

48　　J.A. Brito et al.

15. Vigotski, L.S.: A formação social da mente. Martins Fontes 2007, São Paulo (2012)
16. Huang, Y.M., Chiu, P.S., Liu, T.C., Chen, T.S.: The design and implementation of a meaningful learning-based evaluation method for ubiquitous learning. Comput. Educ. **57**(4), 2291–2302 (2011)

Susceptibility of Users to Social Influence Strategies and the Influence of Culture in a Q&A Collaborative Learning Environment

Ifeoma Adaji$^{(\boxtimes)}$ and Julita Vassileva

Department of Computer Science, University of Saskatchewan,
110 Science Place, Saskatoon, Saskatchewan, Canada
Ifeoma.adaji@usask.ca, jiv@cs.usask.ca

Abstract. Q&A collaborative learning environments such as Stack Overflow are more effective when its users actively participate by asking one another for information, providing good answers to existing questions, and evaluating others. One way to encourage participation is to allow cooperation between users in order to improve question and answer posts and allow users to learn from one another. Research has shown that cooperation between users results in high quality question and answer posts which are required to keep the network active. In order to better understand what influences users to cooperate, we investigate the susceptibility of users to social support influence principles in a Q&A collaborative learning environment, and what factors persuade users to keep using the network. Using Stack Overflow as a case study and a sample size of 282 Stack Overflow users, we develop and test a global research model using partial least-squares structural equation modelling (PLS-SEM) analysis. We further investigate any possible differences in the effect of these social support strategies between cultures by testing two cultural subgroups for collectivist and individualist cultures. Our results show that of all the constructs measured, only social learning significantly influences cooperation in Stack Overflow at the global level. However, at the cultural subgroup level, recognition influences collectivists to cooperate, while social facilitation influences individualists to cooperate. These findings suggest possible design guidelines in the development of Q&A collaborative learning environments that encourage participation through cooperation.

Keywords: Social influence · Persuasive strategies · Collaborative learning

1 Introduction

With the increasing number of programing languages and the dynamic nature of information technology, many people look up to question and answer (Q&A) collaborative learning environments for answers to their IT questions. The advantage of using a Q&A network like Stack Overflow is that users can ask specific questions addressed to other users in the community and will likely receive up to date answers. In addition, users can communicate with the answerer of their questions if they need further

© Springer International Publishing AG 2017
C. Gutwin et al. (Eds.): CRIWG 2017, LNCS 10391, pp. 49–64, 2017.
DOI: 10.1007/978-3-319-63874-4_5

clarification, while possible answerers can also contact them if the question asked was not clear enough [1].

One way to keep Q&A collaborative learning environments active is by posting quality answers [2]. If users consistently get good answers to their questions, it is likely that such users will remain in the network. Collaboration between users has been shown to produce high quality answers [3]. Collaboration in Stack Overflow exists in the form of editing existing question and answer posts to make them better [3]. Since high quality answer posts results in an active Q&A network [2], it is important to identify what influences users to cooperate in Q&A collaborative environments in order to motivate other users to collaborate more and keep the network active.

Stack Overflow implements influence strategies to encourage participation by users in the network [4]. For example, users can earn reputation points, rewards and privileges for being especially helpful in the community. Research has shown that to increase the efficacy of persuasive strategies, they have to be personalized [5, 6]. The use of culture has been identified as a reliable approach to group-based personalization [6]. Its use has been explored in other domains like finance [7] and health [6]. However, the effect of culture on social support influence strategies in a Q&A collaborative learning social network has not been explored.

Research in information seeking suggests that social relationships are often strong indicators of the choice of who one cooperates with [8]. This research aims to (1) understand what social support influence strategies motivate users in a Q&A collaborative learning environment to cooperate and (2) explore any differences in the effect of these social support influence strategies based on the culture of the users.

Using Stack Overflow as a case study and a sample size of 282 Stack Overflow users, we studied the effect of social support influence strategies on the participants. We used the social support influence strategies of the Persuasive Systems Design (PSD) framework [9] which include social facilitation, social comparison, normative influence, social learning, cooperation, competition and recognition. We used these strategies because they motivate users in a system by leveraging social influence.

We developed and tested a global research model using partial least-squares structural equation modelling (PLS-SEM) analysis and the six social support determinants listed above. We further investigated any possible differences that exist between cultures by testing two cultural subgroups for collectivist and individualist cultures. The result of our analysis shows that of all the constructs measured, social learning significantly influences cooperation in Stack Overflow in the global model. In addition, cooperation and competition influence the perceived persuasiveness and use of Stack Overflow. However, at the cultural subgroup level, recognition influences the decision of collectivists to cooperate with others in the network, while social learning influences their perceived persuasiveness of the system and their desire to continue using the system. On the other hand, social facilitation influences individualists to cooperate, while cooperation influences their perceived persuasiveness of the system and their desire to continue using the system. These findings suggest possible design guidelines in the development of successful personalized Q&A collaborative learning environments that encourage participation through cooperation.

2 Related Work

2.1 Stack Overflow

Stack Overflow[1] is a typical Q&A collaborative learning environment where users participate by asking and answering specific IT related questions. Users can earn incentives such as reputation score, badges and privileges by providing high quality answers. While all users can upvote or downvote other users' questions and answers, only the user that asked a question can select the best answer to his/her question. Comments can also be upvoted or downvoted. Upvotes and downvotes contribute towards the reputation score of users. Badges in Stack Overflow are earned by users who are especially helpful in the community. Badges are awarded in several categories including question, answer, participation, tag and moderation badges. Users can collaborate with other users by editing existing questions and answers in order to improve them. However, in order to do so, users have to earn the privilege. Users can also cooperate with others by commenting on answers posted by others to improve them or to seek clarification [3].

This study was carried out using Stack Overflow because it currently has over seven million registered users[2] making participant recruitment possible.

2.2 Social Influence Strategies of the PSD Framework

The Persuasive Systems Design (PSD) framework [9] is a framework for designing and evaluating persuasive systems. It describes the content, software functionality and design principles that are required in the development and evaluation of persuasive systems. It consists of 28 persuasive principles that are highly recommended by the authors when designing, implementing and evaluating persuasive systems. These principles are categorized into four based on the task they aim to accomplish: primary task support principles support users of a system in achieving their primary objective or goal, dialogue support principles support computer-human dialogue that provides feedback to users while moving them towards their target behavior, system credibility support principles which persuade users through the design, look and feel of a system, and social support principles which influence users by leveraging social influence. Since Stack Overflow is a Q&A network where users learn from others, we carried out our study using only the social influence strategies of the PSD framework. These strategies are: social facilitation, social comparison, normative influence, social learning, cooperation, competition and recognition.

Social facilitation principles influence users to perform a target behavior by providing a means for discerning that other users are performing that behavior [10]. In a social context, people learn from others by observing them. This can lead to people evaluating each other, which can improve performance, speed and accuracy of

---

[1] www.stackoverflow.com.

[2] https://data.stackexchange.com/StackOverflow/revision/325050/420211/count-of-all-users-all-questions-and-all-answers.

well-practiced tasks [11]. Hence, social facilitation can influence behavior change in a social setting. Social comparison principles influence users to carry out a target behavior by allowing them compare their performance to others. People look to others for self-enhancement when comparing themselves to others who they are better than, or self-improvement when comparing themselves with others that are better than them [12]. Normative influence strategies leverage peer pressure, the influence of others, to persuade a person to carry out a target behavior. Because people tend to conform to the behavior of their peers in social settings in order to be liked and accepted, normative influence can lead to behavior change [13]. Social learning principles persuade users to perform a target behavior while observing others. Because people tend to learn from others by observing their behavior, social learning can lead to behavior change [14]. People typically cooperate in social settings when trying to achieve similar goals, therefore, they are likely to cooperate if it will help them in achieving a target behavior [15]. Humans compete when trying to gain what others are striving for. Providing measures through which different people can compare their performance in a social setting can lead to competition [16]. Recognition can be earned by gaining approval or acceptance from others. By being recognized in a social setting, a person is likely to be influenced to carry out a target behavior [9].

Because Stack Overflow is a Q&A collaborative learning network where users compete, cooperate and learn from others in a social context, we carried out our study using only the social influence strategies of the PSD framework.

3   Research Design and Methods Used

In order to investigate what influences users in Stack Overflow to cooperate and continue using the system, we developed a hypothetical path model using the social support influence principles of the PSD framework [9]. Our research model is made up of seven hypotheses and eight constructs shown as nodes in Fig. 1.

For all 8 constructs, we adopted previously tested and validated scales of Stibe and Oinas-Kukkonen [17]. The constructs are described in the following section.

3.1   Constructs and Hypotheses Definition

The constructs we used for this study are derived from the social influence strategies of the PSD framework and they include social facilitation, social comparison, normative influence, social learning, cooperation, competition and recognition.

Because Stack Overflow is a Q&A collaborative learning environment where people learn by asking and answering specific IT questions [18], we hypothesize that users are persuaded to use the system because they can learn from fellow IT professionals. People cooperate when they are working together to attain similar goals [15]. Since learning is the goal of several users in the network, we hypothesize that learning influences cooperation in Stack Overflow. Cooperation further influences the persuasiveness of the system to users because they cooperate when working to achieve the same goals [15]. Thus we propose the following hypotheses:

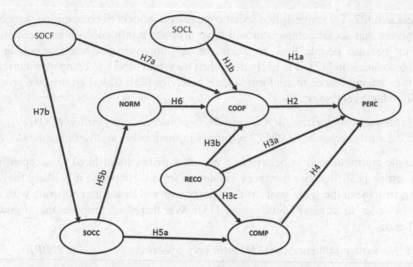

Fig. 1. Research model. All paths are assumed positive. SOCL = Social learning, SOCC = Social comparison, NORM = Normative influence, SOCF = Social facilitation, COOP = Cooperation, COMP = Competition, RECO = Recognition, PERC = Perceived persuasiveness

H1a: Social learning (SOCL) positively affects the perceived persuasiveness (PERC) of users in Stack overflow.
H1b: Social learning (SOCL) positively affects cooperation (COOP) among users in Stack overflow.
H2: Cooperation (COOP) positively affects the perceived persuasiveness (PERC) of users in Stack overflow.

Because recognition has been shown to result from competition and cooperation with others [19], we hypothesize that recognition influences the decision of users in Stack Overflow to compete and cooperate with others. In addition, recognition in Stack Overflow motivates users to use the network [20]. Hence, we propose the following hypotheses:

H3a: Recognition (RECO) influences perceived persuasiveness (PERC)
H3b: Recognition (RECO) positively influences cooperation (COOP)
H3c: Recognition positively (RECO) influences competition (COMP)

Competition in Stack Overflow is influenced by rewards users can earn [4]. For example, the "enlightened badge" is rewarded to the first person to answer a question with a score of at least 10 points and also accepted by the asker of the question as the best answer. Research shows a relationship between such rewards in Stack Overflow and the desire of users to participate in the network [21]. We therefore hypothesize that competition influences user's decision to use the network and propose the following hypothesis:

H4: Competition (COMP) positively affects the perceived persuasiveness (PERC) of users

Research [22, 17] suggests that social comparison influences competition, hence we hypothesize that social comparison will have a positive influence on competition. In addition, because people look at others for self-improvement when searching for positive comparison [12], it is likely that when they find others to compare themselves with, they are influenced to conform to their behavior [23]. Based on this, we propose the following hypotheses:

> H5a: Social comparison (SOCC) positively influences competition (COMP)
> H5b: Social comparison (SOCC) positively influences normative influence (NORM)

People are influenced to behave in a way that makes them liked or accepted in a social setting [13]. Because they seek validation from their peers, it is likely they are striving to achieve the same goals as their peers and will therefore cooperate with said peers in order to achieve those goals [15]. We therefore propose the following hypothesis:

> H6: Normative influence (NORM) positively affects cooperation (COOP)

According to Stibe and Oinas-Kukkonen [17], social facilitation has a direct influence on social comparison. According to the authors, in social settings, people tend to observe others and work with them or compare themselves to others. Hence we propose the following hypothesis:

> H7a: Social facilitation (SOCF) positively influences cooperation (COOP)
> H7b: Social facilitation (SOCF) positively influences social comparison (SOCC)

In addition to determining the validity or otherwise of these hypotheses, we also aim to explore any differences in the effect of these social influence strategies on culture.

3.2 Measurement Model of Constructs

To measure the eight constructs of interest described above, we adopted previously tested and validated scales of Stibe and Oinas-Kukkonen [17]. Each construct measured three items on a five-point Likert scale (1 = strongly disagree, 5 = strongly agree). The scale measure social learning using questions such as "Using Stack overflow has helped me learn from others". One of the questions measured by cooperation is "Stack Overflow allows users to cooperate". An example of a social comparison question asked is "I am able to compare others' performances in the system". Recognition includes questions such as "Users of Stack Overflow are publicly recognized for their participation". An example of a question measuring the perceived persuasiveness of the system is "Stack Overflow motivates me to participate". The complete list of constructs and questions were not included in this paper due to space constraints.

3.3 Description of Participants

We recruited participants for this study through Amazon's Mechanical Turk (AMT). AMT has become an accepted means of soliciting users' responses [24]. Before the main study, we conducted pilot studies to validate our study instruments. In order to ensure that they were truly Stack Overflow users, the first question we asked in the survey was if the participant was a Stack Overflow user. If they answered no, the survey immediately terminated. If they tried a second time, their responses were excluded from the study because the system already stored their AMT user ids as being non-Stack overflow users. The responses of 282 participants were accepted. Participation was voluntary and the study was approved by the ethics board of the University of Saskatchewan. Asians represented our collectivist culture subgroup while North Americans represented our individualist culture subgroup. This is in line with previous studies on culture [6]. 27% of our participants were female while 72% were male. 21% were between 18 and 25 years, while 59% were between 25 and 34 years. 20% were over 34 years. 41% of our participants were Asians while 45% were North Americans.

4 Data Analysis and Results

We analyzed our data using Partial Least Squares Structural Equation Modelling (PLS-SEM) with the SmartPLS tool. We present the result of our analysis in the following section along with validation of the global measurement and structural models used.

4.1 Evaluation of Global Measurements

As suggested by Wong [25], in order to complete the examination of our structural model, it is necessary to establish the reliability and validity of the latent variables or constructs we used, using reliability and validity items such as indicator reliability, internal consistency reliability, convergent validity and discriminant validity.

Indicator Reliability. All indicators have individual indicator reliability values larger than the minimum acceptable threshold for exploratory research of 0.4 [26]. Hence, reliability criteria was met.

Internal Consistency Reliability. In measuring internal consistency, composite reliability has been suggested as a replacement to Cronbach's alpha because Cronbach's alpha tends to provide a conservative measurement in PLS-SEM [27]; we therefore used composite reliability in this study. The composite reliability values for all latent variables were higher than the preferred threshold of 0.7 [25], hence high levels of internal consistency reliability were established among all latent variables.

Convergent Validity. To check for convergent validity, we evaluated each latent variable's Average Variance Extracted (AVE) as suggested by [25]. All of the AVE values are greater than the acceptable threshold of 0.5, so convergent validity is confirmed

Discriminant Validity. To establish discriminant validity, Fornell and Larker [28] suggest that the square root of the AVE of each latent variable can be used if it is larger

Table 1. Latent variable correlations with square root of AVE

	COMP	COOP	NORM	PERC	RECO	SOCC	SOCF	SOCL
COMP	**0.861**							
COOP	0.319	**0.801**						
NORM	0.486	0.273	**0.754**					
PERC	0.421	0.495	0.355	**0.838**				
RECO	0.529	0.387	0.420	0.520	**0.837**			
SOCC	0.378	0.427	0.519	0.385	0.528	**0.862**		
SOCF	0.339	0.397	0.481	0.373	0.452	0.471	**0.861**	
SOCL	0.251	0.560	0.203	0.396	0.364	0.412	0.275	**0.825**

SOCL = Social learning, SOCC = Social comparison, NORM = Normative influence, SOCF = Social facilitation, COOP = Cooperation, COMP = Competition, RECO = Recognition, PERC = Perceived persuasiveness

than other correlation values among the latent variables. As shown in Table 1, the square roots of AVE, in bold on the diagonal of the table, is greater than the other correlation variables along the rows and columns. This indicates that discriminant validity is well established.

4.2 Description of Structural Model

The partial least square path model (Pl-SM) for our research model is shown in Fig. 2. It shows the path coefficients, β, (between the various constructs) that explain how strong the effect of the exogenous variables are on the endogenous variables. The model also indicates how much the variance of the endogenous variables are explained by the exogenous variables. Finally, we used the number of asteriks to indicate the significance of each direct effect. The number of asteriks ranges from 1 to 4, and this corresponds with the p-value of <0.05, <0.01, <0.001 and <0.0001 respectively.

While recognition has the strongest effect (β value) on perceived persuasiveness, social learning has the least effect. This suggests that recognition is a good predictor of perceived persuasiveness. In addition, social learning has a strong effect on cooperation compared to social facilitation normative influence and recognition. This suggests that social learning is a strong predictor of cooperation. Similarly, recognition has a stronger effect on competition compared to social comparison, making recognition a good predictor of competition. Because of the insignificant effect of social learning on perceived persuasiveness, we conclude that social learning does not influence the perceived persuasiveness of the system by users. In addition, because of the insignificant effect of normative influence and recognition on cooperation, we conclude that normative influence and recognition do not influence cooperation between users in the system. Because the acceptable threshold for path coefficient is 0.20 [25], we conclude that social comparison doesn't not affect competition, neither does recognition influence cooperation. In addition, normative influence does not influence cooperation, and social learning does not influence the perceived persuasiveness of the users.

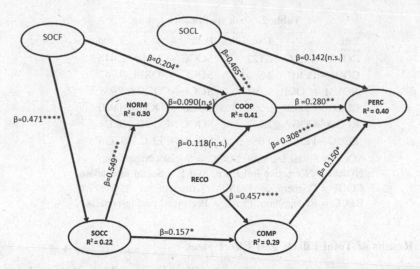

Fig. 2. Structural model with results of PLS-SEM analysis. SOCL = Social learning, SOCC = Social comparison, NORM = Normative influence, SOCF = Social facilitation, COOP = Cooperation, COMP = Competition, RECO = Recognition, PERC = Perceived persuasiveness, n.s. = Not Significant

Going by the PLS-SEM standard [29], a coefficient determination (R^2) value of <0.30 is considered low, while $0.30 < R^2 < 0.60$ is moderate, and $R^2 > 0.60$ is regarded as high. Since R^2 is 0.41 for cooperation, this suggests that social learning, social facilitation, normative influence and recognition moderately explain 41% of the variance in cooperation. In addition, social learning, cooperation, recognition and competition together moderately explain 40% of the variance of perceived persuasiveness.

4.3 Path Significance Testing

In order to determine if the path coefficients between the latent variables of our model are significant, we calculated the T-value for significance testing of the structural paths between constructs in our model as recommended by [25]. This was done by running bootstrap analysis using PLS-SEM. Bootstrapping is a recommended nonparametric procedure that allows testing the statistical significance of various PLS-SEM results such as path coefficients [25]. The bootstrapping result as shown in Table 2 suggest that all paths between constructs are significant except for NORM→COOP, RECO→COOP and SOCL→PERC which did not meet the minimum acceptable threshold of 1.96. This validates our previous findings when looking at the visual PLS-SEM results in Fig. 2.

Table 2. Path significance testing

Path	T-statistics	Path	T-statistics
COMP→PERC	2.122	SOCC→COMP	2.448
COOP→PERC	2.590	SOCC→NORM	9.747
NORM→COOP	1.294	SOCF→COOP	1.987
RECO→COMP	6.564	SOCF→SOCC	8.960
RECO→COOP	1.772	SOCL→COOP	8.027
RECO→PERC	4.088	SOCL→PERC	1.736

SOCL = Social learning, SOCC = Social comparison,
NORM = Normative influence, SOCF = Social facilitation,
COOP = Cooperation, COMP = Competition,
RECO = Recognition, PERC = Perceived persuasiveness

4.4   Results of Total Effects and Effect Sizes

To determine how much an exogenous latent variable contributes to an endogenous latent variable, for example, in our model, how much cooperation contributes to perceived persuasiveness, we calculated the total effects and the corresponding effect sizes of our model. The effect sizes show the strength or degree of the relationship between the various constructs or latent variables [21]. This is in line with the recommendations of Chin et al. [25], who suggest that computing path significance between constructs is not enough to determine the strength of the relationship between the constructs. We adopted effect sizes of 0.02, 0.15 and 0.35 to indicate small, medium and large effect sizes respectively as recommended by [25]. Table 3 describes the total effects and effects sizes between the 8 constructs of our model.

4.5   Validation of Hypotheses

In this section, we verify or discredit the hypotheses defined in Sect. 3.1 based on the results of analyzing our model.

Based on the significant path coefficient, the strength of the path significance and the significant effect size as shown in Fig. 2, Tables 2 and 3 respectively, we are able to validate H1b, H2, H3a, H3c, H5b, H7a and H7b.

On the other hand, because of the low path coefficient (Fig. 2), the low strength of the path significance (Table 2) and the insignificant effect size (Table 3) between social learning and perceived persuasiveness, recognition and cooperation, competition and perceived persuasiveness, social comparison and competition and between normative influence and cooperation, we concluded that our hypothesis were invalid for H1a, H3b, H4, H5a, and H6. For example, we hypothesized in H1a, that social learning will significantly influence perceived persuasiveness, however, as shown in Fig. 2, the path coefficient between SOCL and PERC is not statistically significant and is lower than the acceptable minimum ($\beta = 0.142$ whereas the minimum acceptable value for $\beta = 0.2$). In addition, the path significance of SOCL→PERC (1.736) as shown in Table 2 is lower than the acceptable minimum of 1.96. We therefore concluded that H1a is not valid.

Table 3. Total effects and effect sizes in parenthesis

	COMP	COOP	NORM	PERC	SOCC
COMP				0.150*	
				(0.026)	
COOP				0.280*	
				(0.082)	
NORM		0.034			
		(0.010)			
PERC					
RECO	0.457****	0.114		0.399****	
	(0.213)	(0.015)		(0.101)	
SOCC	0.137*		0.519****		
	(0.026)		(0.432)		
SOCF		0.212**			0.471****
		(0.047)			(0.285)
SOCL		0.455****		0.221****	
		(0.300)		(0.021)	

SOCL = Social learning, SOCC = Social comparison, NORM = Normative influence, SOCF = Social facilitation, COOP = Cooperation, COMP = Competition, RECO = Recognition, PERC = Perceived persuasiveness, n.s. = non-significant. * = $p < 0.05$, ** = $p < 0.01$, *** = $p < 0.001$, **** = $p < 0.0001$

Similarly, we hypothesized in H3b that recognition will significantly influence cooperation. However the path coefficient as shown in Fig. 2 is low and statistically insignificant ($\beta = 0.118$ whereas the minimum acceptable value for $\beta = 0.2$). Also, the path significance between RECO→COOP is significantly low at 1.772. We therefore concluded that H3b is not valid. The same applies for H4, H5a and H6.

4.6 Sub-group Analysis Based on Culture

To determine the effect of the social support influence principles on culture, we split the data into two subgroups; one for the North American participants (the individualists) and the other for the Asian participants (the collectivists). This classification of cultures is in line with the research of Hofstede [30]. We then carried out multi-group analysis between the two subgroups to determine if there were any significant differences in the effect of the social support influence principles between these groups. Table 4 shows the result of the subgroup analysis, in particular, the path coefficients between the constructs described in Sect. 3 and the significance or otherwise of these path coefficients.

The result of the multi group analysis between the two subgroups, individualist and collectivist, shows four significant differences between the two cultures. Individualists are more persuaded by cooperation (COOP) to continue using the system (PERC), unlike collectivists who are influenced by social learning (SOCL) to continue using Stack Overflow (PERC). In addition, while recognition (RECO) influences the decision

Table 4. Path coefficients and significance of the models for Asians (collectivists) and North Americans (individualists)

Path	Global model (Fig. 2)	Collectivist	Individualist	Between group sig.
COMP→PERC	0.150*	0.099	0.093	n.s.
COOP→PERC	0.280**	0.154	0.425****	<0.05
NORM→COOP	0.090	0.145	0.007	n.s.
RECO→COMP	0.457****	0.386****	0.332**	n.s.
RECO→COOP	0.118	0.313***	0.006	<0.05
RECO→PERC	0.308****	0.141	0.371*	n.s.
SOCC→COMP	0.157*	0.367****	0.219****	n.s.
SOCC→NORM	0.549****	0.600****	0.601****	n.s.
SOCF→COOP	0.204*	0.058	0.352****	<0.05
SOCF→SOCC	0.471****	0.501****	0.617****	n.s.
SOCL→COOP	0.465****	0.350****	0.453****	n.s.
SOCL→PERC	0.142	0.430****	-0.091	<0.001

SOCL = Social learning, SOCC = Social comparison, NORM = Normative influence, SOCF = Social facilitation, COOP = Cooperation, COMP = Competition, RECO = Recognition, PERC = Perceived persuasiveness, n.s. = non-significant. * = $p < 0.05$, ** = $p < 0.01$, *** = $p < 0.001$, **** = $p < 0.0001$

of collectivists to cooperate (COOP) with others in the system, social facilitation (SOCF) influences individualists to cooperate (COOP).

5 Discussion

This paper explores the social support factors that influence cooperation between users in Stack Overflow and what persuasive strategies persuade them to keep using the network. In addition, we explored the effect of these strategies on culture. A significant finding from the global model analysis is that of the social influence strategies defined in the PSD model, social learning has the highest significant influence on cooperation. This suggests that the desire of people to learn from others in a social context results in them cooperating in the network. This finding is in line with that of [17] which suggests that if users can observe how others contribute to the network, they can unravel new ways of collaborating in order to improve the network.

Another significant result is that social learning, cooperation, recognition and competition can explain about 40% of the variance in perceived persuasiveness of the system. Of these, recognition has the most influence on the perceived persuasiveness and future use of the system. Thus, recognition motivates people to generate more content [17]. This result suggests that recognition is more important to users in determining the persuasiveness and future use of the system. Another significant finding is that recognition significantly influences competition in the network and not cooperation, as suggested by [17]. This finding is in line with that of [19] which suggests that individuals who strive to be recognized are likely competitive in nature.

In line with this finding, we suggest that Q&A network developers should incorporate ways of recognizing the effort and contribution of their users in the network in order to promote competition in the network. In Stack Overflow, the profile of users is visible on every post they make. This profile includes the rewards they have earned and their reputation score. Hence, the contribution of users in the network is easily recognized.

The influence of social facilitation on social comparison and subsequently on normative influence is another significant finding. Our result suggests that social facilitation (observing other users participate in the network) significantly influences social comparison which in turn significantly influences normative influence (leveraging peer pressure to carry out a target behavior). This is in line with social facilitation theory [11] which suggests that people tend to perform better when they think they have something to prove and are being compared to others in a social setting. This result suggests that when users observe others carrying out a target behavior, they are influenced to compare themselves with others and this leads to them being influenced to carry out the target behavior. Hence Q&A networks should provide a means through which users can observe other users in the network.

With respect to differences in cultures, our result suggest that for individualists, social facilitation influences cooperation and individualists are more persuaded by cooperation to continue using Stack Overflow. This result is not in line with past research which suggests that individualists are more self-interested and less cooperative than collectivists [31]. We suggest that this behavior of individualists in Stack Overflow could be as a result of rewards. Cooperation in Stack Overflow leads to better quality posts, and better quality posts could earn users rewards in the network [32]. Because individualist culture rewards people who stand out [33], it could be that individualists cooperate in Stack overflow in order to be rewarded. This theory will be investigated in our future studies.

Regarding collectivists, our result suggests that recognition significantly influences collectivists to cooperate with other users in the system. However, recognition does not influence collectivists to continue using the system. This is in line with current research where the authors suggest that collectivism discourages individuals from standing out [33]. Hence it is possible that collectivists would rather cooperate with other users in the system to improve existing posts than take the glory for rewards earned themselves. This will be investigated in details in future studies. Our results also suggest that for collectivists, social learning significantly influenced their perceived persuasiveness of Stack Overflow and their intention to continue using the system. This suggests that learning from other members of a group is important to collectivists. This result is in line with Hornik and Tupchiy [34] who suggest that social behavior is established by the roles of the group, and collectivists' willingness to learn is influenced by the group they recognize with.

The results of our study suggest several design implications for Q&A collaborative learning environment developers. Selecting persuasive strategies based on culture could lead to a better personalized experience for the users as there are significant differences to the susceptibility of social support influence strategies between cultures. Collectivists prefer to learn from other users in the system rather than learning on their own, hence, creating a platform through which users can cooperate while learning from others could elicit participation from collectivists. Furthermore, recognizing their contributions in the network could make collectivists cooperate with others in the network. Recognition could be in the form of special rewards based on achievement.

The significant findings in our global model also have some implications for developers. These findings could be applied when the culture of users is not known. First, social learning significantly influences cooperation, which suggests that as long as users in Stack Overflow are learning, they can be influenced to cooperate with other users in the network. This is important because cooperation has been found to improve the quality of answers posted in the network and quality answers keep Stack Overflow active [3]. Secondly, helpful users should be recognized in the network as this significantly influences competition and the perceived persuasiveness and use continuance of the system. Recognition can be accomplished by designers using virtual rewards that users have to earn when they are especially helpful in the community. Finally, since users can be influenced by their peers, Q&A systems should be designed in such a way that users can observe others in the system and be able to compare their performance to that of others.

There are some limitations to this study. First, we cannot guarantee that the participants in our study are actual Stack overflow users. We are however confident to a large extent that our participants are Stack Overflow users because of the popularity of the network (with over seven million registered users online as at May 2017) and because of the control we put in place at the beginning of the survey which terminates the study if the user answers "no" to the question asking if they are Stack Overflow users. Second, the number of participants used in the study (282) might not reflect a significant fraction of the total users on Stack Overflow, or it could be a biased sample, since possibly only particular types of users are active on both AMT and Stack Overflow. We plan to carry out this study on a larger scale in the future with more Stack Overflow users to validate our findings. The main strength of our study is that, to the best of our knowledge, no other research exists that addresses the social influence strategies that affect collaboration and persuasiveness of a Q&A collaborative learning network and examines the effect of culture on the effect of these strategies on Stack Overflow users.

6 Conclusion

In order to keep a Q&A collaborative learning environment active, it is important to encourage participation among users. Cooperation between users has been shown to improve question and answer posts and allows users to learn from one another. In this paper, we investigate the social support factors that influence cooperation between users in a typical Q&A collaborative network, Stack Overflow and what persuades them to keep using the network. Using a sample size of 282 Stack Overflow users, we developed and tested a research model using partial least-squares structural equation modelling (PLS-SEM) analysis. We further investigated the effect of cultural differences on the susceptibility of users to these social support principles by testing two subgroups for collectivist and individualist cultures. Our results show that of all the constructs measured, only social learning significantly influences cooperation in Stack Overflow at the global level. In addition, cooperation and competition influence the perceived persuasiveness and use of Stack Overflow. However, at the cultural subgroup level, individualists are more persuaded by cooperation to continue using the system, unlike collectivists who are influenced by social learning. In addition, while recognition influences the decision of collectivists to cooperate with others in the network, social facilitation influences individualists to cooperate. These findings suggest the importance of personalization in the development of successful Q&A collaborative networking sites and some guidelines for tailored design based on culture.

References

1. Bouguessa, M., Dumoulin, B., Wang, S.: Identifying authoritative actors in question-answering forums: the case of Yahoo! answers. In: Proceedings of the 14th ACM SIGKDD International Conference on Knowledge Discovery and Data Mining, pp. 866–874 (2008)
2. Dror, G., Pelleg, D., Rokhlenko, O., Szpektor, I.: Churn prediction in new users of Yahoo! answers. In: Proceedings of the 21st International Conference on World Wide Web, pp. 829–834 (2012)
3. Adaji, I., Vassileva, J.: Modelling user collaboration in social networks using edits and comments. In: Proceedings of the 2016 Conference on User Modeling Adaptation and Personalization - UMAP 2016, pp. 111–114 (2016)
4. Adaji, I., Vassileva, J.: Persuasive patterns in Q&A social networks. In: International Conference on Persuasive Technology, pp. 189–196 (2016)
5. Park, J.-H.: The effects of personalization on user continuance in social networking sites. Inf. Process. Manag. **50**(3), 462–475 (2014)
6. Orji, R.: The impact of cultural differences on the persuasiveness of influence strategies. In: Adjunt Proceedings of the 11th International Conference on Persuasive Technology, pp. 38–41 (2016)
7. Khaled, R., Barr, P., Noble, J., Fischer, R., Biddle, R.: Our Place or Mine? Exploration into Collectivism-Focused Persuasive Technology Design, pp. 72–83. Springer, Heidelberg (2006)
8. McDonald, D.W.: Recommending collaboration with social networks. In: Proceedings of the Conference on Human Factors in Computing Systems - CHI 2003, p. 593 (2003)
9. Oinas-Kukkonen, H., Harjumaa, M.: A systematic framework for designing and evaluating persuasive systems. In: Oinas-Kukkonen, H., Hasle, P., Harjumaa, M., Segerståhl, K., Øhrstrøm, P. (eds.) PERSUASIVE 2008. LNCS, vol. 5033, pp. 164–176. Springer, Heidelberg (2008). doi:10.1007/978-3-540-68504-3_15
10. Torning, K., Oinas-Kukkonen, H.: Persuasive system design: state of the art and future directions. In: Proceedings of the 4th International Conference on Persuasive Technology, p. 30 (2009)
11. Zajonc, R.: Social facilitation. Sci. New Ser. **149**(3681), 269–274 (1965)
12. Wilson, S., Benner, L.: The effects of self-esteem and situation upon comparison choices during ability evaluation. Sociometry **34**, 381–397 (1971)
13. Deutsch, M., Gerard, H.: A study of normative and informational social influences upon individual judgment. J. Abnorm. Soc. **51**(3), 629–636 (1955)
14. Bandura, A.: Social Foundations of Thought and Action: A Social Cognitive Theory. Prentice-Hall, Englewood Cliffs (1986)
15. Mead, M.: Cooperation and Competition Among Primitive Peoples (2002)

16. Malone, T., Lepper, M.: Making learning fun: A taxonomy of intrinsic motivations for learning - Google Scholar. Aptitude Learn. Instr. **3**, 223–253 (1987)
17. Stibe, A., Oinas-Kukkonen, H.: Using social influence for motivating customers to generate and share feedback. In: International Conference on Persuasive (2014)
18. Doan, A., Ramakrishnan, R., Halevy, A.: Mass collaboration systems on the World-Wide Web. Commun. ACM **54**(4), 86–96 (2010)
19. Schoenau-Fog, H.: Teaching serious issues through player engagement in an interactive experiential learning scenario. Eludamos J. Comput. Game Cult. **6**(1), 53–70 (2012)
20. Anderson, A., Huttenlocher, D., Kleinberg, J., Leskovec, J.: Steering user behavior with badges. In: Proceedings of the 22nd International Conference on World Wide Web - WWW 2013, pp. 95–106 (2013)
21. Anderson, A., Huttenlocher, D., Kleinberg, J.: Discovering value from community activity on focused question answering sites: a case study of stack overflow. In: Proceedings of the 18th ACM SIGKDD International Conference on Knowledge Discovery and Data Mining, pp. 850–858 (2012)
22. Festinger, L.: A theory of social comparison processes. Hum. Relat. **7**, 117–140 (1954)
23. Cialdini, R., Kallgren, C., Reno, R.: A focus theory of normative conduct: a theoretical refinement and reevaluation of the role of norms in human behavior. Adv. Exp. Soc. **24**(20), 1–243 (1991)
24. Mason, W., Suri, S.: Conducting behavioral research on Amazon's mechanical turk. Behav. Res. Methods **44**(1), 1–23 (2012)
25. Wong, K.: Partial least squares structural equation modeling (PLS-SEM) techniques using SmartPLS. Mark. Bull. **24**, 1–32 (2013). Technical note 1
26. Hulland, J.: Use of Partial Least Squares (PLS) in strategic management research: a review of four recent studies. Strateg. Manag. J. **20**(2), 195–204 (1999)
27. Hair Jr., J., Hult, T., Ringle, C., Sarstedt, M.: A Primer on Partial Least Squares Structural Equation Modeling (PLS-SEM). Sage Publications, Thousand Oaks (2016)
28. Fornell, C., Larcker, D.: Evaluating structural equation models with unobservable variables and measurement error. J. Mark. Res. **18**(1), 39–50 (1981)
29. Sanchez, G.: PLS path modeling with R. Trowchez Editions, Berkeley (2013)
30. Hofstede, G., Hofstede, G.: Culture's Consequences: Comparing Values, Behaviors, Institutions and Organizations Across Nations (2001)
31. Hemesath, M., Pomponio, X.: Cooperation and culture: students from china and the united states in a prisoner's dilemma. Cross-Cult. Res. **32**, 171–184 (1998)
32. Vargo, A., Matsubara, S.: Editing Unfit Questions in Q&A. In: 2016 5th IIAI Informatics (IIAI-AAI), (2016)
33. Gorodnichenko, Y., Roland, G.: Understanding the individualism-collectivism cleavage and its effects: lessons from cultural psychology. In: Institutions and Comparative Economic Development, pp. 213–236. Palgrave Macmillan UK, London (2012)
34. Hornik, S., Tupchiy, A.: Culture's impact on technology mediated learning: the role of horizontal and vertical individualism and collectivism. J. Glob. Inf. **14**(4), 31–56 (2006)

Group Matching for Peer Mentorship in Small Groups

Oluwabunmi Adewoyin Olakanmi[(⊠)] and Julita Vassileva

University of Saskatchewan, Saskatoon, Canada
bunmi.adewoyin@usask.ca, jiv@cs.usask.ca

Abstract. The problem of assigning learners to groups is essential in collaborative venture like group peer mentorship. Usually, in group peer mentorship, the group of peers is focused on one topic or question, and engage in discussion, argumentation, and providing criticism and constructive feedback, related to the individual contributions made by the participants. Therefore, the problem here is how to group peers that provide feedback to each other to ensure that all peers benefit from the venture, and everybody has something to offer. This problem is akin to the group formation problem in the area of computer supported collaborative learning (CSCL). Many group formation algorithms exist in the area of CSCL, but they have problem with limited and fixed constraints, evaluation strategies, their initial grouping mechanism and the goal of the grouping strategy. Therefore, we proposed a grouping algorithm based on some constraints and the principles of the Hungarian algorithm, to achieve a diversified grouping of peers for every mentorship session. Although this algorithm had been used manually in some of our previous small scale studies, in this paper, we evaluated the algorithm using 1080 system generated data, and compared the performance of our algorithm with three other algorithms in CSCL.

Keywords: Peer review system · Group mentorship · Group formation · Collaborative learning

1 Introduction

The problem of assigning learners to groups is essential in collaborative learning platforms like peer review and wikis. For example, in peer review, different systems provide different functionalities to support the review assignment, such as selection of competence areas by reviewers from a predefined list of areas, and selection of areas addressed by the submissions by authors. Thus, the problem of review assignment is treated as semantic matching between the expertise of reviewers and the areas of the papers. Yet this approach has the shortcomings of any taxonomy-based matching approach – the predefined list of areas may not capture well the areas represented in the competences of the reviewers or the submissions, and both reviewers and authors may interpret the areas as they wish, which may lead to inconsistencies and sub-optimal matching. Also the lack of possibility to indicate strength of expertise in an area or degree of relevance leads to treating marginally relevant areas as equally important in computing the matching scores. To avoid these problems, an alternative approach, now implemented by most

© Springer International Publishing AG 2017
C. Gutwin et al. (Eds.): CRIWG 2017, LNCS 10391, pp. 65–80, 2017.
DOI: 10.1007/978-3-319-63874-4_6

conference management systems is to allow reviewers to view the titles and abstracts of the submitted papers and bid on the papers they wish to review. This however, is often a very onerous task, and reviewers end up picking a few papers from the top of the list, while the papers down the list would not be selected by anyone.

The problem of reviewer assignment in a peer-review system for group peer mentorship is not so strongly dependent on the precise area of the submitted document and specific expertise of the reviewer. Usually, in group peer mentorship, the group of peers is focused on one topic or question, and engage in discussion, argumentation, and providing criticism and constructive feedback, related to the individual contributions made by the participants. The main purpose is not quality evaluation or selection of individual contributions, but generally improving both the argumentation and discussion skills of peers in the role of mentees and the skills to provide constructive criticism and feedback for the peers in the role of mentors. The problem of reviewer assignment is transformed into the problem of how to group peers that provide feedback to each other to ensure that all peers benefit from the peer-review process, and everybody has something to offer. This problem is akin to the group formation problem in the area of computer supported collaborative learning (CSCL). Therefore, we explore the related work on group formation for CSCL in Sect. 2.

2 Related Work

Finding perfect combination of peers in a group, in which they can mentor one another, is not as straightforward as in the one-to-one mentorship. Therefore, the scenario here is that of matching peers in groups such that some form of reciprocity is involved in order to ensure that all peers benefit from the mentoring relationship. Reciprocal recommendation has been proposed in the context of matchmaking in dating websites [16]. However, ensuring generalized reciprocity is hard when the recommendation aims to select a group of users (mentors & mentees) rather than just match two users, for two reasons. First, users' preferences are not necessarily linear [13]. That is, it is difficult to represent users' preferences in such a way as to capture their real intention. For example, the difference between user ratings of 7 and 8 might not be the same as the difference between 6 and 7. Second, there is always conflict between transparency and privacy. When modeling groups, it is very important to make the reason for certain decisions transparent to users, most importantly for usability and acceptance. However, not every user will like other group members to be aware of their preferences or capabilities. For example, in group learning, learners need to be aware of the reasons why certain learning materials or tutors are recommended to them. Such reasons originate from the individual preferences and needs of the constituent learners. However, not every learner would be happy when other learners see their weaknesses [13].

The core problem of group recommendation is how to use the information in the individual user models to adapt to the group needs. Group modeling strategies have been inspired by the Social Choice Theory, devised for reaching group decisions from individual opinions [14]. We see group peer mentorship as a form of collaborative learning, where peers with mutual accountability and responsibility work together to achieve their goals using the concepts of social interaction and collaboration.

Researchers in the area of collaborative learning had proposed different group formation algorithms based on some existing algorithms – random [4], stratified [12, 23, 30], genetic [15, 28, 31], multi-agent system [9, 20] and clustering [1, 5, 11, 19] algorithms. One of the basic grouping approaches employed by instructors is random grouping algorithm, which assigns students to groups with no particular pattern. However, a random grouping algorithm can result in unbalanced and ineffective group composition [8, 22]. Another approach is the stratified algorithm, which is an improved version of random algorithm that sorts students in the decreasing order of their competences and grouping is done starting from the top students to the weakest on the list. One drawback of this approach is that it will, in most cases; result in creating homogeneous groups of students, which are less efficient than the heterogeneous groups in yielding the desired learning outcomes [12, 23, 30].

[28] proposed a grouping algorithm called DIANA, which uses the psychological features of students to map them into heterogeneous groups using the traditional genetic algorithm. However, DIANA considered so many features that could make it too generic when determining groups of students. Also since it relies on students to self-report their features, and its accuracy can be affected by error or bias in the students' response. In addition, authors were silent on the scalability of DIANA. [15] also proposed a group formation algorithm based on genetic algorithm, to generate inter-homogeneous and intra-heterogeneous groups. However, the algorithm also relies on self-reported data by students in order to determine the characteristics that are used in grouping them. [31] also proposed crowding evolutionary algorithm that assigns students to nine different roles defined by [3] and based on these roles, students are randomly placed in different groups. These groups reshuffled using mutation and crossover algorithms. The fitness level of each group formed is evaluated until there is an optimal combination of roles in each group, and the group formation algorithm stops. One drawback of this algorithm is that it relies on some random matching for the initial group formation. Also, the report was silent about how students' roles were determined for the initial grouping.

[4] proposed a web-based group formation tool, which relies on learners' features defined by the instructor to map learners into homogeneous and heterogeneous groups, depending on the preferences set by the instructor. However, this tool relies on random grouping algorithm to generate heterogeneous groups. [24] also proposed the Squeaky wheel algorithm, which uses the students' ratings of their willingness to work with their peers to compute their mutual compatibility. Their mutual compatibility is then used to create heterogeneous groups of students. This algorithm relies on the initial ratings of students' willingness to work with their peers, which can result in homogeneous groups and some students, who might not be preferred by their peers end up being orphaned and might be grouped using some neutral default values.

[9] proposed a multi-agent system based algorithm, which models the learning goals of students as agents and negotiates between students' agents to form mutually beneficial groups. However, their report lacks the description of the architecture and evaluation of the system. So, we cannot confirm the scalability and effectiveness of the system over other existing algorithms. [20] also proposed a multi-agent based group formation system called I-MINDS, which represents students and groups by intelligent agents that profile students and the groups respectively. The students' agents negotiate

with the groups' agents, based on their previous performances in the group activities. However, authors were silent about the source of data for the first group activities.

In 2015, [19] proposed an automated group decomposition program, which implements k-means algorithm to classify students into heterogeneous groups. This program creates groups in stages. First, it groups students into initial homogeneous groups using their attributes (e.g. communication skill, fluency in the use of computer and in the group work). Then, students are re-grouped into heterogeneous groups using their knowledge of the subject. One drawback of this program is that the attributes used in forming the initial homogeneous groups are fixed and cannot be changed by instructors. Also, the system has not been evaluated in actual academic projects, and the source of data containing students' attributes is not defined. In 2012, [5] proposed user behavior driven group formation tool. This tool uses case-based reasoning to model learners' behaviors, which also contain their learning strategies. The tool extracts their learning strategies to form the strategies-learners' matrix, which is passed to the clustering algorithm to create homogeneous groups of learners. Although, this tool implements a novel idea that considers learners' strategies, it does not address the specific benefits that learners derive from the groups that they are assigned to. Also, the tool generates homogeneous groups which are less efficient than heterogeneous groups in yielding the desired learning outcomes [12]. [11] also proposed an algorithm based on the heuristic algorithm and uniform k-means clustering. This algorithm uses a cognitive diagnoses model named SDINA to automatically quantify students' skill proficiencies in binary value '0' or '1'. These values are used to generate collaborative learning teams with dissimilar features. The system has only been tested with simulated and pre-defined students' data. In 2014, [1] proposed group formation algorithms for educational settings, which are based on modified clustering algorithm. They assumed that each learner is associated with certain ability. The algorithms, therefore, use learners' abilities in the subject of interest to determine their strengths. The algorithms classify learners as "leader - a learner that has strong capability in the subject of interest" or "follower - a learner that has weak capability in the subject of interest". The algorithms map learners into groups in such a way that there are just few leaders in each group and each group has more followers than leaders, to ensure that leaders are spread across groups and are able to maximize their skills to help followers. Unfortunately, these algorithms consider the learning needs of followers to be more important than the leaders. Also, since the algorithms have only been tested with simulated data with assumed abilities, further testing in classroom settings is still required.

The general limitations of the existing group formation tools/algorithms in collaborative learning are:

1. *Limited (and fixed) constraints:* The existing systems model certain criteria, which are used in grouping learners. For example, DIANA uses a maximum of seven fixed criteria [28]. With this in place, the systems become inflexible and it becomes difficult for the users (instructors/learners) to include criteria outside the space of the criteria modeled in the system. Also, users have to strictly follow the listed criteria in the use of these existing systems, even if the criteria do not fully align with their requirements. In addition, some of the systems require some background information about the learners to do the grouping [11, 26]. This makes it difficult to use

effectively when there is no sufficient information about learners, for example, in the case of new learners.

2. *Manual grouping to support the existing systems:* In certain instances, the grouping criteria might result in "*orphaned learners*", who are stranded learners that remain ungrouped [17, 24, 25]. Therefore, the instructors will have to manually add them to certain groups, which might reduce the effectiveness of the group formation tool.

3. *Evaluation strategies:* Most of the existing grouping strategies rely on self-report by the learners, using questionnaire, to measure their effectiveness. However, research had shown that self-reports can be misleading and loaded with bias [21]. Therefore, evaluation of a group-matching algorithm should be multi-faceted, with log and qualitative data from the system and observation reports from the instructors or teaching assistants used as backup to the self-reports from the learners.

4. *Goal of the grouping strategies:* Most grouping strategies discussed in literature, except few [1, 22], are focused on enhancing collaborative learning activities with no mention of the aggregate gains of peers, in terms of learning or skill enhancement, from the collaboration; whereas the purpose of collaborative learning is to facilitate learning in order to enhance learners' skills.

3 Our Group Matching Approach

Peers have different skill levels. The problem in using a collaborative tool like peer review or wiki system in group peer mentorship concerns how to group peers who provide feedback to each other (i.e. how to do the reviewer assignment or the wiki editors' combination) to ensure that all peers can benefit from the collaborative process, where everybody has something to offer. This problem is akin to the group formation problem in the area of CSCL, where some researchers support having peers that are close in skill level grouped together [10], whereas others believe that grouping a mix of peers with different levels yields a better learning outcome [2, 12, 18]. A lot of research on group formation in CSCL has been influenced by the theory of Vygotsky, and specifically his "*Zone of Proximal Development*" concept, which is the difference between what peers can do without help and what they can do with help from a teacher or more capable peer [27]. According to this theory, peers should be grouped with other peers with varying degrees of ability. Therefore, we propose that peers with abilities ranging from weak to average and strong be grouped together. To ensure that all peers have the opportunity to receive valuable feedback, we propose a matching algorithm[1] using some principles of Hungarian algorithm for assignment problem with the following constraints.

1. Each group should not exceed four peers in number. Research had shown that a group of three to four peers works best because it is easy to coordinate and it also encourages group members to be actively engaged in the group tasks [6, 7]. Also, because peers will be reviewing each other's work or performance and we do not

---

[1] The algorithm is presented in Sect. 3.1.

want any peer to feel overwhelmed by the volume of work, it is important to keep the number of peers in each group to four so peers can handle a reasonable number of reviews at once (three in this case) with which they should be able to give their best effort.

2. We propose peers should be classified as weak peers (*wp*), average peers (*ap*) or strong peers (*sp*) by using an initial calibration task relating to what they are expected to do in the peer review. The feedback from the initial task will be used to temporarily determine their strength, which changes after each peer review iteration. To classify them as strong, average or weak peers, we will calculate the average score from the initial calibration task for all the participants; every participant with a score less than the average score of the group is classified as a *wp*, while every participant with a score equal to the group average is classified as an *ap* and every participant with a score greater than the group average is classified as an *sp*.

3. In each group, the number of *wp* should be less than half of the total number of peers in the group (i.e. number(*wp*) < [number(*wp* + *ap* + *sp*)]/2). This constraint will help ensure that the peers form a bipartite graph, and if not, we have to eliminate the extra link to be able to apply the principles of Hungarian algorithm to match the group of peers.

4. A weak peer cannot review/mentor another weak peer. This will ensure that peers are able to learn from other peers in their zone of proximal development [27]. That is, *wp* should get help from more knowledgeable and more skilful peers.

5. A *sp* or *ap* cannot receive more than one review (be mentored) from a *wp*. This is to ensure that every peer gets more than average and useful feedback overall. Although we would like every peer to be able to see and learn from an example of a not-so-good review, we still want peers to be able to learn from their good peers in order to be able to operate within their zone of proximal development [27].

3.1   Group Matching as Akin to Assignment Problem in Mathematics

We see the group matching problem in CSCL as a bipartite graph. A bipartite graph is a *"special case of k-graph (where k = 2) that the vertices can be decomposed into two disjoint sets such that no two vertices within the same set are adjacent"* [29]. In our case, peers constitute both disjoint sets and can be matched to form collaborative learning group as in a bipartite graph, following the matching constraints mentioned in Sect. 3. We see potential in the algorithms used in solving assignment problems in mathematics, for example, the Hungarian, stable marriage and tournament algorithms. We chose the Hungarian algorithm for two reasons. As much as we would like to keep the constraints in view, every peer should be treated equally. However, in stable marriage algorithm, priority is given to a certain class of nodes over the other. Therefore, stable marriage algorithm is inapplicable here. Also, the tournament organization algorithms require that the teams involved are known ahead of time in order to schedule their resource use in terms of time and other facilities. However, in this case, we can only know the number of peers ahead of time and cannot predict the number of groups that will result from our matching. Also, because we require peers to be treated equally, the Hungarian algorithm is more suitable.

To apply the principles of Hungarian algorithm to a matching problem, the bipartite graph must be regular. In our case, we have a regular graph only if the number of weak peers (*wp*) is not equal to or greater than half of the total number of peers (as stipulated by constraint 3 in Sect. 3). We present the pseudo-code for the modified algorithm below. This algorithm was implemented using MATLAB.

1. *Conduct a calibration test for peers*
2. *The calibration test will be graded by a senior peer. Based on their grades from the calibration test, assign peers into one of the three categories: weak peers wp, average peers ap and strong peers sp. [**constraint 2**: classify peers as wp, ap and sp].*
3. *Cluster peers into smaller groups of four peers in each group and the left-over peers should be treated the same way as the grouped peers. [**constraint 1**: each group should not exceed four peers in number]*
4. *For each group:*
   a. *If number(wp)< (number(wp+ap+sp))/2, go to c [**constraint 3**: to ensure that peers form bipartite graph]*
   b. *else if number(wp) ≥ (number(wp+ap+sp))/2, then check*
      i.! *if number(wp) = (number(wp+ap+sp))/2, then (we will finish with very few matchings) do steps e to i*
      ii.! *else if number(wp) > (number(wp+ap+sp))/2 go to step m*
   c. *Check if number(wp) ≥ 2, do steps e to i*
   d. *else if number(wp) < 2, do e-f, then go to step j*
   e. *Duplicate peers in each group and make them nodes in the two vertices of a bipartite graph*
   f. *Match each node from one vertex to another node in another vertex. No node (peer) should be matched to itself.*
   g. *Check if there is any wp to wp matching [**constraint 4**: a weak peer cannot review / mentor another weak peer]*
      i. *If true, delete all wp to wp matchings*
      ii. *Else, proceed to step h*
   h. *Check if any wp to sp or wp to ap matching occurs more than once. [**constraint 5**: an ap or sp cannot receive review (be mentored) from more than one wp]*
      i. *If true, discard all but the first matching with the combination wp to sp or wp to ap.*
      ii. *else proceed to step i*
   i. *Check if any matching has more than 3 other peers on the list as mentees [**constraint 1**: to prevent peers from being overwhelmed with work]*
      i. *If true, trim down to 3 in each list and proceed to step h*
      ii. *else if false, proceed to step j*
      j. *Compute the peers' gain within each group*
      k. *Compute the time and space consumption*
      l. *Print out the final matching, peers' gain, time and space consumption*
      m. *End*

Algorithm 1. Pseudocode for our group matching algorithm

4   Evaluating the Performance of the Algorithm

We evaluated the performance of our algorithm based on three metrics - the value of the aggregate knowledge gain made by peers in each group formed, time spent to execute and memory space consumed while executing the algorithm.

4.1   Datasets

Our datasets comprised a set of 1,080 synthetic peers (n = 1080) with abilities represented as randomly sampled values from normal, uniform, and Pareto distributions, while we observed their performances when n = 120, 360, 600, 840, and 1080. Peers from the normal datasets were sampled with abilities from a normal distribution with mean 0 and standard deviation 1, while their abilities were sampled uniformly from (0, 1) for the uniform datasets. For the Pareto datasets, peers' abilities were generated from the Pareto distribution with the shape parameter set to 3.

4.2   Knowledge Gain Function

Since our peers were synthetic and there was no real interaction or problem solving in each group formed, we modeled knowledge gain using the linear equation

$$r_{i+1} = a * r_i + b_{i+1} \tag{1}$$

where r_{i+1} refers to the new value of the knowledge level of each peer, r_i refers to the current knowledge level of peers. The difference between r_{i+1} and r_i gives the knowledge gain of peers after each iteration of the algorithm. a is computed by finding the standard deviation of the current knowledge levels of all peers in the group ($a = std$ (r_i)) and b_{i+1} is computed using the quadratic Eq. (2) below.

$$b_{i+1} = a1(1) * b_i^2 + a1 \tag{2}$$

where $a1(1)$ and $a1(2)$ are two values selected from the three random numbers generated from the function $a1(3) = random(3, 1)$. With this approach, we envisaged that there would be an increase in the knowledge gain by each peer, irrespective of the algorithm used, but we expected that there would be differences in the absolute value of gain made by peers using the four grouping algorithms. Therefore, the values of the three performance metrics from our algorithm were compared with the values of the same performance metrics from three other algorithms – random, stratified and grouping algorithm by [1]. For clarity, we will refer to the four algorithms as follows, and these terms will be used interchangeably in the rest of this paper - Random algorithm: *algo1;* Stratified algorithm: *algo2;* algorithm by [1]: *algo3;* Our algorithm: *algo4.*

4.3 Aggregate Knowledge Gains by Peers

For every group formed using the four algorithms, we computed the aggregate knowledge gains of peers in each group formed from the algorithms using Eqs. (1) and (2). As shown in Fig. 1, for the uniform and normal datasets, we observed that all the four algorithms recorded an initial gain in the peers' knowledge across the entire datasets, except for when the gains dropped in *algo1* and *algo2* for the normal datasets from 840. For the two datasets, our algorithm (*algo4*) had similar performance in peers' knowledge gain as with *algo3*. However, for the Pareto datasets, our algorithm outperformed all the three algorithms, with the peak value when n = 840, from which point the total gain starts to diminish for both our algorithm and *algo3*. However, there was no gain observed for peers using *algo1* and *algo2*.

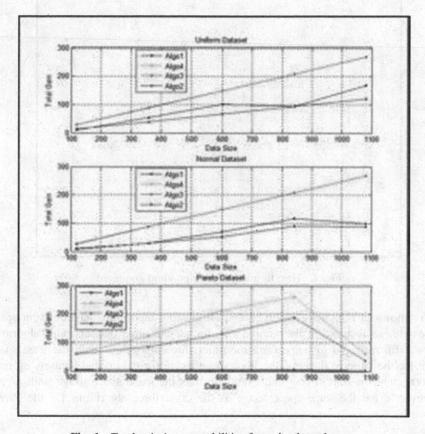

Fig. 1. Total gain in peers abilities from the three datasets

We observed the time and space it took the four algorithms to execute. As shown in Fig. 2, we observed a drop in time for all the four algorithms with the uniform datasets up until when n = 360, and it remains stable until n = 600 when it starts to rise again.

Also, in the normal and Pareto datasets, we observed a steady increase in time for all the algorithms with *algo3* having the highest rate of increase. However, *algo1* and our algorithm had the least time usage for all the datasets, and *algo3* had the highest time usage for all three datasets. On the overall, we observed that our algorithm had a linear time usage.

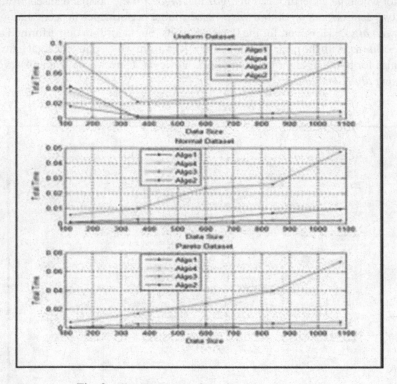

Fig. 2. Time to run the four algorithms compared

As shown in Fig. 3, we observed that all the four algorithms have a rising space usage with an increase in the sample size for all the three datasets. Our algorithm (*algo4*) still managed to outperform the other three algorithms with the least space usage for the uniform datasets, the least space usage for the normal datasets up until n = 600, when it starts rising and eventually has the same space usage with *algo3*. However, it has the same space usage as the other three algorithms for the Pareto datasets.

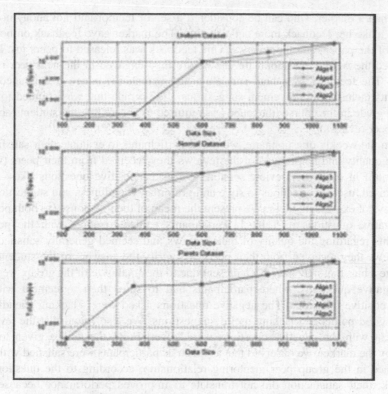

Fig. 3. Space usage by the four algorithms compared

5   The Implementation of Our Grouping Approach in Three Small Scale Studies

Between January 2013 and April 2016, we did three case studies of exploratory nature, in undergraduate and graduate classes of computer science, all which have a strong writing component. Our goal was to find out if group peer mentorship in improving students' writing and argumentation skills can be accomplished within regular coursework with uniform writing assignments. The studies lasted from 6 to 7 weeks, during which students had to submit short weekly essay on a specific topic related to the content discussed during the week in class. Participants were grouped for the peer review session based on their competence in such a way that weak peers were grouped with strong peers in order to ensure diversity and also allow peers to learn within their zone of proximal development (see Sect. 3). We conducted an initial calibration test, a short essay, which was used to judge participants' competence for the first peer review session, and their subsequent competences were derived from their peer ratings from each peer review session, which was used to group them for each peer review session (following the grouping approach in Sect. 3). The students were asked to fill brief questionnaires after every peer-review assignment.

We had a marker, who can be considered a senior mentor and not anonymous, in order to make her feedback more authoritative. The marker gave feedback on both the quality of the papers and the reviews. This feedback was released to peers just before they filled the weekly questionnaire and before they engaged in the next peer review session. The feedback was both formative and summative, since it contained both comments including improvement suggestions and a grade that was counted towards the total grade in the course (the latter was required to ensure that the students actually do the peer-reviews).

From the weekly questionnaire, we asked participants to evaluate their satisfaction with the quality and helpfulness of the reviews they received from their peers (within their group) in each peer review session. We asked positive questions like – good points raised, useful corrections to style and grammar, friendliness and suggestions on good ways of expressing ideas. We present the mean of their responses to both positive and negative questions in Table 1. Participants tended to agree with the positive statements regarding the quality of their reviews and seemed generally satisfied with the reviews they received from their peers. To verify the answers of the students and minimize a bias that may have been present due to the small size of the group, we asked also negative questions, where participants had to show their agreement with the reverse positive questions. The negative questions asked were - lacking friendliness, lacking good points and lacking useful suggestions. We also found that the levels of agreement with the negative questions were lower. From the grades given to their essays by the marker, we observed that as much as participants were satisfied with their experience in the group peer mentoring relationship, according to the questionnaire feedback, their satisfaction did not translate to improved performance because their marks did not show a sustained improvement in their writing skill (see Table 2).

Table 1. Case Studies using our grouping approach

Studies	Number of participants	Number of peer review sessions	Feedback from the survey questions (Average)	
Study 1	6	6	+ve	7.54
			−ve	3.89
Study 2	24	6	+ve	7.5
			−ve	3
Study 3	10	7	+ve	4.6
			−ve	0.8

Table 2. Average marks given to their final essays from each peer review session

Studies	Average marks (out of 10)						
Study 1	Essay	1	2	3	4		5	6
	Marks	8.67	8.17	8.17	7.67		8.5	8.08
Study 2	Essay	1	2	3	4		5	6
	Marks	8.7	8.2	8.78	7.76		7.83	7.23
Study 3	Essay	1	2	3	4	5	6	7
	Marks	7.33	8.1	8.97	8.43	8.5	8.53	8.57

While the results from the three studies were not statistically significant due to the small sample size, they were consistent over time with different classes and types of students. The results from questionnaire feedback supports the hypothesis that the grouping approach is effective in achieving a successful mentoring session. However, we believe that several factors could have contributed to the fluctuating marks in their essays. For example, load of course work, commitment to other courses and their finals. Therefore, further studies would be required to conclude with the marks given to their essays.

6 Limitations of Our Algorithm

Our algorithm has few limitations. First, we have restricted the number of peers in each group to four, in order to balance the workload on peers in each peer review session and also for easy coordination [6, 7]. However, in situations where we have more than four peers (e.g. 5) to be grouped, we will have to trim down the number of peers in order to keep to constraint 1 (see Sect. 3). However, this can result in the trimmed peers having very limited feedback. Also in one of our grouping constraints, we proposed that peers be grouped based on their capabilities measured by an initial calibration task. In case where it is not possible to conduct an initial calibration task for peers, their past course average could suffice. However, the past course average might not in most cases perfectly model the skill that peers are looking at improving using the group peer mentorship. Also, the past course average cannot be used in studies involving professionals. In this case, the algorithm will rely on an initial random approach to grouping, and the peer ratings from the initial group will be used for grouping in the subsequent peer mentorship session. However, data from the initial groups formed from the random approach can be ignored when evaluating the overall group metrics (performance).

7 Conclusion

Peer grouping is a crucial stage in group peer mentorship. A cohesive group is an indication of successful collaboration among the group members. Research had shown that a group with diverse skills will yield a positive learning outcome [9, 23, 30]. In this paper, we discussed a group-matching algorithm that relies on an initial calibration test depending on the purpose of the grouping to initiate peer grouping. Our approach is based on the Hungarian algorithm because it is easy to implement, does not require a prior knowledge of group components, does not give priority to any group member, and is not subjected to manipulation unlike the Gale-Shapley algorithm (stable marriage algorithm), which can be manipulated to give preference to a particular gender or peer.

While the traditional Hungarian algorithm can be computed in a polynomial time $O(n^3)$, our algorithm can be computed in linear time $O(n)$, which offers better performance. We ran experiments with 1,080 synthetic peers with abilities sampled from the uniform, normal, and Pareto distributions. With these datasets, we observed peers' knowledge gain separately for the groups formed by the four algorithms: random, stratified, algorithm by [1], and our group-matching algorithm. On the overall, our algorithm demonstrated good performance with more gain in peers' knowledge from the group formed, and it showed the best time and space consumption on the overall. With our group formation algorithm, we would like to emphasize four important factors for optimum group formation for collaborative learning:

1. Identification of skill levels of peers to ensure they receive appropriate help
2. Heterogeneous groups to enable transfer of skills within the community of peers in each group
3. Small groups to balance the workload on peers and enable them to give quality and helpful feedback to their peers
4. Periodic evaluation of total gains in every group formed to ensure that learning is taking place.

We have manually tested the algorithm in small scale studies with graduate and undergraduate students of Computer Science (Sect. 5) and we found that the algorithm is effective to achieve successful mentoring session. However, there is a need to for further test with large sample size. Some of our results had been presented in our past publications.

References

1. Agrawal, R., Golshan, B., Terzi, E.: Grouping students in educational settings. In: Proceeding of the 20th ACM SIGKDD International Conference on Knowledge Discovery and Data Mining, pp. 1017–1026 (2014)
2. Azimita, M.: Peer interaction and problem solving: when are two heads better than one? Child Dev. **59**, 87–96 (1998)
3. Belbin, R.M.: Team Roles at Work. Butterworth-Heinemann, Oxford (1983)
4. Christodoulopoulos, C.E., Papaniklaou, K.A.: A group formation tool in a e-learning context. In: IEEE International Conference on Tools with Artificial Intelligence, pp. 117–123 (2007)
5. Cocea, M., Magoulas, G.D.: User behaviour-driven group formation through case-based reasoning and clustering. Expert Syst. Appl. **39**, 8756–8768 (2012)
6. Csernica, J., Hanyka, M., Hyde, D., Shooter, S., Toole, M., Vigeant, M.: Practical Guide to Teamwork, version 1.1. College of Engineering, Bucknell University (2002)
7. Davis, B.G.: Tools for Teaching. Jossey-Bass Inc., San Francisco (1993)
8. Henry, T.R.: Creating effective student groups: an introduction to groupformation.org. In: SIGCSE 2013 Proceeding of the 44th ACM Technical Symposium on Computer Science Education, pp. 645–650 (2013)
9. Inaba, A., Supnithi, T., Ikeda, M., Mizorguchi, R., Toyoda, J.: How can we form effective collaborative learning groups? In: Proceedings of the 5th International Conference on Intelligent Tutoring Systems, pp. 282–291 (2000)
10. Kuhn, D.: Mechanisms of change in the development of cognitive structures. Child Dev. **43**, 833–844 (1972)
11. Liu, Y., Liu, Q., Wu, R., Chen, E., Su, Y., Chen, Z., Hu, G.: Collaborative learning team formation: a cognitive modeling perspective. Database Syst. Adv. Appl. **9643**, 383–400 (2016)

12. Manske, S., Hecking, T., Chounta, I., Werneburg, S., Hoppe, H.U.: Using differences to make a difference: a study on heterogeneity of learning groups. In: 11th International Conference on Computer Supported Collaborative Learning (CSCL 2015), vol. 1, no. 2, pp. 182–189 (2015)
13. Masthoff, J.: Modeling a group of television viewers. In: Proceedings of the Future TV: Adaptive Instruction in your Living Room Workshop, Associated with ITS02, pp. 34–42 (2002)
14. McLean, I., Hewitt, F. (eds.) Condorcet: Foundations of Social Choice. Edward Elgar Publishing, Aldershot (1994)
15. Moreno, J., Ovalle, D.A., Vicari, R.M.: A genetic algorithm approach for group formation in collaborative learning considering multiple student characteristics. Comput. Educ. **58**, 560–569 (2012)
16. Pizzato, L., Rej, T., Chung, T., Koprinska, I., Kay, J.: RECON: a reciprocal recommender for online dating. In: Amatriain, X., Torrens, M., Resnick, P., Zanker, M. (eds.) Proceedings of the 2010 ACM Conference on Recommender Systems, RecSys 2010, pp. 207–214 (2010)
17. Redmond, M.A.: A computer program to aid assignment of student project groups. In: Proceedings of the 32nd SIGCSE Technical Symposium on Computer Science Education, Charlotte, NC, USA (2001)
18. Rogoff, B.: Social interaction as an apprenticeship in thinking: guided participation in spatial planning. In: Resnick, L., Levine, J., Teasley, S. (eds.) Perspectives in Socially Shared Cognition, pp. 349–364 (1991)
19. Sarkar, A., Seth, D., Basu, K., Acharya, A.: A new approach to collaborative group formation. Int. J. Comput. Appl. **128**(3), 7–14 (2015)
20. Soh, L.K., Khandaker, N., Liu, X., Jiang, H.: A computer-supported cooperative learning system with multiagent intelligence. In: Proceedings of the 5th International Joint Conference on Autonomous Agents and Multiagent Systems, pp. 1556–1563. ACM, New York (2006)
21. Sorensen, J.: Measuring emotions in a consumer decision-making context – approaching or avoiding. Working Paper Series, Department of Business Studies, Aalborg University (2008)
22. Srba, I., Bielikova, M.: Dynamic group formation as an approach to collaborative learning support. IEEE Trans. Learn. Technol. **8**(2), 173–186 (2015)
23. Strnad, D., Guid, N.: A fuzzy-genetic decision support system for project team formation. J. Appl. Soft Comput. **10**(4), 1178–1187 (2009)
24. Tanimoto, S.L.: The squeaky wheel algorithm: automatic grouping of students for collaborative projects. In: Workshop on Personalisation in Learning Environments at Individual and Group Level in Conjunction with 11th International Conference on User Modeling, pp. 79–80 (2007)
25. Tobar, C.M., de Freitas, R.L.: A support tool for student group definition. In: The 37th ASEE/IEEE Frontiers in Education Conference, Milwaukee, WI, USA, 10–13 October (2007)
26. Vivacqua, A., Lieberman, H.: Agents to assist in finding help. In: Proceedings of the ACM Conference on Computers and Human Interface (CHI-2000), The Hague, Netherlands, pp. 65–72 (2000)
27. Vygotsky, L.S.: Mind in Society: The Development of Higher Psychological Processes. Harvard University Press, Cambridge (1978). Cole, M., John-Steiner, V., Scribner, S., Souberman, E. (eds.)
28. Wang, D.Y., Lin, S.S.J., Sun, C.T.: DIANA: a computer-supported heterogeneous grouping system for teachers to conduct successful small learning groups. Comput. Hum. Behav. **23**(4), 1997–2010 (2007)

29. Weisstein, EW.: Bipartite Graph. MathWorld–A Wolfram Web Resource (2014). http://mathworld.wolfram.com/BipartiteGraph.html. Accessed 28 July 2014
30. Wessner, M., Pfister, H.R.: Group formation in computer-supported collaborative learning. In: International ACM SIGGROUP Conference on Supporting Group Work (GROUP 2001), pp. 24–31 (2001)
31. Yannibelli, V., Amandi, A.: A deterministic crowding evolutionary algorithm to form learning teams in a collaborative learning context. Expert Syst. Appl. **39**, 8584–8592 (2012)

Practice of Skills for Reading Comprehension in Large Classrooms by Using a Mobile Collaborative Support and Microblogging

Gustavo Zurita[1], Nelson Baloian[2(✉)], Oscar Jerez[3], and Sergio Peñafiel[2]

[1] Department of Information Systems and Management Control, Faculty of Economics and Business, Universidad de Chile, Diagonal Paraguay 257, Santiago, Chile
gzurita@fen.uchile.cl
[2] Department of Computer Sciences, Universidad de Chile, Beaucheff 851, Santiago, Chile
{nbaloian,spenafie}@dcc.uchile.cl
[3] Economics and Business Faculty, Teaching and Learning Centre, Universidad de Chile, Diagonal Paraguay 257, Santiago, Chile
ojerez@fen.uchile.cl

Abstract. Reading comprehension is essential for students, because it is a predictor of their academic or professional success, however, it is challenging for many students, even more if they are part of large classrooms. This paper presents a work which uses Design-Based Research with the purpose of combining theories, methods and techniques of the educational sciences to design a collaborative learning activity including peer evaluation to develop the skills of reading comprehension, oral and written communication. It also presents an application for iPads supporting teacher and students performing this activity. The most relevant contributions of the proposed design are two: (1) teachers can in real time automatically configure the members of the work teams using 3 different criteria: random, individual performance hitherto achieved by the student achieved in previous stages of the same activity, or the learning styles of each student prefers; and (2) the prior calibration of an evaluation rubric in order to ensure the quality of the application of the peer evaluation method in order to grade the answers students produce to an individual reading comprehension test. In addition, other methods and techniques are incorporated, such as: monitoring students' performance in real time; active learning based on peer instruction to support the strategy of reading comprehension implemented.

Keywords: Reading comprehension · Large classrooms · Collaborative learning

1 Introduction

Reading comprehension is an essential ability for students at any level, because it is a predictor of their future academic or professional success, [1]. However, reading comprehension is challenging for many students, who struggle in reading due to having difficulty with it [2]. Research suggests that the use of collaborative activities supported by appropriate technology [3, 4], can help to improve students' reading skill by

© Springer International Publishing AG 2017
C. Gutwin et al. (Eds.): CRIWG 2017, LNCS 10391, pp. 81–94, 2017.
DOI: 10.1007/978-3-319-63874-4_7

supporting various of the activities involved in the required learning activities, such as delivering content, support students' practice, and introduce the level of participation, guidance and motivation needed in order to become successful in reading comprehension [2, 5, 6]. After all, most of today's students are digital natives; thus it would be natural for them to use technology as a tool to promote their engagement and achievement during reading comprehension.

On the other hand, large classrooms are a fact at any educational level, bringing disadvantages regarding attention, discipline, and learning [7]. In such situations, technological tools which allow collecting students' answers, (i.e. a classroom responder system) to problems or questions proposed by the teacher, are one of the most used technique to give interactive feedback by the teacher to their students, [8].

This paper presents a learning activity whose design requirements are based on validated learning methodologies which aims at improving Reading Comprehension skills of the students, supported by a technological tool named RedCoApp (described in detail in Sect. 3). The learning activity can be performed in large classrooms, using a method which collects the answers using technology which collects the answers of at least 60 students. The learning activity has been designed with the purpose of developing in students the skills of reading comprehension, oral and written communication, and teamwork. The RedCoApp application (described in Sect. 3) has been implemented with JavaScript, HTML5 and libraries that allow it to run in any browser of a desktop computer or mobile devices (iPad, SmartPhones) that are connected to the Internet.

The research method used was Design-Based Research [9], Which is characterized by being: (1) **Pragmatic**: the central objective corresponds to the design of effective learning activities based on learning theories. Design-based research refines both theory and practice. The value of theory is appraised by the extent to which principles inform and improve practice. (2) **Grounded**: Design is theory-driven and grounded in relevant research, theory and practice; conducted in real-world settings and the design process is embedded in, and studied through, design-based research. (3) **Interactive, iterative, and flexible**: designers are involved in the design processes and work together with participants. Processes are an iterative cycle of analysis, design, implementation, and redesign. (4) **Integrative**: Mixed research methods are used to maximize the credibility of ongoing research. Methods vary during different phases as new needs and issues emerge and the focus of the research evolves. And (5) **Contextual**: The research process, research findings, and changes from the initial plan are all documented. Research results are connected with the design process and the setting.

The difference between Design-Based Research and applied research in engineering or exact sciences areas is that in their "design", "experimentation" and "transformation" processes, there are overlaps and relationships between them, rather than conceive results of each process as products bound to their environment and previously established objectives. The Design-Based Research method relates experimentation and design through feedback cycles, in order to construct effective learning activities that the study of complex education systems require, [10].

The content of this article is organized as follows. Section 2 explains the relevant theories, methods and techniques used as design requirements for the reading comprehension activity. Specifically, they detail: (a) a learning support technology to be used in large classrooms (a Classroom Response System), (b) the advantages of using short messages, (c) real-time monitoring techniques by the teacher regarding the level of progress of the students, (d) learning theories and methods based on collaborative learning, (e) peer instruction and active learning, (f) techniques for configuring work team members, and (g) methods of peer evaluation among the students themselves. Section 3 details the design of the reading comprehension activity, along with the description of the RedCoApp support application. Finally, Sect. 4 describes the following stages of our work, and the most relevant contributions of the proposed design: (a) teachers can in real time automatically configure the members of the work teams using 3 different criteria: random, individual performance hitherto achieved by the student achieved in previous stages of the same activity and (b) the prior calibration of an evaluation rubric in order to ensure the quality of the application of the peer evaluation method in order to grade the answers students produce to an individual reading comprehension test, along with the description of the following stages.

2 Theories, Methods and Techniques to Support Learning

2.1 Classroom Response Systems in Large Classrooms

Nowadays, large classrooms are a fact at any educational level, bringing drawbacks regarding students' attention, discipline, and learning, [7]. Attempts to overcome common problems of lectures in large classes include introducing learning activities like recitation sections, case study teaching in labs, peer instructions, and the use of technology that allows to capture the students' answers. They are usually named Classroom Response Systems (CRS) [8]. Collecting students' answers introduce positives experiences by using interactive feedback systems that transform the traditionally passive classroom into an interactive experience, [8].

The popularity of CRS technologies has increased in large classrooms as a means to improve engagement and motivation, feedback to understanding, improve participation, to be a scaffold of collaborative learning [11, 12], and enhance learning [13]. It is a powerful and flexible tool for teaching, and has been used in a variety of subjects with students of almost any level of academic training, [11]. CRS change the student feelings of being disconnected in large classrooms [7], and changing the classroom traditional format of a lecture-style to let teachers provide feedback to the student and vice-versa as to how well a concept is understood.

According to [14], four different CRS-type technologies have been applied in large classrooms to improve classroom learning: (1) low-cost tools such as hands, flashcards, color cards, or whiteboards to give their responses; (2) instant response devices with numeric keypads, interconnected by hard-wired equipment; (3) wireless radio frequency or infrared devices; and (4) wireless interconnected systems that use desktop or mobile devices to collect students' answers. CRS can be used with many styles of questions, and new technologies allow other formats than multiple-choice questions, [15]. The only "rule" for question design is that each question's structure and content should reflect specific learning goals. Questions may have a single correct answer or be designed without any "right" answer in order to encourage debate and discussion. Furthermore, there are positive effects of CRS on student's high-level cognitive abilities: critical thinking, problem solving, metacognition, CRS can be applied for immediate feedback, interactive feedback, classroom monitoring, peer instruction, equal participation, and formative assessment, [16].

Based on what has been mentioned in this section, and considering that the number of students where the reading comprehension activity will be applied is large (at least 60 students), the RedCoApp application will be of the CRS type. We consider that a CRS adequately supports the implementation of the reading comprehension strategy (described in the next section) consisting of the execution of a sequence of stages. Each stage requires students to perform tasks that yield specific intermediate results. Each intermediate result will be collected and managed by RedCoApp, to be arranged as relevant information to be analyzed by the teacher, in a simple and easy to operate computational interface. The result of the analysis of the information will allow the teacher to make decisions such as: provide feedback to his students, set up work teams, or continue with the next stage.

2.2 Reading Comprehension

Students who use reading comprehension strategies (such as prediction, think-aloud, text structure, visual representation of text, key words selection, etc.), improve their understanding of the message read, identify the essential and relevant message of the text, and/or are able to express opinions [1]. The strategy of selecting 3 to 5 key words (KW) or main ideas of the text [6, 17] consists of following a series of elementary stages that the teacher should manage: (1) The teacher provides a texts to be read and establish the purpose (objective) of what is to be read, which is also known as the detonating factor; (2) students select the relevant KWs and justify them by means of brief comments corresponding to annotations providing justifications that support the achievement of the purpose of what is being read; (3) students make connections between KW; and (4) students examine and reflect on the KW and its associated brief comments in order to finally respond to the purpose established in the initial stage.

If in addition, steps 2 to 4 mentioned above can be carried out collaboratively between 2 to 5 students. In this way the understanding of what they are reading is favored through conversations, exchange of various opinions or points of view, and discussion on the selected KWs and their comments, [1, 6]. Brief comments facilitate the exchange of information, discussion and convergence among students.

According to the above, the RedCoApp design that we propose (see Sect. 3), besides considering the implementation of a reading comprehension strategy based on the selection of KW, will use: (1) the advantages of the use of **short messages** (microblogging); (2) **real-time monitoring** to manage the follow-up of the elementary stages; And (3) the incorporation of activities of **collaborative learning** between 2 to 5 students who will work together in the selection process of the KW. Although students will work collaboratively in the process of identifying KW and its associated comments, each individual student will have to submit an answer regarding the purpose of the reading comprehension activity. By making each student responsible, the achievement of the detonating factor or purpose associated with reading can be measured individually.

In an educational context, **short messages** (microblogging, or tweets) can be used to express ideas, paraphrase or critique a concept, [18]. Short messages provide support for the collaborative work of the students, as they facilitate posing questions, share ideas and send answers. All this while practicing and learning by doing (**active learning**), that is in this case reading and writing, [19]. The educational activities that use short messages allow increased interactions, favor the discussion processes, and improve the commitment in the learning process of students, whether they are working through computer technologies in different places, or face to face, [20–22].

One of the main contributions of software applications as a scaffolding for learning activities is the real-time monitoring that the teacher can have on the level of progress and achievement of his students, allowing her to act as a catalyst to produce changes in the educational activity or in pedagogy [23]. For example, in [24] the teacher can review student responses, achievement levels, etc., and select one for the purpose of initiating a discussion involving the teacher and students. In this way, a computer application can implement immediate feedback to the teacher and the students, with the consequent contribution in the teaching-learning processes. Real-time monitoring is "the true heart of learning that allows students to converse with others on the basis of the dissonance revealed by the screens," [25] which is a shared zone where divergences and reconciliations occur, necessary for the processes of reformulation of ideas, [26].

Nowadays, university leaders are recognizing the need for **collaborative learning** inside of classroom, to bolster student success [27]. The goal of collaborative learning technique is to support learning for a specific educational objective through a coordinated and shared activity, by means of social interactions among the group members [28]. Research has shown that the proper design of collaborative learning tasks can improve motivation levels, facilitate communication and social interaction [29], support coordination and increase the level of students' learning achievement [12, 19], and facilitate face-to-face work supported by mobile devices [29–31]. Computational technology can help organize the information, do real-time monitoring, control and favor divergence and convergence processes, and support the coordination and communication of members of the collaborative work team [24, 28, 32]. On the other hand, **peer instruction** is an interactive and collaborative teaching technique that promotes classroom interaction to engage students and addresses difficult aspects of the material, [33, 34]. By providing opportunities for students to discuss concepts in class, peer instruction allows them to learn collaboratively from each other, [12]. It modifies the traditional lecture format to include questions designed to engage students and uncover difficulties with the material.

Active learning is any learning method that gets students actively involved; collaborative learning is one variety of active learning which structures students into groups with defined roles for each student and a task for the group to accomplish. Active and/or collaborative learning techniques involve the students in the class and increase retention of information following the class period. Individual active learning techniques are easier to apply and take less class time, while collaborative learning techniques require more advance planning and may take an entire class period, [35].

2.3   Choosing Members of Teamwork and Size of Team Works

According to [29, 36], technology can assist the configuration of working teams in order to apply various criteria with the aim of gaining more efficiency for achieving the proposed learning goals. In the literature we can find few examples of this when this has to be done by the teacher while the learning activity is taking place, and furthermore, it considers performance results from previous stages. Most common criteria used for forming work teams, in addition to random selection, are based on the selection of students by academic achievement (resulting from the assessment of the level of learning achieved for a specific educational objective) [37] and learning styles, [38]. Another criteria are based on social characteristics of the members; or group goals and a theory as an intelligent guidance that helps teachers to create theory-based CL scenarios, [39].

Configuring team works according to the student's **performance** is a well-known collaborative learning best practice. A sample of representative research suggests that task relevant, skill-homogeneous groups are good at narrowly defined analytical tasks, while heterogeneous groups perform better in extended synthetic tasks requiring learning, creativity and ideation, [32, 40]. According to [41], homogenous groups can be more motivating for students while heterogeneous ones can offer better learning opportunities. Liu et al. [36], say that the heterogeneity tends to achieve better learning levels in certain scenarios.

Learning styles are classifications of the different ways of learning that are more suitable to each student, whose use leads to an improved results. Using objects or learning elements that fit best with students' learning styles [42], Kolb developed a questionnaire to identify them that later Honey and Mumford modified it to be used with Spanish speaking students, [43]. Honey and Mumford classified learning styles in four groups: active, reflective, theoretical, and pragmatic. Since the learning objects that will be used in the reading comprehension activity will be the same, we consider that it will be more useful to bring together students who have heterogeneous learning styles. Regarding the size of groups, in [44] 2 to 3 members are recommended, in order to raise the levels of motivation among the members and avoid the formation of subgroups when the number of members is greater. According to [45], in a team of four members there will always be more simultaneous interaction than in a team of five or three. If the number of components of a computer is odd (3 or 5), it is more likely that one member will not interact with another at any point in time and will be out of activity.

2.4   Evaluation in Large Classrooms: Peer Evaluation

Another main problem with large classrooms, for both face-to-face and online scenarios is giving timely and systematic feedback to students or evaluation of their performance, because it takes a great amount of time and resources, [46]. One approach to solve the problem mentioned above is involving students as peer evaluators of their classmates in order to generate positive effects in the educational process, not only because it may help to overcome this problem by passing to the students most of the burden which traditionally has been taken by the teaching staff, but also because it has other positive effects on the learning process such as engagement, [47]. However, in order to be effective, peer evaluation should be positive correlated with that made by the teaching staff [48]. In other words, the peer student evaluation should be similar to those made by the teaching staff. For achieving this, we will introduce the previous calibration method, which consists in students practice the application of an evaluation rubric on sample examples before applying it to the work produced by their peers.

3 Design of the Reading Comprehension Activity: RedCoApp

This section describes the design of the collaborative activity supported by the RedCoApp application, which can be used under two roles: teacher (described in Sects. 3.1 to 3.3) and student (described in Sect. 3.4). The role of teacher allows access to specific functionalities which display real-time information that reflects the state of progress of the learning activity that students are performing at each stage (see Sect. 2, real-time monitoring). The information presented to the teacher will be shown by easy to understand graphic interfaces, such as comparative tables or matrices, bar charts, etc. (See Figs. 2 and 3). The teacher role allows to manage the learning activity of reading comprehension by activating in sequence each of the 6 stages that students must follow (see Sect. 3.4). These are: (1) The creation of activities on reading comprehension, and assigning them to students who will perform the tasks. (2) Real-time monitoring of the task progress, which will allow the execution in sequence of each stage of the task as they are completed; or identify at each stage the feedback that students need to receive in order to advance at each stage and advance to the next. And (3) the assignment of the student members that make up the work teams.

3.1 Reading Comprehension Task Creation – Teacher's Role

This stage consists of the creation of the Reading comprehension activity where the teacher performs following actions using the setup option (see Fig. 1): (a) inputs the name of the activity and specifies the detonating factor (DF) corresponding to the text students have to produce individually based on the Reading task; (b) uploads the documents students have to read; (c) identifies the relevant key words (KW) and its alternatives associated to the specified detonating factor in order to compare them with the ones identified by the students for measuring their achievement level; (d) assigns the students that will participate in the task (using the "Users" labelled button in Fig. 1); (e) specifies the rubric associated to the detonating factor (using the "Rubric" labelled button in Fig. 1) which students will use to evaluate the answers of their peers. The information required for each student is their names and preferred learning style previously identified based on the answers given to the questionnaire designed by Honey and Mumford [43], see Sect. 2.3.

Each task may have 2 or 3 associated documents with a length of a half page which are related according to the instructions given for the Reading task. The corresponding detonating factor will require from each participating student to identify and mark three keyword for each document ordered by relevance and write a small text justifying their selection.

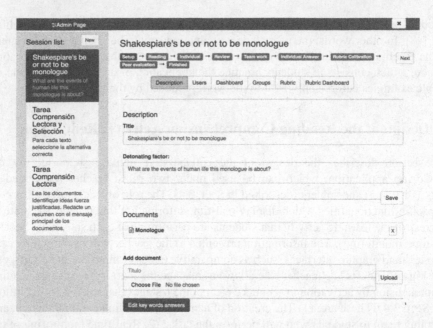

Fig. 1. View of the RedCoApp application's interface for the teacher role to upload documents to read (in the example, Shakespeare's Monologue), specify the detonating factor (what are the events of human life this text is about?). On the left there are three activities of reading comprehension.

The KW specified by the teacher can then be compared with those produced by the students thus generating relevant information about their performance. This information is presented in a simple, clear visual way when the teacher presses the "Dashboard" button in her application's interface. (see Fig. 2). This information can be used by the teacher in order to decide about: (a) going to the next stage; (b) provide feedback to the students in order to better accomplish the task; (c) assign members to working groups for the next working stages.

The evaluation rubric consists of 2 to 5 criteria for 4 levels of achievement, each of them described in detail and specified by the teacher. In addition, the weighting of each criterion should be specified and a final comment will be made to the proposed rubric. Before requesting the students to perform a peer evaluation of their responses, a calibration process will be performed for the rubric. For this, the teacher introduces three possible answers, which will be used as examples. After completing the specification and determination of the data and instructions necessary for each task, the teacher can start the learning activity (using the "Reading" button of Fig. 2) at the beginning of the class, and to continue with the following stages.

3.2 Real Time Monitoring of the Task Development – Teacher's Role

As already said, using the RedCoApp application the teacher has access to relevant information during the learning activity in order to: (1) Identify the state of progress of

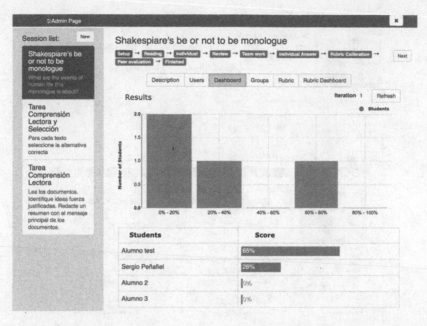

Fig. 2. View of the teacher's interface, showing a bar diagram with students' performance, based on comparing keywords chosen by the students and those proposed by the teacher.

the students in each of the stages of the learning activity. For example, the teacher can know how many students have chosen the correct keywords (see the bar diagrams of Fig. 2), or how many work teams have already completed the selection of the keywords (using the "Dashboard" button during the "Team work" stage). Figure 1 shows all steps in the upper part of the interface. This information will be used to decide whether to move to the next stage or wait for a significant number of students to complete the current activity stage; (2) identify the level of achievement of students in each stage according to keywords correctly chosen by the students. For example, if at the individual keyword selection stage, there less than 1/3 of the students have successfully completed the task the teacher may proceed to intervene the class, offering feedback to explain the detonating factor, how to identify relevant keywords, explain the context of the texts, etc.

3.3 Configuring Work Teams – Teacher's Role

Using the application, the teacher determines the configuration of the work teams, each one composed of 2 to 4 students (see Sect. 2.3), or 3 in case the total number of students is odd. Three criteria can be applied: (1) randomly; (2) based on performance (correct selection of keywords during the "Individual" stage); and (3) based on the learning style of each student. For the last two criteria, the teacher can also choose to group those students who had similar or different performance or learning styles (see Fig. 3).

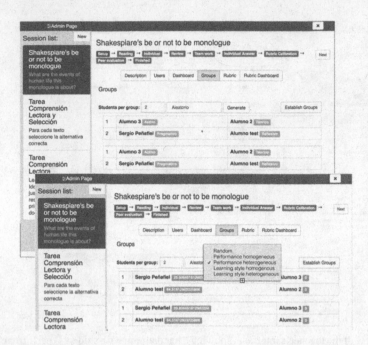

Fig. 3. Interfaces used by the teacher for the selection of the team members of a working group. The top view generated a random proposal; The bottom one is generated based on performance, with heterogeneous criterion: students with a good performance with others who did not perform well.

3.4   Stages in the Learning Activity – Student's Role

This section describes the 8 stages students should take with RedCoApp to accomplish the reading comprehension learning activity. The 8 stages are performed in 2 regular classes of 90 min (stages 1 to 5 in the first class). RedCoApp was developed to be used on iPads that will be provided to at least 60 students in a classroom. Stages 3 and 4 correspond to collaborative activities (see Sect. 2.2). Stages 2 to 7 correspond to active learning activities (students are developing and applying reading comprehension strategies to develop this activity, see Sect. 2.2). Stage 4 corresponds to activities of the peer instruction type (allows students to learn collaboratively from each other, see Sect. 2.2).

Stage 1: Read instructions and texts ("Reading" stage of Fig. 1); time: 10 min. And Stage 2: Start performing the task individually ("Individual" stage of Fig. 1); time: 20 min. By entering the application and logging using a personal account, each student receives the activities assigned by the teacher on their respective iPads. At this stage, each student will read the instructions, the detonating factors, the documents, and generate a keywords ranking individually. To choose a keyword, the student selects 1 to 3 words from the document, and write a short comment that justifies this selection. The student can at any time modify or eliminate an already specified keyword, as well as the associated comment. During this stage, the student can change the order of the keywords ranking. At the end of this stage, each student must identify between 6 and 9 keywords (3 for each of the 2 or 3 documents) ranked by relevance, justified by short messages.

Stage 3. Re-elaborate the task individually ("Review" stage of Fig. 1); time: 20 min. Anonymously, and individually, each student accesses the keywords and comments proposed by the other members of his team, with whom they will work in a non-anonymous way in the next stage. On the basis of these keywords, the student re-elaborates its initial keywords ranking proposal of ranking. Its original proposal remains accessible. It is expected that the processing will generate between 6 and 9 new KW.

Stage 4. Re-elaborate the task collaboratively ("Team Work" stage of Fig. 1); time: 25 min. The application shows each student the names of the members of his/her work team. Each student can see the ranked list of keywords and their feedback of the other members of their work team. Trough face-to-face interaction they must re-elaborate a proposal for a new keywords ranking, based on those developed in stages 1 and 2. They can identify new keywords and their respective comments/justifications together, which will be used in the next stage.

Stage 5. Answering to the detonating factor individually ("Individual Answer" stage of Fig. 1); time: 15 min. Each student answers individually and in written form to the detonating factor, based on the documents read, the ranking and comments/justifications of the keywords. The written document should refer to the keywords identified, and their comments/justifications.

Stage 6. Rubric Calibration ("Rubric Calibration" state of Fig. 1); time: 40 min. Around three texts are evaluated with a specific rubric, for which students must: (a) read the text to be evaluated, and their detonating factor; (b) apply the rubric individually (the text can be shown whenever the students want it), along with writing the general comment; (c) analyze the results contrasting their own answers with the correct one issued by the teacher. The teacher will be able to analyze statistical data (mean, frequency distribution, etc.) in order to be sure that students are correctly "calibrating" their assessment skills, and can therefore activate the next stage. Calibration is a stage that we foresee that needs special attention, because text examples for each learning task depending on students' prior achievements should be carefully chosen and commented by the teacher.

Stage 7. Peer evaluation ("Peer evaluation" stage of Fig. 1); time: 30 min. At this stage, students evaluate the responses of two other students anonymously and based on the evaluation rubric proposed by the teacher. Each student receives 2 answers to evaluate, which requires: (a) to read the text to be evaluated and its detonating factor; (b) apply the evaluation rubric, together with the writing of a general commentary associated with its evaluation.

Stage 8. Analysis of the results and closure of the activity ("Finished" stage of Fig. 1); time: approximately 20 min. In this stage the teacher analyses the students' performance in front of the students presenting some data. The data are: general performance comparing the answers of the students with the "correct" ones introduced by the teacher, frequency distribution of the results associated with the detonating factor, the best answers of the students, example of "interesting" answers, etc. It is expected that at this stage the teacher will close the activity, provide feedback and assessment to the students.

4   Conclusions and Next Steps

Following the Design-Based Research method, this section describes in general the experiences that led to the design proposal explained in Sect. 3. The design was developed during 4 months by a team of experts from different areas, such as educators, psychologists, computer scientists, and teachers. Coordination meetings were held together for 4 h per week, along with at least 4 h on average of individual work that each expert invested to explore, analyze and propose educational theories, methods and techniques, and their possible combinations to specify an educational activity. The decision about which would be the most appropriate reading comprehension strategy to be used in large classrooms was most essential outcome to design a collaborative reading comprehension activity and its RedCoApp support tool, which used several benefits and advantages that were identified in the literature on related applications.

From our experience and having reviewed the literature, we consider that the most relevant contributions of the design of the presented activity to support reading comprehension and RedCoApp, are following two aspects, which are not present in other approaches: (1) the teacher can configure in groups in real time based on 3 criteria: random, individual performance achieved by students during previous stages of the activity, or the learning styles of each student (see Sect. 3.3); and (2) the prior calibration of an evaluation rubric in order to ensure the quality of the peer evaluation application to individual reading comprehension responses that are asked of each student (see description of stages 5 and 6 of the learning activity and Sect. 3.4).

It is also important to highlight other aspects of the design, which have been used in other applications already but not in the context of reading comprehension: (1) Classroom Response System as a method for solving problems that arise in large classrooms; (2) monitoring of students' performance in real time; and (3) active collaborative learning and peer evaluation.

The following steps of this research work envisage the implementation in large classrooms and using it with real students, in order to implement the experimental process associated with the aforementioned design contributions. Results are expected to feedback the design processes, and introduce improvements in learning activity and the RedCoApp application.

Acknowledgements.   This paper was supported by Fondecyt Regular 1161200.

References

1. Duke, N.K., Pearson, P.D.: Effective practices for developing reading comprehension. J. Educ. **189**(1/2), 107–122 (2008)
2. Weber, C.L., Cavanaugh, T.W.: Promoting reading: using eBooks with gifted and advanced readers. Gifted Child Today **29**(4), 56–63 (2006)

3. Hannafin, M.J., Land, S.M.: The foundations and assumptions of technology-enhanced student-centered learning environments. Instr. Sci. **25**(3), 167–202 (1997)
4. Azzam, A.M.: Digital opportunity. Educ. Leadersh. **63**(4), 89 (2005)
5. Cheung, A.C., Slavin, R.E.: Effects of educational technology applications on reading outcomes for struggling readers: a best-evidence synthesis. Reading Res. Q. **48**(3), 277–299 (2013)
6. McNamara, D.S.: Reading Comprehension Strategies: Theories, Interventions, and Technologies. Psychology Press, New York (2012)
7. Herreid, C.F.: "Clicker" cases: introducing case study teaching into large classrooms. J. Coll. Sci. Teach. **36**(2), 43 (2006)
8. Mazur, E.: Peer Instruction: A User's Manual. Prentice-Hall, Upper Saddle River (1997)
9. Wang, F., Hannafin, M.J.: Design-based research and technology-enhanced learning environments. Educ. Teach. Res. Dev. **53**(4), 5–23 (2005)
10. Bannan-Ritland, B.: The role of design in research: the integrative learning design framework. Educ. Res. **32**(1), 21–24 (2003)
11. Caldwell, J.E.: Clickers in the large classroom: current research and best-practice tips. CBE-Life Sci. Educ. **6**(1), 9–20 (2007)
12. Blasco-Arcas, L., et al.: Using clickers in class. The role of interactivity, active collaborative learning and engagement in learning performance. Comput. Educ. **62**, 102–110 (2013)
13. Katz, L., et al.: Considerations for using personal Wi-Fi enabled devices as "clickers" in a large university class. Act. Learn. High. Educ. (2017). doi:10.1177/1469787417693495
14. Liu, C., et al.: The effects of clickers with different teaching strategies. J. Educ. Comput. Res. (2016). doi:10.1177/0735633116674213
15. Barber, M., Njus, D.: Clicker evolution: seeking intelligent design. CBE-Life Sci. Educ. **6**(1), 1–8 (2007)
16. Deal, A.: Classroom response systems, a teaching with technology. White Paper, Office of Technology for Education, Carnegie Mellon (2007)
17. Thiede, K.W., Anderson, M., Therriault, D.: Accuracy of metacognitive monitoring affects learning of texts. J. Educ. Psychol. **95**(1), 66 (2003)
18. Prestridge, S.: A focus on students' use of Twitter–their interactions with each other, content and interface. Act. Learn. High Educ. **15**(2), 101–115 (2014)
19. Carpenter, J.P.: Twitter's capacity to support collaborative learning. Int. J. Soc. Media Interact. Learn. Environ. **2**(2), 103–118 (2014)
20. Tur, G., Marín, V.I.: Enhancing learning with the social media: student teachers' perceptions on Twitter in a debate activity. J. New Approaches Educ. Res. **4**(1), 46 (2015)
21. Evans, C.: Twitter for teaching: can social media be used to enhance the process of learning? Br. J. Educ. Technol. **45**(5), 902–915 (2014)
22. Luo, T., Gao, F.: Enhancing classroom learning experience by providing structures to microblogging-based activities. J. Inf. Technol. Educ. Innov. Pract. **11**, 1 (2012)
23. Dufresne, R.J., et al.: Classtalk: a classroom communication system for active learning. J. Comput. High. Educ. **7**(2), 3–47 (1996)
24. Alvarez, C., et al.: Collboard: fostering new media literacies in the classroom through collaborative problem solving supported by digital pens and interactive whiteboards. Comput. Educ. **63**, 368–379 (2013)
25. Woodford, K., Bancroft, P.: Using multiple choice questions effectively in information technology education. In: ASCILITE (2004)
26. Miao, Y., et al.: An activity-oriented approach to visually structured knowledge representation for problem-based learning in virtual learning environments. In: Proceedings of Fourth International Conference on the Design of Cooperative Systems (2000)

27. Adams Becker, S., Cummins, M., Davis, A., Freeman, A., Hall Giesinger, C., Ananthanarayanan, V.: NMC Horizon Report: 2017. NMC Horizon Report, H.E. edn. The New Media Consortium, Austin (2017)
28. Zurita, G., Nussbaum, M.: Computer supported collaborative learning using wirelessly interconnected handheld computers. Comput. Educ. **42**(3), 289–314 (2004)
29. Baloian, N., Zurita, G.: MC-supporter: flexible mobile computing supporting learning though social interactions. J. UCS **15**(9), 1833–1851 (2009)
30. Zurita, G., Baloian, N., Baytelman, F.: A face-to-face system for supporting mobile collaborative design using sketches and pen-based gestures. In: 10th International Conference on Computer Supported Cooperative Work in Design, CSCWD 2006. IEEE (2006)
31. Zurita, G., Baloian, N.: Handheld-based electronic meeting support. In: International Conference on Collaboration and Technology. Springer (2005)
32. Zurita, G., Nussbaum, M., Salinas, R.: Dynamic grouping in collaborative learning supported by wireless handhelds. Educ. Technol. Soc. **8**(3), 149–161 (2005)
33. Crouch, C.H., Mazur, E.: Peer instruction: ten years of experience and results. Am. J. Phys. **69**(9), 970–977 (2001)
34. Crouch, C.H., et al.: Peer instruction: engaging students one-on-one, all at once. In: Research-Based Reform of University Physics, vol. 1, no. 1, pp. 40–95 (2007)
35. Keyser, M.W.: Active learning and cooperative learning: understanding the difference and using both styles effectively. Res. Strateg. **17**(1), 35–44 (2000)
36. Liu, D.M., et al.: Smart grouping tool portal for collaborative learning. In: Frontiers in Education Conference (FIE), vol. 32614. IEEE (2015)
37. Amara, S., et al.: Using students' learning style to create effective learning groups in MCSCL environments. In: 1st National Conference on Embedded and Distributed Systems, EDiS 2015 (2015)
38. Felder, R.M., Silverman, L.K.: Learning and teaching styles in engineering education. Eng. Educ. **78**(7), 674–681 (1988)
39. Isotani, S., et al.: A semantic web-based authoring tool to facilitate the planning of collaborative learning scenarios compliant with learning theories. Comput. Educ. **63**, 267–284 (2013)
40. Paredes, P., Ortigosa, A., Rodriguez, P.: A method for supporting heterogeneous-group formation through heuristics and visualization. J. UCS **16**(19), 2882–2901 (2010)
41. Yacef, K., McLaren, B.M.: Supporting Learners' Group Formation with Reciprocal Recommender Technology (2011)
42. Kolb, A.Y., Kolb, D.A.: Learning styles and learning spaces: enhancing experiential learning in higher education. Acad. Manag. Learn. Educ. **4**(2), 193–212 (2005)
43. Honey, P., Mumford, A.: The Learning Styles Helper's Guide. Peter Honey Maidenhead, Berkshire (2000)
44. Sadeghi, H., Kardan, A.A.: A novel justice-based linear model for optimal learner group formation in computer-supported collaborative learning environments. Comput. Hum. Behav. **48**, 436–447 (2015)
45. Kagan, S.: The structural approach to cooperative learning. Educ. Leadersh. **47**(4), 12–15 (1989)
46. Saunders, F.C., Gale, A.W.: Digital or didactic: using learning technology to confront the challenge of large cohort teaching. Br. J. Educ. Technol. **43**(6), 847–858 (2012)
47. Oncu, S.: Online peer evaluation for assessing perceived academic engagement in higher education. Eurasia J. Math. Sci. Technol. Educ. **11**(3), 535–549 (2015)
48. Sahin, S.: An application of peer assessment in higher education. TOJET: Turk. Online J. Educ. Technol. **7**(2), 1–5 (2008)

Promoting Active Learning in Large Classrooms: Going Beyond the Clicker

Claudio Álvarez[1], Nelson Baloian[2(✉)], Gustavo Zurita[3], and Fabio Guarini[1]

[1] Facultad de Ingeniería y Ciencias Aplicadas, Universidad de los Andes, Santiago, Chile
calvarez@uandes.cl, fguarini@miuandes.cl
[2] Department of Computer Sciences, Universidad de Chile, Beaucheff 851, Santiago, Chile
nbaloian@dcc.uchile.cl
[3] Department of Information Systems and Management Control,
Faculty of Economics and Business, Universidad de Chile,
Diagonal Paraguay 257, Santiago, Chile
gzurita@fen.uchile.cl

Abstract. Teaching and learning in most current university lectures has remained unchanged for centuries and nowadays, large lecture classes are a fact at universities. Technologies such as Classroom Response Systems have been designed to ease the adoption of new pedagogical practice in these contexts; however, these pose technological, economic and pedagogical limitations to teachers, students and institutions. In this paper, we present a feasibility study of a system that allows students to take snapshots of paper-based, handwritten solutions to a given task with their devices, and then converts this input to vector graphics that are automatically hosted in a cloud-based storage service, such as Google Drive. The teacher can then discuss students' solutions and provide elaborate formative feedback in class. We report on the findings of a feasibility study with engineering students in Chile, which validate the practicality of the approach. After this validation we plan to integrate optical character recognition capabilities in the system, in order to support programming and physics education.

Keywords: BYOD · Classroom Response System (CRS) · Active learning

1 Introduction

The educational process carried out in brick and mortar university classrooms has remained almost static for the last couple of centuries [1]. This obliviously neglects a wealth of research evidence indicating that not all students can learn effectively through the same learning experiences and at the same pace [2]. In addition, ascertaining students' mastery of the expected learning outcomes requires conducting effective assessment [3]. With regard to assessment, high-stakes testing that is usually conducted in Chilean university education poses two major problems:

1. The time span between successive assessments is too long (i.e., many weeks or months), thus the teacher remains unaware of students' learning performance for most of the academic term.

© Springer International Publishing AG 2017
C. Gutwin et al. (Eds.): CRIWG 2017, LNCS 10391, pp. 95–103, 2017.
DOI: 10.1007/978-3-319-63874-4_8

2. It is common that teachers themselves do not revise and grade students' summative tests due to the large amount of time this process requires. Instead, teaching assistants usually conduct this work for them. As a result, teachers do not become aware of students' common misconceptions, errors and lack of learning, thus continue to repeat ineffective teaching strategies term after term.

Both problems mentioned above, together with the assumption that all students do not learn at the same pace, calls for solutions that can provide the university teacher continuous awareness on students' learning progress, and the possibility for him/her to provide the students timely feedback that can effectively address learning issues. One way in which such solutions can be implemented is through embracing Active Learning (AL) in the classroom [2]. With AL the teacher conducts hands-on activities with the students, improving their motivation and understanding compared to traditional lecturing [4]. Moreover, through observation of students' results in the classroom, the teacher is able to discern the extent to which students have mastered expected learning outcomes. It is therefore a common practice to conduct formative assessment activities in AL contexts, enabling the teacher to become aware of students' common misconceptions, errors and lack of learning, and take prompt remedial action. According to the literature [1, 3], formative assessment activities in university classrooms consist of low-stakes tests conducted with following procedure: (1) The teacher presents the problem statement to the students. (2) The students try to solve the problem either mentally if the problem's cognitive requirements are low, or by sketching the solution on paper and pencil if more complex knowledge representations are needed to solve it. (3) The teacher will have a quick look at students' responses and spot any common misconceptions or errors. (4) The teacher provides feedback addressing learning shortcomings through further explanation and examples.

Analyzing this procedure, we can see the limitations that arise when embracing active learning and conducting formative assessment activities with large cohorts and no technological support. Firstly, management issues arise, as the teacher requires quick collection of students' responses and selecting those that can provide evidence for learning misconceptions and shortcomings. Secondly, the teacher needs to draw on students' responses to show and comment on students' own mistakes or achievements, and s/he has no convenient way to display (project) students' solutions at a large size in the classroom, and to edit and combine students' responses.

In the past, various systems have been developed allowing students to work on computer-based "documents" or "electronic worksheets". These technologies enable the teacher to monitor students' in-class work [5–7]. However, most of these systems have been used with small cohorts, as the activities require 1:1 computer-student settings which are difficult to scale to large classrooms [6]. Classroom Response Systems (CRS) [8, 9] have been used for fostering students' participation in class, by introducing some kind of technological device for the student to deliver an answer to a question or problem posed by the teacher. Commonly, closed-ended or multiple-choice questions are posed to the students, rather than open-ended questions and tasks that prompt for more elaborate responses requiring more sophisticated knowledge representations [10].

In this work, we present a feasibility study of a CRS system that allows students to submit pictures of their work to the teacher by using the camera on their mobile phone.

The system transforms the handwriting and sketches contained in the pictures to Scalable Vector Graphics (SVG), which the teacher can further edit and combine with a tablet device or an interactive whiteboard, to provide feedback to the students in formative assessment activities. Furthermore, SVG facilitates enabling automatic handwriting recognition, which could be used to input students' responses to third-party applications, such as simulation software, or a programming language. The abovementioned process can be implemented in a technology-enhanced manner as follows: (1) The teacher presents the problem statement to the students. (2) The students try to solve it using pencil and paper. (3) Upon completion of the exercise or the time set for the exercise, students capture an image of the response with their smart phones and send it to the system for processing. (4) Once the images have been processed, the teacher reviews the answers on his tablet, selecting a set of them that can serve as a basis for carrying out the next step. (5) The teacher proceeds to the discussion, feedback, evaluation, analysis and storage of students' responses and elaborates feedback for the students.

The following sections present a review of related literature, an account of our feasibility study that includes a description of the system, the results of the study and prospects for future work.

2 Related Work: Active Learning in Large Classrooms

Although large classrooms are cost effective, they have many disadvantages for learning [8]. Attempts to offset these problems include implementing participative learning methods, such as in-class problem solving, case studies, and peer discussion. Technology has been used to support these efforts. In particular, the term Classroom Response Systems (CRS) [9] refers to technology which allows a teacher to present a question or problem to the class, students to enter their answers using some kind of device, and then aggregates and summarizes students' answers instantly. An interesting example is Eric Mazur's experience with Peer Instruction in physics education at Harvard [11, 12]. Regarding CRS, studies have reported greater levels of student motivation [13], better student understanding [13], increased classroom attendance, higher student performance, improved student participation in class [4, 12], support for collaborative learning activities [12], and enhanced learning in the classroom [10, 15]. The main goal of a CRS has been to increase student engagement, especially in large classes where students may feel disconnected and anonymous [8, 16].

According to [14], four different CRS-type technologies have been applied in large classrooms to collect students' instant responses: (1) low-cost, low-technology tools such as hands, flashcards, color cards, or whiteboards (2) instant response systems: such as numeric keypads, interconnected by hard-wired equipment. (3) wireless radio frequency or infrared devices, which resemble a TV remote control. (4) wireless network-based systems and so-called *Bring Your Own Device* (BYOD) settings [17], i.e., smartphones can be used as answer devices, and an application can quickly scan and collect students' answers. Positive effects of CRS on student's cognitive abilities like critical thinking, problem solving and metacognition have been reported in [14].

Despite the significant benefits reported, CRS have some disadvantages too. Despite the ease of use of the technology and the benefits that they provide, faculty members may be reluctant to introduce new technologies in class and may perceive high costs in terms of time and effort investments. In addition, similar to other advanced technologies, CRS can generate frustration and unsatisfactory situations due to technical issues like failures or bugs [10].

Nowadays, the need for collaborative learning inside of classroom, around data-sharing, is understood as a fundamental basis to incorporate suitable collaborative learning activities, to bolster student success [17]. The BYOD movement calls for enabling students to perform learning activities by using the technology with which they are already familiar. This permits students a greater sense of ownership over their learning, brings productivity gains and fosters ubiquitous learning.

3 Feasibility Study

The system here proposed is illustrated in Fig. 1, and it works as follows: The teacher poses a task for the students to work on in class (step 1), then the students write down their solutions to the task on paper and take a picture of it with their mobile phones (step 2). Thereafter the students submit the solution to a web application (step 3). The web application issues an asynchronous processing job to an image processing RESTful service that corrects (i.e. crops, rotates, and adjust image levels) and converts (i.e. binarizes and vector-izes) the original bitmap image. When the resulting vector image is ready, the web application is notified by the service and then the vector image is uploaded by the web application to a cloud-based storage service, such as Google Drive or Dropbox. In step 4, the teacher can review the solutions submitted by the students, and then conduct a discussion viewing, editing, combining different solutions using any vector illustration application available in his/her mobile device (step 5).

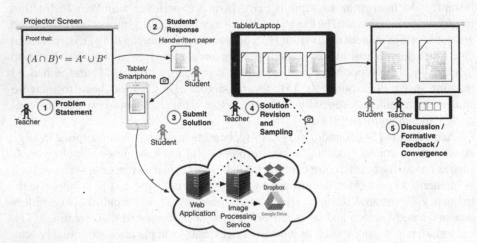

Fig. 1. The system is composed of a web application that hosts the user frontend, and an image processing service that corrects and enhances the source image, and cloud-based storage.

We conducted an initial trial of the system involving a cohort engineering students at Universidad de los Andes, Santiago, Chile. The trial comprised two activities based on logic problems, which were conducted with the intent to evaluate technological features and pedagogical usability of the tool; namely, we sought to assess the quality of the SVG digital sketches produced by the image processing algorithm embedded in the system, the practicality of the tool in the classroom from the students' standpoint, and validating the digital affordances offered by the tool to the teacher, to conduct discussions examining students' sketches on a tablet device.

The trial was conducted in a classroom equipped with a full HD projector, a WiFi access point, an AppleTV device and mobile chairs with swivel tablet arm.

3.1 Sample Description

Seven engineering students attended the trial activity. Six of them majored in computer science, and one in electrical engineering. All the students were male with ages between 22 and 25 years. The mean age of the group was 23.9 years. Every student in the sample owned an iOS or Android smartphone with photo camera.

An engineering thesis student took the teacher role in the activity. He used a 12-inch iPad Pro device to monitor students' activity and discuss their solutions to the tasks comprised in the trial. The AppleTV device in the classroom was used to stream the iPad's screen contents to the projector in the classroom.

3.2 Procedure

Firstly, a short briefing was delivered by the teacher to the students, which included an overview of the system and an explanation about the learning flow of the activity. The students were also given some hints on how to take appropriate pictures of their handwriting on paper, with suitable lighting and framing. Then they were instructed to open the solution submission site in the web browser in their smartphones.

After the briefing, the teacher presented the first task to the students on paper. The task was based on a puzzle problem based on the popular game Strimko. The students had to solve the puzzle with paper and pen, which involved drawing a graph with several numbered nodes and edges. When a student finished writing his solution, he was required to take a picture with his smartphone and submit it through the online submission form. In the meantime, the teacher automatically received the students' solutions as SVG illustrations in a Google Drive folder (see the conversion process in Fig. 2), which he could check on his iPad device with a vector illustration application. Once all the students submitted their solutions, the teacher continued to present and discuss the students' different approaches to solve the problem. He managed to edit students' solutions in the application, with digital handwriting on the iPad device.

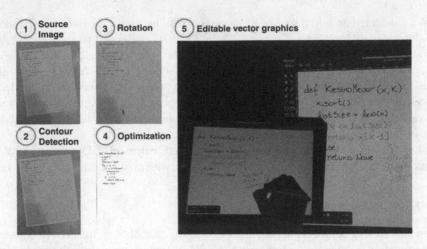

Fig. 2. Steps to students' automatic response digitalization and conversion to vector graphics.

The second task of the trial was about solving a logic puzzle. The puzzle was presented to the students in narrative form, which included a partial solution. It was the students' job to find an explanation for such solution, and state the explanation in either verbal language, formal logic or both. The same learning flow described above was conducted, with the activity ending with a discussion mediated by the teacher.

At the end of the activity a survey was administered, with the aim to collect students' appraisal and impressions about the trial and practicality of the tool in the classroom.

3.3 Results

The items and results of the survey conducted at the end of the trial are shown in Table 1. The responses to the first two questions were unanimously affirmative and ascertain that the initial instructions in the briefing were clear to all the students. The responses to questions 3 and 4 show that some students had difficulty taking a good picture with the smartphone, however, uploading the picture to the system once taken was easy. The quality of the processed images displayed on the projector screen was very good (question 5), and the students liked the methodology and considered its implementation in engineering lectures feasible and desirable (questions 6–8, and 10–12). However, only 5 of 7 students had their solutions selected for at least one of the discussions and therefore displayed on the projector screen (question 9). The students consider that the system could be useful for both regular lectures and recitations (question 13), and that keeping the original solution submitted by the student and the solution modified by the teacher would be beneficial for learning (question 14).

Table 1. Results of students' survey.

#	Question	Answers	M (SD)
1	Were you able to understand the instructions given at the beginning of the trial for taking pictures with your smartphone?	No (0), Yes (1)	1.0
2	Were you able to understand the instructions given at the beginning of the trial for submitting your responses to the teacher	No (0), Yes (1)	1.0
3	What is the difficulty level of taking a picture of a handwritten solution on paper with your smartphone?	Five-point Likert Scale (LS) 0: Very difficult 5: Very easy	3.86/5.00 (0.49)
4	What is the difficulty level of submitting pictures taken with your smartphone to the teacher?	Five-point LS 0: Very difficult 5: Very easy	4.29/5.00 (0.76)
5	How does the digital version of your response presented by the teacher in the discussion resemble the original response you wrote on paper?	Four-point LS 0: Very poorly 4: Very well	3.71/4.00 (0.49)
6	Did you like the activity?	No (0), Yes (1)	1.0
7	Do you think the methodology used in the activity could be implemented in engineering classrooms?	No (0), Yes (1)	1.0
8	Would you like to participate in regular classes with this methodology?	No (0), Yes (1)	1.0
9	Was any of your responses selected in the discussions conducted in the activity?	No (0), Yes (1)	0.71
10	Do you think this methodology could facilitate teacher-student communication in the classroom?	No (0), Yes (1)	1.0
11	Do you think this methodology could facilitate student-student communication in the classroom?	No (0), Yes (1)	1.0
12	Do you think this methodology can improve learning of certain contents?	No (0), Yes (1)	1.0
13	In which of the following contexts do you think this methodology could be beneficial? (1) Problems in class about new contents, (2) Problems in class about previous contents, (3) Recitation problems	Multiple-choice	Choice frequency: 1:3 2:5 3:5
14	Which of the following solutions can be useful for students' further analysis and study after discussion? (1) Only the original version, (2) Only the modified version, (3) Both versions	Multiple-choice	Choice frequency: 1:0 2:2 3:5

The teacher was able to conduct the activity with no technical issues or errors. He could access the students' solutions automatically copied by the system to his personal Google Drive folder and display them in the illustration application on the iPad Pro device with ease. The students' solutions were highly legible.

4   Conclusions and Future Work

The CRS system presented here allows students to submit solutions to open-ended problems proposed by the teacher using their own smartphones, and in a very simple fashion. The teacher has the possibility to review (at least a sample of) students' solutions and provide elaborate feedback in the classroom to address students' common misconceptions, errors, and analyze different ways to solve a given problem. This procedure is easily scalable to large classrooms, allowing students to actively participate in lectures. At this stage of our work we successfully tested the system with a small cohort of engineering students, evincing that the technology can support active learning activities with formative feedback with use of student-owned smartphones. In addition, the technology supports the teacher in elaborating feedback based on students' handwritten responses.

After completing our first proof of concept, through which we have managed to digitize students' handwritten responses, obtain clearly legible and editable vector graphics, and have the solutions automatically stored in a cloud-based storage service, our future efforts will aim at applying optical character recognition to students' handwriting, in order to use students' handwritten text and sketches as input for a programming language interpreter, such as Python, or a physics simulation software. In the case of programming education, the system opens the possibility to lively test students' original handwritten code on paper, modify the code (e.g. merge code from different solutions, or debug the code), and distribute the code back to the students. On the other hand, mechanics simulation could be possible by means of stating movement equations and sketching the bodies in motion on paper. From a more general point of view, we envision that our system will evolve towards becoming a general means for seamlessly converting students' and teachers' contents generated with paper and pen to digital learning objects, and in this way augment teacher's possibilities to elaborate formative feedback for students in lectures, beyond what is possible with the conventional clicker-based CRS.

Acknowledgements.   This research has been partially funded by the Chilean Science and Technology Commission (CONICYT) through grant FI-11160211.

References

1. Biggs, J.B.: Teaching for Quality Learning at University: What the Student Does. McGraw-Hill Education, Maidenhead (2011)
2. Freeman, S., et al.: Active learning increases student performance in science, engineering, and mathematics. Proc. Natl. Acad. Sci. **111**(23), 8410–8415 (2014)
3. Black, P., Wiliam, D.: Developing the theory of formative assessment. Educ. Assess. Eval. Account. **21**(1), 5 (2009)
4. Deslauriers, L., Schelew, E., Wieman, C.: Improved learning in a large-enrollment physics class. Science **332**(6031), 862–864 (2011)
5. Baloian, N., Pino, J.A., Hoppe, H.U.: Dealing with the students' attention problem in computer supported face-to-face lecturing. Educ. Technol. Soc. **11**(2), 192–205 (2008)

6. Baloian, N., Pino, J.A., Hardings, J., Hoppe, H.U.: Monitoring student activities with a querying system over electronic worksheets. In: Baloian, N., Burstein, F., Ogata, H., Santoro, F., Zurita, G. (eds.) CRIWG 2014. LNCS, vol. 8658, pp. 38–52. Springer, Cham (2014). doi: 10.1007/978-3-319-10166-8_4

7. Yoon, S.A., Koehler-Yom, J., Anderson, E., Lin, J., Klopfer, E.: Using an adaptive expertise lens to understand the quality of teachers' classroom implementation of computer-supported complex systems curricula in high school science. Res. Sci. Technol. Educ. **33**(2), 237–251 (2015)

8. Herreid, C.F.: "Clicker" cases: introducing case study teaching into large classrooms. J. Coll. Sci. Teach. **36**(2), 43 (2006)

9. Chien, Y.T., Chang, Y.H., Chang, C.Y.: Do we click in the right way? A meta-analytic review of clicker-integrated instruction. Educ. Res. Rev. **17**, 1–18 (2016). http://doi.org/10.1016/j.edurev.2015.10.003

10. Blasco-Arcas, L., et al.: Using clickers in class. The role of interactivity, active collaborative learning and engagement in learning performance. Comput. Educ. **62**, 102–110 (2013)

11. Mazur, E.: Peer Instruction: A User's Manual. Prentice-Hall, Prentice-Hall (1997)

12. Crouch, C.H., Mazur, E.: Peer instruction: ten years of experience and results. Am. J. Phys. **69**(9), 970–977 (2001)

13. Camacho-Miñano, M.-D.-M., del Campo, C.: Useful interactive teaching tool for learning: clickers in higher education. Interact. Learn. Environ. **24**(4), 706–723 (2016)

14. Liu, C., et al.: The effects of clickers with different teaching strategies. J. Educ. Comput. Res. (2016). doi:10.1177/0735633116674213

15. Deal, A.: Classroom response systems, a teaching with technology. White Paper, Office of Technology for Education, Carnegie Mellon University (2007)

16. Trees, A.R., Jackson, M.H.: The learning environment in clicker classrooms: student processes of learning and involvement in large university-level courses using student response systems. Learn. Media Technol. **32**(1), 21–40 (2007)

17. Adams Becker, S., et al.: NMC/CoSN Horizon Report: 2016K (2016)

Sequence Patterns in Small Group Work Within a Large Online Course

Dorian Doberstein[✉], Tobias Hecking, and H. Ulrich Hoppe

COLLIDE Research Group, University of Duisburg-Essen,
Lotharstr. 63, 47057 Duisburg, Germany
doberstein@collide.info

Abstract. A recent challenge in online learning courses is to establish collaboration in small groups. Group work in such courses often has to take place asynchronously, which puts additional requirements on communication and coordination to organise work in a productive way. This paper presents analyses of sequences of actions performed by such small learning groups during collaborative editing of texts in an online tool as part of a university-level online course. There were no face-to-face sessions and coordination between group members was supported by providing discussion forums. Actions of the group members in the forum or the writing tool were encoded as different contribution types, namely coordination, monitoring, minor contribution, and major contribution. Sequences of those actions derived for particular groups were used to explore the differences in the working process between the groups. It is partially possible to attribute those differences in the action sequences to the type of group composition (heterogeneous vs. homogeneous groups). Furthermore, initial evidence could be found that groups with inactive members had difficulties with coordination and tend to start the work late. These insights can be used to design mechanisms to diagnose defective group work and to generate interventions in online learning courses.

Keywords: Sequence analysis · Learning groups · Online courses · Collaboration patterns

1 Introduction

In MOOCs and other types of current online learning courses the main activities are video watching and regular assignments such as self-test quizzes. The intention is to support individual learners in self-directed knowledge acquisition independent of time and place. Collaboration only plays a minor role and is often restricted to discussion forums. Typical of those courses is a low level of retention due to users who access only specific course elements or users who are lost due to the lack of individual support and possible incentives arising from a shared social environment. It has been argued that online courses should be further adapted to individual learner needs by offering learning activities and assistance taking into account specific problems or profiles of learners or learner types [1]. However, this is difficult to realise because of the high number and high diversity of course participants and the limited availability and capabilities of tutors to focus on individual users. Thus, another approach for improving the learning

© Springer International Publishing AG 2017
C. Gutwin et al. (Eds.): CRIWG 2017, LNCS 10391, pp. 104–117, 2017.
DOI: 10.1007/978-3-319-63874-4_9

experience in large online courses is to facilitate collaboration and group work [2–4]. While it is known that group work can be beneficial in general [5], in online courses it can also help to establish an effective learning community in which the lack of individual support is compensated by decentralised peer-help and self-organised discussions. Recent research provides evidence that collaboration and a sense of an active community can also reduce attrition in online courses [6]. Furthermore, the heterogeneity of background knowledge and point of views in a large audience can be exploited for different kinds of group compositions and to facilitate knowledge exchange and critical discourse between participants [2].

Despite the opportunities and possible advantages of small-group learning in online courses there are several challenges: In addition to studying the effect of different strategies for composing small learning group based on individual learning experiences or student models, also the issue of establishing well-functioning and productive learning groups in general has to be addressed. I.e., strategies for group composition have to be combined with strategies for supporting group work, and the latter may even be more crucial. In pure online courses group work often takes place asynchronously and communication is mediated and constrained by technology. This requires additional effort in coordination in collaborative task solving. Furthermore, typical problems of group work such as social loafing and a lack of commitment of the members can be more salient in online courses due to anonymity and limitations of communication facilities [7]. This is very problematic since low productivity or even inactivity of single members negatively affects the learning experience of the other members. Longer periods of inactivity can cause uncertainty about the willing of group members to participate. Limitations of social presence in online courses further complicates this issue [8, 9].

The problem of establishing effective and productive learning groups in large-scale online courses is widely unexplored. In a recent study, it was investigated whether different group compositions impact the overall productivity of the working groups. Indications could be found that the informed composition of learning groups based on previous course activity of the participants influence the productivity of the groups [2]. In particular, it was observed that heterogeneous groups in terms of the previous activity of their members are more productive than groups of learners who had a similar level of activity in preceding group works. Based on these initial findings, this paper aims at a more fine grained analysis of different types of learning groups in an online course with a particular focus on temporal aspects analysing time series of actions performed by group members in group discussions and collaborative writing. The goal is to identify characteristic patterns in those collaboration sequences using sequence analysis, and to relate the sequential patterns to different group compositions and levels of participation. Corresponding methods of sequence analysis were first designed in bioinformatics to analyse DNA, RNA or peptide sequences and have since been used in a variety of applications, including social interactions [16]. Especially in the context of CSCL, temporal aspects play an important role [15]. The results of the analysis described in this paper are supposed to contribute to a better understanding of group work in online courses and to highlight possible starting points for the development of proper intervention mechanisms and support mechanisms based on early identification of collaboration problems.

The remainder of this paper is organized as follows: The next Sect. 2 describes the background of this study in more detail and relates it to existing research. Section 3 outlines the approach for our analysis, Sect. 4 presents the results and the last Section discusses the findings and possible future work.

2   Background: Group Work in Large Online Courses

As stated in the beginning there is a lack of experience regarding the applicability of small-group work in learning courses taking place solely online. In order to test different concepts of group work in such courses two subsequent online courses on the topic of "computer mediated communication" (mainly from a psychology perspective) were conducted. These courses were open to students of different study programs from two universities. The design of the courses was inspired by contemporary MOOCs. The course platform based on Moodle[1] was adapted to the needs of collaborative online courses. In each course section students were provided with a short instructional video, literature, and self-test quizzes to acquire theme specific knowledge. In addition, the students were supposed to apply their knowledge in assignments that had to be solved in small groups of four participants each. The goal of these assignments was to collaboratively create a short text based on a given scenario. Two existing Moodle plugins were adapted to support the groups in solving the tasks. For text creation students had to use the collaborative editor Etherpad, which was integrated in the learning platform and enables real-time collaboration. Discussions and coordination activities were supported by separated discussion forums for each group. Discussion forums and Etherpads were linked such that the students could constantly switch between the two. A snapshot of the coupled discussion and writing tool is depicted in Fig. 1.

One of the experiences of the first course was that it is challenging to maintain an adequate level of activity of the learning groups. Activity gaps (longer inactive periods) in the group work could be identified as a serious problem. These activity gaps occur due to a lack of coordination, inactive group members and, different time schedules and working habits of group members. In worst cases particular group members felt uncertain whether there are other members in the group even if the list of group members was visible all the time. Furthermore, a relationship between satisfaction with group work and overall satisfaction with the course could be found based on survey data [10]. Based on these first experiences, significant improvements in course satisfaction could be achieved in the second instance of the course by a clearer structuring of the group activities and more strict guidelines for solving group tasks [11].

Apart from testing different structures and types of group assignments, one major research question was to what extend the compositions of learning groups has an effect on the productivity of the groups. In two group tasks the groups were assembled based on activity data collected during the previous group task. On this basis, students were classified into three levels, i.e. high, average, or low activity, based on the amount of text they contributed in the discussion forums of the preceding group work. The basic

---

[1] http://moodle.org.

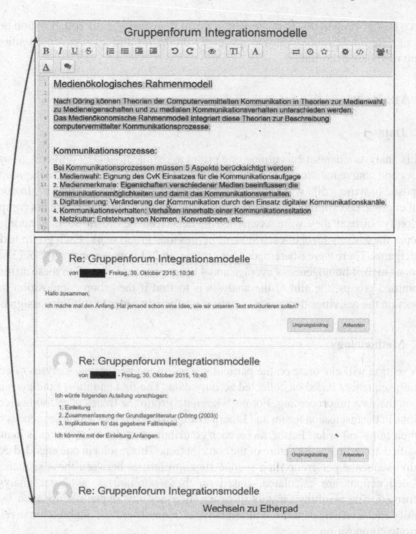

Fig. 1. Combined activity in Etherpad (top) and group coordination in a forum (bottom).

hypothesis was that heterogeneous groups with users of different previous activity levels produce more text and are more engaged in forum discussions than homogeneous groups (all high, all average, or all low). Differences in the productivity between heterogeneous and homogeneous groups could partially be observed [2]. While homogeneous groups solely composed of students who were classified as highly active in the preceding group work were most productive in the current group work, heterogeneous groups were slightly worse but better than homogeneous groups with students classified as average or low. These initial results are taken as evidence that informed group formation can be a means for course managers to maintain an adequate productivity of learning groups.

To further support this hypothesis it is worth to investigate the collaboration behaviour of different learning groups more deeply on the level of concrete contributions of group members over time.

3 Analysis

3.1 Dataset

In this analysis a dataset concerning one group assignment with 19 different groups, in the second course mentioned in Sect. 2, was used. For this assignment each group was supposed to write a 500 word wiki article on the topic of "Brainstorming". In contrast to other group tasks during this course, the groups for this assignment were not composed randomly. Instead they were assembled as described before in Sect. 2, taking into account the activity level of each student in previous group work. Each group had four participants. There were 8 heterogeneous groups, and 11 homogeneous groups (3 homogeneous high, 4 homogeneous average and 4 homogeneous low). With these artificially assembled groups, the aim of the analysis is to find if the group composition has an impact on the activities that group members perform in order to fulfil the assignment.

3.2 Methodology

This section will elaborate on the particular steps in the performed analyses of collaboration sequences based on collected activity data. The first and most time-consuming step is the data preprocessing. For each learning group the traces of individual contributions in the discussion forum and Etherpad are assembled into action sequences based on their temporal order. Furthermore, each contribution in these sequences is manually classified according to the nature of the contribution. This results in one encoded collaboration sequence per group. In a second step similarities between these sequences of encoded actions are calculated. Based on these similarities, a cluster analysis is performed. The resulting clusters of resembling activity sequences are then uses to identify characteristic patterns of different types of small-group collaboration in relation to group composition.

Data Pre-processing
The first step selects the contributions in the group forum and the text written in the Etherpad editor which are logged in the database for each group and orders them temporally. Since the Etherpad is a real-time editor, and thus, there are no revisions all characters written by a single user subsequently without a break of more than 60 min are subsumed as a single contribution. The results are action sequences of forum posts and text snippets contributed in the collaborative editor for each group in chronological order.

Next, the single actions of each sequence are classified into four main categories to make them comparable across different groups. Contributions in the Etherpad can either be *major contributions* or *minor contributions*. Major contributions add a considerable amount of text and extend the semantic content of the text. Minor contributions are small improvements in spelling or smaller text modifications. Posts in the forum can be of type *coordination*, *monitoring*, *major contribution* or *minor contribution*. Major contributions are posts in the forum which concern the subject of the assignment and which are meant to be posted in the Etherpad afterwards. Minor contributions are short content-related post, i.e. posts concerning the text outline. Posts in the forum are classified as coordination if they are dedicated to organising the groupwork. These are messages with a prospective character, for example planning or work distribution. On the other hand, retrospective posts are classified as monitoring. These are for example reports regarding own contributions to the Etherpad, the status of the groupwork or technical problems. This classification of the actions has to be done manually which is time consuming, since every single post in the forum has to be classified. Occasionally there are also actions that are not related to the group task. These *other* actions are deleted from the data. The concrete coding scheme for post classification is listed in Table 1.

Table 1. Coding scheme for contributions.

Contribution type	Description	Examples
Coordination	Forum posts of prospective character, e.g. planning, distribution of work, commitments for envisaged contributions according to own time schedule	"I could write something in the introduction but I won't have the time until tomorrow" "Do you have some ideas how to structure the text?"
Monitoring	Retrospective forum posts, e.g. reports of contributions, reflection on the progress, technical problems	"I wrote something in the discussion part. Could you have a look if it fits?"
Major contribution	Contributions in Etherpad with more than 600 characters that significantly expand the content of the text Posts in the group forum if text is posted that is supposed to be integrated into the Etherpad text	
Minor contribution	Small improvements such as restructuring of the text, correction of typos, and other small text additions below 600 characters, or drafting an outline	
Other	Forum posts that cannot be considered as relevant for the group work In addition, sometimes there can be activity logs that refer to deletions of spaces at the end of the text, or accidentally deletion and restoring of characters	"The text looks good to me, I have nothing more to contribute" "Thank you for the good work"

The resulting encoded collaboration sequences only contain actions of the group members but do not reflect inactive phases during which no group member showed any activity in the forum or the Etherpad. These passive phases are of special interest since they have a negative impact on the group work (see Sect. 2). In order to reflect these phases of inactivity a new *gap* action is inserted into the collaboration sequences whenever there is an inactive period of 24 h. To identify inactive periods before the first activity of a group member takes place, a *start* element is added as first item in each sequence with a timestamp that corresponds to the start time of the assignment. The resulting encoded collaboration sequences of the groups can then be interpreted as characteristic fingerprint of the collaboration activities of each group during an assignment. Figure 2 shows such a sequence for one group. Each action is coloured according to its class (see Table 1). The sequence begins with the *start* element. Subsequently two *gaps* follow. After that all different contribution types appear in the sequence, which ends with a minor contribution.

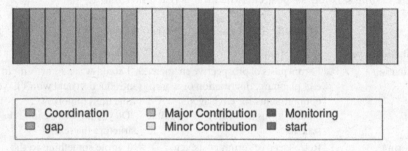

▨ Coordination	▨ Major Contribution	■ Monitoring
▨ gap	☐ Minor Contribution	■ start

Fig. 2. The complete collaboration sequence for one group.

In the next step, the final group sequences can be compared, to find similarities between them.

Sequence Matching and Clustering
The aim of the sequence matching is to group the sequences into different clusters where each cluster is composed of similar group activity patterns. Hereon, it is necessary to introduce a notion of similarity (or distance) for those sequences first. A proper measure of the distance of two collaboration sequence is the optimal matching distance [12] which generates edit distance similar to the Levenshtein distance. The idea of optimal matching is to calculate the minimal costs of transforming one sequence into another by insertion, deletion and substitution of sequence elements. The cost for the transformation sequence elements can be application specific and different depending on the types of elements and performed operation. For the collaboration sequences analysed in this work, the cost for insertion and deletion is 1 while the cost for substitution is dependent on if a gap action is part of the substitution or not. The substitution of a gap by any contribution or vice versa comes at a cost of 2, while all other substitutions have a cost of 1. The reason is to emphasise the difference between inactivity and active contributions of users. For example, changing a minor contribution into a major contribution to match one sequence to another does not make a big difference considering the course of actions in the development of a shared document. However, changing a gap into an action or an action into a gap should be more expensive since inactive periods can be

an indicator for problems in the group work and as such substituting them should be weighted accordingly.

The resulting distance matrix is used to group the sequences into clusters. For the clustering two different methods are compared. The first method is *Partitioning around medoids with estimation of number of clusters (PAM)* [13]. The second method is *Affinity Propagation (AP)* [14].

The idea of PAM is to search for k representative objects (medoids) for a given k and build the clusters around these medoids such that the dissimilarities between all objects and their closest medoid is minimised. To find a proper clustering, the algorithm first searches for a suitable set of representatives (build phase). Then it matches the object to the representatives until no switch of objects between clusters could improve the results (swap phase). The clustering is performed with different number of clusters k, ranging from 2 to 4. To determine which clustering is the best fit for this dataset, the measures of diameter of the clusters, average distance inside the clusters and average distance between the clusters were taken into account. The clustering for $k = 4$ performs best in all categories.

The idea of a clustering based on Affinity Propagation, similar to PAM, is to find so called "exemplars" which are representatives for the clusters. In contrast to PAM the algorithm does not require a k for clusters as input. Applied to the dataset the AP clustering results in two clusters. Comparing these two clusters to the two clusters that are generated by PAM k = 2 shows that, considering the mentioned measuring categories, PAM generates the better clustering. Since PAM with $k = 4$ shows the better results compared to PAM clusterings with a different value for k, this clustering was chosen as the most appropriate for the dataset.

4   Results

For a first overview, the distribution of the contribution types over days of the group assignment across groups is depicted in Fig. 3.

It can be seen that independent of group type, the most active day was the last day of the assignment. In fact, the amount of activity tends to increase with the least activity on day one (except for the homogeneous high groups) and the most activity on the final day. Especially the homogeneous low groups show very little activity in the first 4 days. In addition, there is only little coordination in the homogeneous low groups and if it occurs only on the last day. Furthermore, the major contributions are distributed over the whole time of the assignment for the heterogeneous groups and for the homogeneous groups with high performers. Whereas most of the major contributions were made relatively late by homogeneous low and average groups. 7 out of the 19 groups had one group member which was inactive for the entire duration of the assignment and one group had two inactive members. These group members showed neither activity in the Etherpad nor in the forum. All groups with inactive members were of one of the homogeneous types. One homogeneous high, two homogeneous average and four groups with inactive members were homogeneous low.

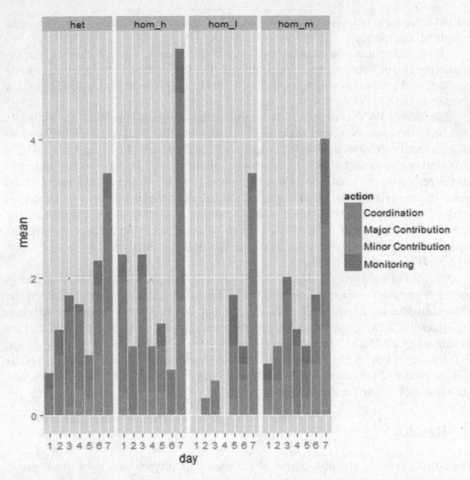

Fig. 3. The distribution of activities for the four different group types. (het = heterogeneous, hom_h = homogeneous high, hom_l = homogeneous low, hom_m = homogeneous average)

While Fig. 3 shows the distribution of each group types' activities during the assignment, there is no information about the chronological order of the activities of single groups. Thus, in the following a more detailed view based on the collaboration sequences of the groups is presented.

The analysis of the group sequences results in 4 clusters (see Fig. 4). While cluster 2 (Type 2) contains 9 sequences, cluster 4 (Type 4) only consists of 1 sequence, and consequently can be considered as an outlier group which should be further investigated. Sequences are arranged horizontally and each action in a sequence is coloured depending on their classification. The length of the sequences depends on the amount of actions that the groups performed during the assignment. While the shortest sequence in Type 1 only consist of 9 activities excluding the start element, the longest sequence (cluster 4) contains 24 activities.

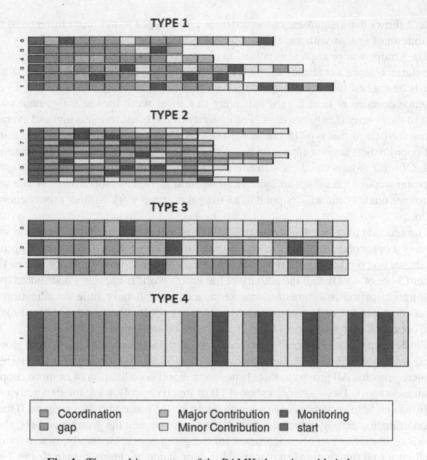

Fig. 4. The resulting groups of the PAMK clustering with 4 clusters.

As stated before, each group is assigned a group type based on their composition. Groups that include only one type of group member (high, average, low) are homogeneous, while groups that included members of different types are heterogeneous.

Table 2. Placement of the different group types into the 4 cluster types as result of the PAM with k = 4 clustering. Most likely cluster for each group type in bold face.

Cluster Type / Group Type	Type1	Type2	Type3	Type4
Heterogeneous	1	**5**	1	1
Hom. High		1	**2**	
Hom. Average	**2**	**2**		
Hom. Low	**3**	1		
w. inactives	**4**	2	1	
w.o. inactives	2	**7**	2	1

Table 2 shows the assignment of the different group types to the four clusters and the distribution of groups with and without inactive members.

The groups whose sequences belong to cluster 1 in Fig. 4 can be categorised as the "late starters" since a characteristic pattern for them is that the majority do not show any activity on the first two days. Only two groups start the work before the third day. Every sequence contains at least 5 gaps indicating that most work for the assignment takes place in the course of only two days. The majority of the homogeneous low and average groups are part of this type (5 out of 8). There is little coordination in the beginning. First coordination actions appear on day 4 or later and 3 groups show no coordination at all. Of the 7 groups which have inactive members, 4 can be found in Type 1. Overall the group work of the groups in Type 1 can be summarised as problematic. A late start and longer phases of inactivity point to an irregular group work without proper coordination.

The second cluster contains groups of all types. All groups with one exception start on the first or second day. Only one group starts later (day 5). This is also the only group that shows no coordination activity. Most of the heterogeneous groups are part of this cluster (5 out of 8). Overall the activity of the group work is unevenly distributed over the duration of the assignment. Some sequences exhibit only little coordination (5 sequences contain 2 or less coordination activities) while other groups showed much more coordination (2 sequences contain 5 or more coordination activities).

Cluster Type 3 includes three sequences. Two of the sequences originate from groups which are composed only of members classified as high. The other group is classified as heterogeneous. All groups in this cluster show good coordination (4 or more coordination messages). Two sequences show 48 h of inactivity following the first activity.

However, both sequences have a coordination action preceding the two gaps. If there is a coordination activity which distributes the work between the group members, short periods of inactivity can be insignificant for the group work. Generally, inactivity is a sign for not well functioning group work. However, it can be clearly seen in cluster Type 2 and Type 3 that longer activity gaps do not have such a strong impact as in Type 1 since gaps are most of the time preceded by coordination activities. Consequently, if the work is distributed and there is awareness of the group members about everyone's task, the gaps do not pose a problem. In contrast to this, there are no coordination activities preceding the gaps in cluster 1. The work is not distributed and the lack of communication leads to uncertainty whether the other members of the group will take part in the assignment or if they will be inactive.

Only one sequence is in cluster 4 which is not similar to all other sequences. This sequence is based on the activities of a heterogeneous group. After inactivity in the first two days the members of this group coordinate the availability of each group member and distribute the work accordingly. At the beginning the group shows the characteristic patterns of type 1 groups (no activity and no coordination). Taking a closer look into the concrete activity protocols, however, the Type 4 group could recover in a self-organised way having two very active members who take over the coordination. This group can be seen as an example of how one or two group members with high activity can lead to a well-functioning group work by distributing the work and organising the work schedule.

5   Discussion and Conclusion

In conclusion, we found evidence for an effect of group composition on collaboration. Homogeneous groups of members categorized as low and average performing tend to start the work late and exhibit longer periods of inactivity for all group members. Homogenous groups of high performers as well as heterogeneous groups show better coordination and more continuous group work. This gives further evidence to the claim made in [2], that learning groups should be formed heterogeneously based on previous activity since in homogeneous conditions all low or all average groups are problematic in terms of productivity.

Groups with long periods of inactivity are likely groups that start late with the group work and suffer from a lack of coordination. Recovery of a group returning to productive collaboration seems to be only possible in exceptional cases, when some active users take over the coordination and work distribution (see Type 4 group in Sect. 4). More concretely, it can be said, two days of inactivity at the beginning leads to low productivity in total, except coordination has taken place beforehand. One reason could be that some students are reluctant in making the first contribution. If nobody shows visible activity this goes along with uncertainty about the potential knowledge and motivation of the groupmates. However, if the groupmates show more "presence" and share their time schedule and structure their group work beforehand, activity gaps are not a big issue and can be overcome.

Our findings lead to the following suggestions for establishing and supporting productive group work in large online courses:

- Group assignments have to be clearly structured. Too many degrees of freedom increase the coordination effort for groups which can be a source of problems as our results showed. Deadlines has to be adjusted such that students with different time schedules have the chance to make adequate contributions (c.f. [11]).
- Students should be assembled in heterogeneous groups since at least one member classified as high active might facilitate the group work reducing the risk of longer activity gaps.
- Scaffolding mechanisms for group work should be offered, for example, guidelines for students highlighting the importance of early coordination.
- Intervention systems have to be developed that trigger messages for groups showing uncoordinated activity gaps of more than two days or other critical patterns such as unevenly distributed contributions. Tutors could be equipped with monitoring tools that help tutors to turn their attention to those groups.

This study has the limitation that the analysed dataset is relatively small, comprising data from only 19 groups. However, the findings give plausible indications and encourage further research in this direction to confirm our initial results.

As for the analysis methods and techniques, the extraction of coordination sequences from data could be further automated. Assessing the individual contributions and assigning them to the categories major, minor, coordination, and monitoring contribution is a work-intensive task. Development of sophisticated algorithms for automatic classification will be a major challenge in future works to scale the proposed analysis approach and make it applicable to larger online courses.

Acknowledgement. This study is based on data collected in the context of the project "Pädagogische und technologische Konzepte für kooperatives Lernen in Massive Open Online Courses (MOOCs)" funded by the Mercator Foundation, 2014–2016. The project was conducted cooperatively at University Duisburg-Essen and Ruhr University Bochum. We thank all our collaborators for their contributions.

References

1. Grünewald, F., Meinel, C., Totschnig, M., Willems, C.: Designing MOOCs for the support of multiple learning styles. In: Hernández-Leo, D., Ley, T., Klamma, R., Harrer, A. (eds.) EC-TEL 2013. LNCS, vol. 8095, pp. 371–382. Springer, Heidelberg (2013). doi: 10.1007/978-3-642-40814-4_29
2. Wichmann, A., Hecking, T., Elson, M., Christmann, N., Herrmann, T., Hoppe, H.U.: Group formation for small-group learning: are heterogeneous groups more productive? In: Proceedings of the International Symposium on Open Collaboration (OpenSym 2016) (2016)
3. Ferschke, O., Howley, I., Tomar, G., Yang, D., Rosé, C.P.: Fostering discussion across communication media in massive open online courses. In: Proceedings of the 11th International Conference on Computer Supported Collaborative Learning, Gothenburgh, Sweden, vol. 451, pp. 459–466 (2015)
4. Staubitz, T., Pfeiffer, J., Renz, C., Willems, C., Meinel, C.: Collaborative learning in a MOOC environment. In: Proceedings of the 8th International Conference of Education, Research and Innovation, pp. 8237–8246. IATED, Seville (2015)
5. Ludwigsen, S.: Sociogenesis and cognition. The struggle between social and cognitive activities. In: Schwarz, B., Dreyfus, T., Hershkowitz, R. (eds.) Transformation of Knowledge Through Classroom Interaction, pp. 302–318. Routledge, New York (2010)
6. Tomar, G.S., Sankaranarayanan, S., Rosé, C.P.: Intelligent conversational agents as facilitators and coordinators for group work in distributed learning environments (MOOCs). In: AAAI 2016 Spring Symposium at Stanford University, Palo Alto, CA, USA (2016)
7. Piezon, S.L., Donaldson, R.L.: Online groups and social loafing: understanding student-group interactions. Online J. Dist. Learn. Admin. **8**, 1 (2005)
8. Roberts, T.L., Lowry, P.B., Sweeney, P.D.: An evaluation of the impact of social presence through group size and the use of collaborative software on group member "Voice" in face-to-face and computer-mediated task groups. IEEE Trans. Prof. Commun. **49**, 28–43 (2006)
9. Weinel, M., Bannert, M., Zumbach, J., Hoppe, H.U., Malzahn, N.: A closer look on social presence as a causing factor in computer-mediated collaboration. Comput. Hum. Behav. **27**, 513–521 (2011)
10. Kyewski, E., Krämer, N., Christmann, N., Elson, M., Erdmann, J., Hecking, T., Hermann, T., Hoppe, H.U., Rummel, N., Wichmann, A.: Is small group collaboration beneficial in large scale online courses? An investigation of factors influencing satisfaction and performance in group MOOCs. In: The 12th International Conference of the Learning Sciences (ICLS), pp. 918–922. ISLS (2016)

11. Erdmann, J., Rummel, N., Christmann, N., Malte Elson, R., Hecking, T., Herrmann, T., Hoppe, H.U., Krämer, N.C., Kyewski, E., Wichmann, A.: Challenges in implementing small group collaboration in large online courses. In: 12th International Conference on Computer Supported Collaborative Learning (CSCL), Philadelphia, PA, USA, vol. 2, pp. 625–628 (2017)

12. Abbott, A., Tsay, A.: Sequence analysis and optimal matching methods in sociology review and prospect. Sociol. Meth. Res. **29**, 3–33 (2000)

13. Kaufman, L., Rousseeuw, P.: Clustering by means of medoids. In: Statistical Data Analysis Based on the L1-Norm and Related Methods. North-Holland, New York (1987)

14. Frey, B.J., Dueck, D.: Clustering by passing messages between data points. Science **315**, 972–976 (2007)

15. Reimann, P.: Time is precious: variable- and event-centred approaches to process analysis in CSCL research. Int. J. Comput. Support. Collaborative Learn. **4**(3), 239–257 (2009)

16. Cornwell, B.: Social Sequence Analysis: Methods and Applications. Cambridge UP, New York (2015)

Susceptibility of Graduate Assistants to Social Influence Persuasive Strategies

Humu-Haida Selassie[✉] and Julita Vassileva

Department of Computer Science, University of Saskatchewan, Saskatoon, Canada
{hus447,yiv905}@mail.usask.ca

Abstract. Persuasive Technology which leverages technology to accomplish the art of persuasion has been successfully used to motivate people into adopting desirable target behaviours in many domains including workplaces. This success informed the decision to use persuasive technology to promote workplace engagement and collaboration among Graduate Assistants. This will result in a more effective and efficient learning process for students as well as creating a sense of relatedness among Graduate Assistants. An effective way of implementing Persuasive Technology is to tailor persuasive strategies to user groups and/or individuals. This study was therefore carried out to investigate the persuasive strategies Graduate Assistants are most susceptible to. A survey was conducted with 55 Graduate Assistants from the University of Saskatchewan. A Three-Way Mixed ANOVA with persuasive strategy as a within-subjects factor and Gender and Continent of Origin as a between-subjects factors was run. The results showed that in general, Graduate Assistants are most susceptible to Trustworthiness, followed by Reward and Competition and least susceptible to Social Learning and Social Comparison. Also, African and Asian females were found to be more susceptible to Trustworthiness than North American females. Also, African males were more susceptible to Social Learning than North American males. Designers must therefore consider Gender and Continent of Origin when choosing Social Learning and Trustworthiness as persuasive strategies to promote collaboration among Graduate Assistants.

Keywords: Persuasive technology · Gamification · Workplace · Personalization · Persuasive strategy · Persuadability · Graduate Assistants

1 Introduction

Testing has been viewed by previous literature to be reliable and effective, however, it has also been identified to measure inconsequential and distorted learning. This has caused students to use their own strategies to focus on what they think teachers are after and avoid or ignore whatever is left. Despite this problem, assessment has also been viewed as a driver of active learning and valuable learning outcomes. Assessment is one of the essential aspects of higher education because it shapes learning and provides an orientation for all frames of the learning cycle [1]. Assessments happen after students have been tested on some form of acquired knowledge. The end result of an assessment is usually the provision of feedback which is also an undeniably significant aspect of the learning cycle

© Springer International Publishing AG 2017
C. Gutwin et al. (Eds.): CRIWG 2017, LNCS 10391, pp. 118–131, 2017.
DOI: 10.1007/978-3-319-63874-4_10

of students. Providing feedback promptly to students has been identified as one of the seven principles of good practices required to achieve a successful and productive under-graduate education [2]. Tutorials on the other hand, constitute another component of the learning process that have been used by institutions especially higher education to provide a mentoring system to guide students. This strategy has been adopted by university lecturers all around the world as a teaching strategy to increase the learning success rates of students [3].

Much like other universities, the University of Saskatchewan, Canada, leverages the availability of graduate students to carry out tasks such as tutorials and assessments to ensure that lecturers can dedicate more time to developing and maintaining workable course contents. Graduate Assistants (Teaching Assistants and Markers) collaborate to shape the learning cycle of students by executing their respective tasks in exchange for funding and/or hourly wages. Despite the significance of assessments, it is known to consume a considerable amount of time to execute effectively [1]. Also, the system of assessing many perspectives of solutions provided by students to the same questions, makes assessment a somehow repetitive and tedious task that is not inherently enjoyable. Monotonous tasks are known to lead to a workforce that is not engaged with their respon-sibilities at work [4]. This implies that Graduate Assistants usually execute the minimum amount of work required of them to have access to their funding. It is in view of this that a study was carried out to investigate the work motivation of Graduate Assistants and how Persuasive Technology can be leveraged to produce intrinsically motivated workforce that is engaged with their responsibilities. This will inform the design and implementa-tion of a platform that will facilitate collaboration among Graduate Assistants to make them more engaged, productive and specifically for markers, provide quality feedback that students can understand and act on.

A Requirements Focused-Design Science Research (DSR) [5] approach was adopted to find a practical solution to this real-world problem. As part of the DSR approach adopted, a survey was administered to 55 Graduate Assistants to understand their moti-vation and their susceptibility to various persuasive strategies. We found out that although Graduate Assistants placed their relationship with each other as part of their top five motivating factors, they did not perceive themselves to have a strong social relationship with each other. In addition to this, they did not perceive themselves to act effectively in the accomplishment of their responsibilities as Graduate Assistants. Also, Graduate Assis-tants did not perceive the execution of their responsibilities to be self-determined. This means that their basic psychological needs of Relatedness, Competence and Autonomy are not satisfied. The satisfaction of these needs is quintessential in intrinsically moti-vating individuals. Per the Self-Determination Theory, intrinsic motivation stems from the execution of a task because of the inherent will to do so [6]. Research has shown that a satisfaction of the basic psychological needs leads to individual well-being and behav-iour engagement whilst a frustration of these needs leads to individual ill-being and lack of engagement in responsibilities [6–8].

Persuasive systems and gamified applications are implemented using persuasive strat-egies. Implementing an effective and meaningful persuasive system has been shown by previous literature to require tailoring of persuasive strategies to user groups or individ-uals [9, 10]. One way to achieve this is understanding the susceptibility of groups and/or individuals to various persuasive strategies and implementing a persuasive system based on this knowledge. The most susceptible persuasive strategies are implemented to effectively tap into the core drives of target groups or individuals. We present in this document, the method, results and implications of the susceptibility of Graduate Assistants to five persuasive strategies of social influence measured using Busch et al.'s [11] Persuadability Inventory. The social influence strategies measured in this scale are Reward, Competition, Social Learning, Social Comparison and Trustworthiness. Social Influence has been proven by previous research to be the most effective way of causing desirable behaviour change in people [12] and helps foster and maintain social relationships when implemented well.

Our findings show that Graduate Assistants are most susceptible to trustworthiness as a persuasive strategy, followed by Reward and Competition and least susceptible to Social Learning and Social Comparison. However, Continent of Origin and Gender influenced the susceptibility of Graduate Assistants to some of these social influence persuasive strategies. Asian females were more susceptible to Trustworthiness as a persuasive strategy than North American females. Also, African and Asian males were more susceptible to Social Learning than North American males. We therefore propose a careful consideration of Continent of Origin and Gender when selecting persuasive strategies to apply to Graduate Assistants.

2 Background

Busch et al. [11] developed an instrument that measures the susceptibility of individuals or groups to five social influence persuasive strategies selected from Torning and Kukkonen's [13] collection of persuasive strategies. This instrument is called the Persuadability Inventory and it is a 9-point 25-item scale. It contains five constructs, with each construct measuring one of the five social influence strategies. It was empirically validated using 167 participants [11]. The five persuasive strategies the scale measures are:

- **Rewards:** Involves the use of virtual rewards to cause people to continue in the path of performing desirable behaviors.
- **Competition:** Provide an avenue or system that allows individuals to compete towards the achievement of an anticipated reward.
- **Social Comparison:** Allows individuals to compare their performance to their peers. Social comparison can either be upward or downward. In upward comparison, an individual is informed on the proportion of their peers that performed better than them whilst downward comparison informs them of the proportion of their friends who they performed better than.
- **Social Learning:** This involves the demonstration of a behaviour by a real or fictional character. One way of implementing this is with cues by prompting an individual to perform an activity because other people in their social group are doing it.
- **Trustworthiness:** This strategy has to do with providing a way to make individuals trust the system and mechanisms that have been implemented to achieve persuasion. People need to believe that gamified persuasive system provides the right information and is unbiased.

3   Related Work

The significance of personalizing persuasive strategies to individuals and user groups has received much attention and has been studied extensively by previous literature [9, 10, 14–17]. This is because people are different in the way they respond to motivating factors such as persuasive strategies. For example, Orji et al. in their previous works have shown that individuals or groups respond differently to Cialdini's persuasive principles based on factors like culture, gender, and personality [18, 19]. In their study with 1108 respondents (48% females and 52% males), they explored the impact of gender and age of individuals on their susceptibility to Cialdini's persuasive principles. Orji et al. found out that females were more susceptible to Reciprocity, Commitment and Consensus than males [18]. A later and recent study by Orji [19] explored the differential susceptibility of collectivist and individualists to Cialdini's persuasive principles. This study disclosed that both collectivist and individualist are most susceptible to commitment. However, whilst collectivists were least susceptible to Scarcity, individualists were least susceptible to Authority [19].

Also, a recent study by Oyibo et al. [20] investigated the susceptibility of North Americans to social influence persuasive strategies in persuasive technology and the influence of gender and age. They carried out a study among 323 Canadians using the Persuadability Inventory [11] instrument discussed above. They found that males and females respond differently in their susceptibility to Reward and Social Comparison. They also found that younger adults (18–24 years old) were more persuadable by Competition, Social Comparison and Social Learning than older adults (above 24 years old). Another study by Oyibo and Vassileva [21], which investigated the predictors of Competition among North Americans, found that the strongest predictor of a competitive behaviour is Reward.

In both studies investigating social influence [20, 21] in the later paragraph, the susceptibility of individuals to Trustworthiness was omitted although it is a part of the Persuadability Inventory, the same instrument used in this study. The pervasive role of Trustworthiness in social cohesion and integration cannot be underestimated. It is a significant element for the survival of social relationships through social cohesion and integration [22]. Also, the social influence studies described above only explored the independent impact of gender and age on the susceptibility to the social influence strategies measured. The sample used also came from one continent; North America. Culture has however been identified to impact and shape social behaviour significantly as proved by Orji's [19] study discussed previously. Therefore, in a workplace which brings together individuals (Graduate Assistants) who are different in terms of gender, culture, and education, it is empirical to investigate their susceptibility to these social influence persuasive strategies.

So far, there is no work that has studied the influence of both gender and culture on susceptibility of individuals or groups to these social influence persuasive strategies especially among Graduate Assistants in the field of Persuasive Technology.

4   Study Design and Methods

As discussed in the introduction, this paper presents a part of a study that was carried to study work motivation and susceptibility to persuasive strategies among Graduate Assistants. This is aimed at informing the development of design and implementation guidelines to promote workplace engagement among graduate assistants. Here, we discuss the tools, participants and data analyses that were used to measure the susceptibility to the persuasive strategies; Reward, Competition, Social Learning, Social Comparison, and trustworthiness.

4.1   Tool

The tool used for the study is Busch et al.'s [11] scale for measuring persuadability which has been discussed briefly in Sect. 2 above. Although it is originally a 9-point 25-item scale, we used a 7-point Likert scale (1-Completely Disagree; 7-Completely Agree) to ensure a scale consistency with other instruments in the study that used a 7-point Likert scale. Participants were asked a series of questions and asked to express their level of agreement with them on a scale of 1 (Completely Disagree) to 7 (Completely Agree). Some of the items used in the scale are shown in Table 1.

Table 1.   Sample items from the Busch et al. Persuadability Inventory [11]

Reward
• *"It is important to me that my actions are rewarded"*
• *"I put more ambition into something, if I know I am going to be rewarded for it"*
Competition
• *"I push myself hard, when I am in competition with others"*
• *"I would like to participate in Quiz shows, where I need to assert myself against other people"*
Trustworthiness
• *"I trust information better when the source is specified"*
• *"It is important for me to be precisely informed about things that I need to do, before I do them"*
Social Comparison
• *"It is important to me, what other people think of me"*
• *"I adapt my style to the way my friends dress"*
Social Learning
• *"I adapt my behavior to other people around me"*
• *"I take other people as role models for new behaviors"*

4.2   Participants

An email containing a link to the questionnaire was sent to Graduate Assistants in the Department of Computer Science, University of Saskatchewan. Also, a link was posted on University of Saskatchewan's public bulletin board inviting Graduate Assistants to participate. Clicking on the link took a respondent to Fluid Survey where the questionnaire was hosted. It took an average of ten minutes to provide responses to this questionnaire. Participants were asked to provide their emails to be entered into a draw for a chance to win a \$50 gift card. 71 responses were received but 55 were used for analyses because the remaining 16 responses were less than half completed. Respondents were from Africa (25.5%), Asia (38.2%), Middle East (9.1%), and North America (25.5%). There were 24 males (43.6%) and 30 females (56.4%). 83.6% of the participants were between the ages of 16–34 years old and 10.9% were between the ages of 35–44. These age groups were used because of the initial intention to explore the debated topic of generational differences, although no differences were found with respect to susceptibility to the persuasive strategies measured in this document.

4.3 Data Analysis

A Kaiser-Meyer-Olkin (KMO) and Bartlett's test of Sphericity were run on the responses to test for sampling adequacy and to reject the null hypothesis that there are no correlations between the variables measured. KMO was measured at 0.64 and Bartlett's test for Sphericity rejected the null hypothesis ($BTS = (\chi^2(300) = 777.37, p < 0.0001)$). These results show that the responses were valid for a factor analysis. Also, to establish internal validity, a Cronbach's alpha test was run and all the constructs passed this test (Rewards = 0.91; Competition = 0.79; Social Learning = 0.62; Social Comparison = 0.73; Trustworthiness = 0.51). The low Cronbach's alpha value of 0.51 was accepted for Trustworthiness because it contained only 3 items [19].

A Three-Way Mixed ANOVA (BBW) was used to analyze the data with persuasive strategies as a Within-Subjects factor and Gender and Continent as a Between Subjects factors. The 35 cells of the study design were checked for outliers. There were two outliers in one of the cells (Gender = Female, Continent = North America) from the same respondent in the Reward category. However, these outliers were not removed because the results of the Three-Way ANOVA were not statistically different with or without the outliers. All cells of the study design were normally distributed as tested by a Kosmogorov-Smirnov test (p > 0.05). There was homogeneity of variances (assumption that variance of the dependent variable is equal for all groups of the Between-Subjects factor) in all constructs measured (p > 0.05). However, Mauchly's test of Sphericity showed that the assumption of Sphericity had been violated ($\chi^2(9) = 33.245$, p < 0.001). Since Epsilon (ε) was lower than 0.75, a Greenhouse-Geisser correction was used to correct the results of the Three-Way Mixed ANOVA. Epsilon is the degree to which Sphericity is assumed in a data with an Epsilon of 1 indicating an exact assumption of Sphericity. The less, the value of epsilon, the greater the violation of Sphericity [23].

5 Results

5.1 General Susceptibility to Persuasive Strategies

There were main effects of susceptibility to persuasive strategies and this was statistically significant ($F(4, 184) = 28.23$, p < 0.01, partial $\eta^2 = 0.38$). Graduate Assistants were most susceptible to Trustworthiness (M = 5.82, SE = 0.11), Reward (M = 5.17,

SE = 0.19), Competition (M = 4.71, SE = 0.17), Social Comparison (M = 3.84, SE = 0.15) and Social Learning (M = 3.90, SE = 0.14) in that order. There were significant differences between susceptibility to Trustworthiness and Reward, and, Trustworthiness and Competition (p < 0.05). There was no statistically significant difference between Reward and Competition (p > 0.05). The difference between susceptibility to Social Learning and Social Comparison was also not statistically significant (p > 0.05) (Fig. 1).

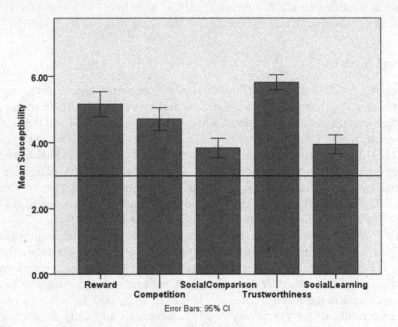

Fig. 1. Bar graph of Graduate Assistants' susceptibility to persuasive strategies measured (rewards, competition, social comparison, trustworthiness and social learning)

5.2   Gender, Continent of Origin and Persuasive Strategy Interaction

The results of the Three-Way Mixed ANOVA also showed a statistically significant three-way interaction between susceptibility to persuasive strategies, Gender and Continent of Origin (F(12, 184) = 2.45, p = 0.015, partial η^2 = 0.14). Continent of origin and Gender of Graduate Assistants did not significantly impact susceptibility to the persuasive strategies independently.

Statistical significance for simple two-way interactions and simple simple main effects were accepted at a Bonferroni-adjusted alpha level of 0.025 and 0.05 respectively. Bonferroni corrections were made with comparisons within each simple simple main effect considered as a family of comparisons. Bonferroni corrected adjusted p-values are reported for pairwise comparisons.

5.3   Gender, Continent of Origin and Social Learning

There was a simple two-way interaction between Gender and Continent of Origin in susceptibility to Social Learning ($F(3.46) = 3.64$, $p = 0.019$) and this interaction was statistically significant. There was a statistically significant simple simple main effect of Gender for North America with regards to susceptibility to Social Learning ($F(1.46) = 6.41$, $p = 0.015$). Also, there was a statistically significant simple simple main effect of Continent for Males with regards to susceptibility to Social Learning ($F(1.46) = 1.22$, $p = 0.018$) but not for females (Fig. 2).

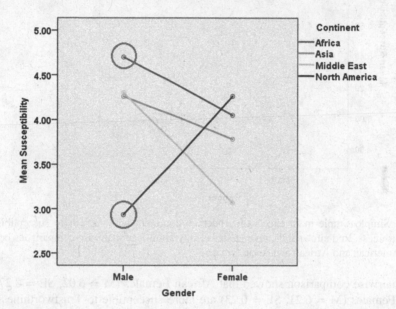

Fig. 2. Simple simple main effects of gender on continent with regards to susceptibility to social learning. Red circles indicative of statistically significant pairwise comparisons between North American and African males.

A pairwise comparison for statistically significant simple simple main effects indicated that mean susceptibility to Social Learning was higher in African ($M = 4.7$, $SE = 0.19$) than North American Males ($M = 2.933$, $SE = 0.30$). However, there was no statistically significant difference between African Males, Asian Males ($M = 4.27$, $SE = 0.31$) and Middle Eastern Males ($M = 4.3$, $SE = 0.09$) (Fig. 2).

5.4   Gender, Continent of Origin and Trustworthiness

There was also a statistically simple two-way interaction between Gender and Continent of Origin in susceptibility to Trustworthiness ($F(3.46) = 4.11$, $p = 0.012$). There was a statistically significant simple simple main effect of Gender for North America with regards to susceptibility to Trustworthiness ($F(1.46) = 9.45$, $p = 0.004$). Also, there was a statistically significant simple simple main effect of Continent for Females with regards to susceptibility to Trustworthiness (F(3.46) = 4.69, p = 0.006) but not for Males (Fig. 3).

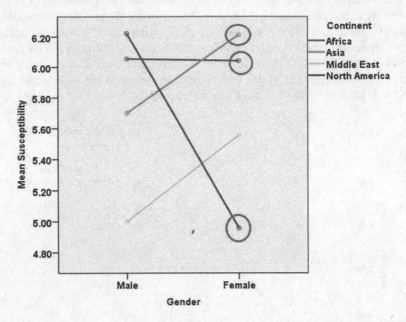

Fig. 3. Simple simple main effects of gender on continent with regards to susceptibility to trustworthiness. Red circles indicative of statistically significant pairwise comparisons between North American and African and Asian females.

A pairwise comparison showed that African Females (M = 6.02, SE = 0.27) and Asian Females (M = 6.21, SE = 0.23) are more susceptible to Trustworthiness as a persuasive strategy than North American Females (M = 4.96, SE = 0.26). There was no statistically significant difference between African and Asian Females' susceptibility to Trustworthiness. There was no statistically significant difference between Middle Eastern Females (M = 5.56, SE = 0.23) and females from other continents (Fig. 3).

6 Discussion

Graduate Assistants were most influenced by Trustworthiness as a social influence persuasive strategy. Just as much as trust is important between an organization and its customers or clients, in-house enterprise trust is equally important. Employees must trust each other, management and all other systems or mechanisms that have been implemented at the workplace. The existence of sufficient trust at the workplace fosters a workplace that is set apart by effective communication, teamwork and performance. Trustworthiness within an organization has also been identified to be a prerequisite for increase in productivity and meaning in workplace responsibilities. This is analogous to trust being a precondition for the survival of social relationships through social cohesion and integration [22]. Also, Ethos (communicator credibility), one of the components of the rhetoric triangle, represents the establishment of trust between the persuader and the target audience for effective persuasion to occur [24]. This implies that persuasion is hardly possible without the existence of trust in any setting.

After Trustworthiness, Graduate Assistants were more susceptible to Reward and Competition. Westover and Taylor [25] found out that one of the major drivers of job satisfaction among employees in most countries is rewards especially those that foster intrinsic motivation like interesting work and job autonomy. Intrinsic tasks rewards at the workplace, followed by extrinsic rewards are known to cause employees to become very satisfied with their job and thus exhibit an increase in workplace engagement [26]. Some of these rewards may include but not limited to salary, style of supervision, fringe benefits, working conditions and promotions. Competition on the other hand is a widespread and a remarkable workplace phenomenon which increases effort [27]. It is usually characterized by the effort by employees to outperform each order to receive higher salaries, wages, bonuses or rewards. It is therefore not surprising that there was no statistical significant difference between Graduate Assistants' susceptibility to Reward and Competition. This result is also supported by a previous study which found Reward to be the strongest predictor of a Competitive behaviour [21].

Social learning and Social Comparison ranked the lowest in terms of susceptibility among Graduate Assistants with a mean of 3.84 and 3.90 respectively on a scale of 1 (Completely Disagree) to 7 (Completely Agree). This is also supported by a previous finding by Oyibo and Vassileva [20]. The poor susceptibility of Graduate Assistants to Social Learning and Social Comparison can be explained by previous works which found young adults (16–34, constituting 86.3% of our study participants) to be independently minded and as such like to do things their way [28].

Results from this study are also supported by previous literature that males and females do not have any significant difference in the degree of trust they usually exhibit [29, 30]. However, the introduction of another factor which is Culture/Continent of Origin, brings to light a different view of social influence susceptibility which is also supported by previous literature [31]. The results showed that susceptibility to Trustworthiness was impacted by Graduate Assistants' Gender and their Continent of Origin. North American Females were less susceptible to Trustworthiness than African and Asian Females. However, contrary to previous studies, North American women were discovered to prioritize integrity as opposed to Asian women who prioritized benevolence and cultural similarity at the workplace [31]. North Americans belong to the individualist culture whilst Asians and Africans belong to the collectivist culture [19]. The individualist culture is characterized by people who usually look out for themselves hardly form social relations with members of their community. They are brought up to be independent right form an early age. On the contrary, collectivists form strong social bonds with each other right from birth [19, 32]. African and Asian females might have been most influenced by Trustworthiness because of the importance of trust amongst collectivists. Trust is one of the most important virtues that allows collectivist to achieve a social cohesion.

Also, Males from Africa are more influenced by Social Learning than Males from North America. This result is evident by the collectivist nature of Africans who are innately drawn to social and community integrations. Social Learning which is comparable to consensus was found by Orji [19] to be a more effective strategy to persuade collectivists than individualists. A previous study also discovered females to be more influenced by consensus than males. This probably enlightens why Female Graduate Assistants revealed the same propensity to learn or pick up behaviour (social learning) from each other despite their country of origin.

7   Design Implications

The results of the study suggest the implementation of a persuasive gamified system that will foster relatedness among Graduate Assistants whilst increasing competence and autonomy. One way relatedness can be implemented, is to provide a platform that will support collaboration among Graduate Assistants. This platform could allow Graduate Assistants to fill in for each other when others are not in the position to grade or tutor. Graduate Assistants will be willing to fill in for a colleague if there is a potential benefit to them. This is evident by the fact that benefiting from a social group is one of the most effective ways of achieving the survival of group cohesion [33, 34]. This could be done in exchange for performing less responsibilities at another time or in exchange for virtual rewards such as points or badges. Competition can be implemented by giving rewards (points or badges) for providing feedbacks that are beneficial to students. Students can therefore be asked to rate the quality of feedbacks provided to them. The weight of Rewards provided to Graduate Assistants could be dependent on the rating they receive from students. A leaderboard can then be implemented, so Graduate Assistants can compete against each other. The leaderboard is one way to support Competition and Trustworthiness in a persuasive gamified system. As Trustworthiness is important to Graduate Assistants, they must be assured that their scores/rewards in the persuasive gamified system is representative of their efforts and that other users are not favored over them.

The findings also imply that, in designing and implementing a persuasive system to promote collaboration among Graduate Assistants, designers must choose the right social influence persuasive strategies taking into consideration Gender and Continent of Origin of users. In choosing Reward and Competition as social influence strategies, designers can ignore the impact of Gender and/or Continent of Origin. Social Comparison should sparingly be used to promote collaboration among Graduate Assistants as there is a tendency of persuasion not happening. However, although Trustworthiness was found to be the most influential persuasive strategy, it's influence on North American females is not very strong. Also, Social Learning which was one of the least influential persuasive strategies in the general population appeared to be moderately influential for African Males. However, North American Males are not persuadable by Social Learning. This implies that, Social Learning can be used for African Males but not North American males.

8   Limitation and Future Work

A sample of convenience which was mostly focused on Graduate Assistants from the Department of Computer Science was used. A consideration of how a substantial number of responses from other departments influences these results will be valuable. Also, the relation between susceptibility to these persuasive strategies and employee motivation will provide a more detailed understanding of how employee motivation impacts susceptibility to these persuasive strategies. Future work will therefore use a larger sample size and explore the diverse factors that could impact susceptibility to these social influence persuasive strategies. Future work will also consider making these findings actionable through the provision of design and implementation guidelines as well as the selection of persuasive and game elements that support these strategies when implementing persuasive technology to promote collaboration among Graduate Assistants.

9   Conclusion

To investigate the susceptibility of Graduate Assistants to Rewards, Competition, Social Comparison and Social Learning, respondents were made to express their level of agreement (1-Completely Disagree; 7-Completely Agree) to a 25-item scale measuring these social influence persuasive strategies. In general, Graduate Assistants were persuadable by all the five strategies measured; Trustworthiness, Reward, Competition, Social Comparison and Social Learning. The results also showed that this category of workforce is most persuadable by Trustworthiness. Rewards and Competition were the next most effective strategies, although there was no difference in their influencing power. Social Learning and Social Comparison least persuadable. However, when Gender and Continent of origin were taken into consideration, we found out that, Asian and African females were more susceptible to Trustworthiness than North American females. Also, Asian males were more influenced by social learning than North American males. North American are influenced by Social Learning since the recorded susceptibility was very low. We therefore advise a consideration of individuals' continent of origin and Gender when tailoring social influence persuasive strategies to Graduate Assistants.

Acknowledgements. This research was supported by the NSERC Engage and Discovery grants to the second author.

References

1. Gibbs, G.: How assessment frames student learning. Innov. Assess. High. Educ. **23**, 23–36 (2006)
2. Chickering, A.W., Gamson, Z.F.: Seven principles for good practice in undergraduate education. Am. Assoc. High. Educ. Bull. **39**, 3–7 (1987)
3. Ruiz, N.M., Fandos, M.G.: The role of tutoring in higher education: improving the student's academic success and professional goals. Rev. Int. Organ. RIO. **12**, 89–100 (2014)

4. Cleary, M., Sayers, J., Lopez, V., Hungerford, C.: Boredom in the workplace: reasons, impact, and solutions. Issues Ment. Health Nurs. **37**, 83–89 (2016)
5. Peffers, K., Tuunanen, T., Gengler, C.E., Rossi, M., Hui, W., Virtanen, V., Bragge, J.: The design science research process: a model for producing and presenting information systems research. In: Proceedings of Design Research in Information Systems and Technology DESRIST 2006, pp. 83–106 (2006)
6. Ryan, R.M., Deci, E.L.: Intrinsic and extrinsic motivations: classic definitions and new directions. Contemp. Educ. Psychol. **25**, 54–67 (2000)
7. Gagné, M., Forest, J., Gilbert, M.-H., Aube, C., Morin, E., Malorni, A.: The motivation at work scale: validation evidence in two languages. Educ. Psychol. Meas. **70**, 628–646 (2010)
8. Van Den Broeck, A., Vansteenkiste, M., Witte, H., Soenens, B., Lens, W.: Capturing autonomy, competence, and relatedness at work: construction and initial validation of the work-related basic need satisfaction scale. J. Occup. Organ. Psychol. **83**, 981–1002 (2010)
9. Kaptein, M., Van Halteren, A.: Adaptive persuasive messaging to increase service retention: Using persuasion profiles to increase the effectiveness of email reminders. Pers. Ubiquitous Comput. **17**, 1173–1185 (2013)
10. Orji, R.: Design for Behaviour Change: A Model-driven Approach for Tailoring Persuasive Technologies (2014)
11. Busch, M., Schrammel, J., Tscheligi, M.: Personalized persuasive technology – development and validation of scales for measuring persuadability. In: Berkovsky, S., Freyne, J. (eds.) PERSUASIVE 2013. LNCS, vol. 7822, pp. 33–38. Springer, Heidelberg (2013). doi: 10.1007/978-3-642-37157-8_6
12. Stibe, A., Oinas-Kukkonen, H.: Comparative analysis of recognition and competition as features of social influence using Twitter. In: Bang, M., Ragnemalm, E.L. (eds.) PERSUASIVE 2012. LNCS, vol. 7284, pp. 274–279. Springer, Heidelberg (2012). doi: 10.1007/978-3-642-31037-9_26
13. Torning, K., Oinas-Kukkonen, H.: Persuasive system design. In: Proceedings of the 4th International Conference on Persuasive Technology – Persuasive 2009, p. 1 (2009)
14. Kaptein, M., Lacroix, J., Saini, P.: Individual differences in persuadability in the health promotion domain. In: Ploug, T., Hasle, P., Oinas-Kukkonen, H. (eds.) PERSUASIVE 2010. LNCS, vol. 6137, pp. 94–105. Springer, Heidelberg (2010). doi:10.1007/978-3-642-13226-1_11
15. Kaptein, M., De Ruyter, B., Markopoulos, P., Aarts, E.: Adaptive persuasive systems: a study of tailored persuasive text messages to reduce snacking. ACM Trans. Interact. Intell. Syst. **2**, 1–25 (2012)
16. Lehrer, D., Vasudev, J.: Evaluating a social media application for sustainability in the workplace. In: CHI 2011 Extended Abstracts on Human Factors in Computing Systems, pp. 2161–2166 (2011)
17. Selassie, H.-H., Oyibo, K., Vassileva, J.: Responsiveness to persuasive strategies at the workplace: a case study. In: Seventh International Multidisciplinary Conference on e-Technologies, pp. 273–284 (2017)
18. Orji, R., Mandryk, R.L., Vassileva, J.: Gender, age, and responsiveness to cialdini's persuasion strategies. In: MacTavish, T., Basapur, S. (eds.) PERSUASIVE 2015. LNCS, vol. 9072, pp. 147–159. Springer, Cham (2015). doi:10.1007/978-3-319-20306-5_14
19. Orji, R.: Persuasion and culture: individualism-collectivism and susceptibility to influence strategies. CEUR Workshop Proc. **1582**, 30–39 (2016)
20. Oyibo, K., Orji, R., Vassileva, J.: Investigation of the persuasiveness of social influence in persuasive technology and the effect of age and gender. In: Persuasive Technology (PPT 2017) Workshop (2017)

21. Oyibo, K., Vassileva, J.: Investigation of social predictors of competitive behavior in persuasive technology. In: International Conference on Persuasive Technology, pp. 279–291 (2017)
22. Hodson, R.: Organizational trustworthiness: findings from the population of organizational ethnographies. Organ. Sci. **15**, 432–445 (2004)
23. Laerd Statistics: Three-Way Mixed ANOVA(BBW). https://statistics.laerd.com/premium/spss/mabbw/mabbw-in-spss-14.php
24. Higgins, C., Walker, R.: Ethos, logos, pathos: strategies of persuasion in social/environmental reports. Account. Forum. **36**, 194–208 (2012)
25. Westover, J.H., Taylor, J.: International differences in job satisfaction: the effects of public service motivation, rewards and work relations. Int. J. Product. Perform. Manag. **59**, 811–828 (2010)
26. Mottaz, C.J.: The relative of intrinsic importance rewards as and extrinsic determinants of work satisfaction. Sociol. Q. **26**, 365–385 (1985)
27. Benndorf, V., Rau, H.A.: Competition in the Workplace: An Experimental Investigation (2012)
28. Wong, M., Gardiner, E., Lang, W., Coulon, L.: Generational differences in personality and motivation do they exist and what are the implications for the workplace? J. Manag. Psychol. **23**, 878–890 (2008)
29. Croson, R., Buchan, N.: Gender and culture: international experimental evidence from trust games. Gend. Econ. Trans. **89**, 386–391 (1999)
30. Zak, P.J., Kurzban, R., Matzner, W.T.: Oxytocin is associated with human trustworthiness. Horm. Behav. **48**, 522–527 (2005)
31. Golesorkhi, B.: Gender differences and similarities in judgments of trustworthiness. Women Manag. Rev. **21**, 195–210 (2002)
32. Jones, M.L.: Hofstede - culturally questionable? In: Oxford Business and Economic Conference, p. 9 (2007)
33. Hamari, J., Koivisto, J.: Working out for likes: an empirical study on social influence in exercise gamification. Comput. Human Behav. **50**, 333–347 (2015)
34. Carron, A.V., Brawley, L.R.: Cohesion: conceptual and measurement issues. Small Gr. Res. **31**, 89–106 (2000)

Mediating Intergenerational Family Communication with Computer-Supported Domestic Technology

Francisco J. Gutierrez[1](✉), Sergio F. Ochoa[1], and Julita Vassileva[2]

[1] Department of Computer Science, University of Chile,
Beauchef 851, 3rd Floor, Santiago, Chile
{frgutier,sochoa}@dcc.uchile.cl
[2] MADMUC Lab, Department of Computer Science, University of Saskatchewan,
176 Thorvaldson Building, 100 Science Place, Saskatoon, SK, Canada
jiv@cs.usask.ca

Abstract. The proliferation of social media tools for facilitating interpersonal communication has inadvertently modified the ways in which intergenerational exchanges are supported. However, such technology has generally not acknowledged the complexity of designing social interaction mechanisms involving older adults, where the provided technology services and the actual needs of elderly people are not necessarily aligned. As a way to bridge this gap, we developed SocialConnector, a computer-supported domestic system that facilitates and mediates social interaction among older adults and other family members using their preferred interaction paradigms and communication media. This paper reports on the results of an empirical in-the-wild study evaluating the mediation effect of the proposed system with a sample of nine families over nine weeks. The study results show that older adults using SocialConnector were more engaged in interacting within their close social networks, whereas social awareness notification messages did encourage user participation between family members and their older adults. By addressing the lessons learned in this study, social computing designers and practitioners would be in a better position to identify plausible solutions that would improve user experience and the effectiveness of computer-supported mediation strategies in intergenerational communication settings.

Keywords: Older adults · Intergenerational interaction · Social media · Domestic technology · Empirical study · Computer-mediated communication

1 Introduction

In a world where global population is progressively getting older in both developed and developing economies, there is an increasing interest in deploying domestic supporting technology to encourage active aging in place and promoting sustainable informal elderly caregiving [21]. While family members provide more than 95% of the informal care for older adults who do not live in nursing homes [11], recent surveys show that most adults aged 65 and over express a desire to stay at home as long as possible when

© Springer International Publishing AG 2017
C. Gutwin et al. (Eds.): CRIWG 2017, LNCS 10391, pp. 132–147, 2017.
DOI: 10.1007/978-3-319-63874-4_11

aging [12]. Therefore, this paradigm is highly praised by governments, since it reduces the impact of older adults on public health services [14, 18].

In recent years, the study of intergenerational communication has gained the attention of socio-technical designers, researchers, and practitioners. Previous research shows that as a person gets older, the size of his/her social networks, sense of social connection, and interaction frequency all tend to decrease [3, 10], focusing more on close family members, mainly with their children and grandchildren [19]. This perceived degradation in social exchanges negatively impacts the physical and mental health of older adults, and therefore, their wellbeing. In that respect, one of the most important duties that informal elderly caregivers are expected to fulfill is ensuring that older adults sustain a suitable social health, i.e., favoring the social inclusion within the family network and avoiding potential negative effects of social isolation. Although face-to-face interaction and phone calls between older adults and their family members still prevail, the frequency, quality, and extension of these interactions seem to decrease [6].

The use of information and communication technology (ICT) is in part responsible of the digital divide that isolates the older adults. However, several researchers state that ICTs are also able to enhance and improve the social integration of the elderly (e.g. [1, 2, 4]). Such technologies can play in favor or against a certain target population depending on the ways in which they are designed and used.

To better understand the nuances of intervening in the home of older adults with domestic social technology, we deployed an interactive system named SocialConnector, which aims to monitor and mediate intergenerational family communication between older adults and the rest of their family networks. By analyzing the reports that are automatically generated by the system, we studied the usage of such a system aiming to derive implications for designing social computing systems in this domain.

This article contributes in advancing the field of computer-supported cooperative work in family settings by providing contextualized evidence on the design of computer-based technology to mediate family communication between older adults and their families, simultaneously respecting the preferences and main expectations of the involved parties.

The rest of this paper is structured as follows. Section 2 reviews related work. Section 3 introduces the SocialConnector system and describes its main services. Section 4 frames the empirical study design. Section 5 presents the study results, which are discussed in Sect. 6. Finally, Sect. 7 concludes and provides perspectives on future work.

2   Related Work

Considering older adults in the design of computing systems is complex, since multiple human and cultural factors must be addressed, which go beyond a mere characterization of their limitations caused by age or health conditions [15, 20, 23]. Indeed, older adults might be able to learn and overcome media literacy issues [8], thus effectively evading the negative effects derived from social isolation. We agree that the elderly can become active users of digital technologies. However, the design of these tools should be integrated into their particular sociocultural context, aiming to facilitate their acceptance and appropriation. For instance, the use of common online spaces allows family members to share their values and attitudes, and strengthen the ties across generations [22].

Several authors have conceived domestic systems aimed to encourage the social integration of older adults. For instance, Garattini et al. [4] developed the Building Bridges system, a communication prototype installed in the homes of older adults as a way to enhance social interaction among both friends and strangers. According to the authors, the system facilitates the interaction among socially isolated older adults. The device consists of a 12-inch touch screen computer, embedded in a custom-made stand and incorporating a phone handset with cradle and speakers. Through the system, users can listen to regular broadcasts and, once they are finished, they can engage in group conversations with others. Besides, users can make direct calls to one or more people, write them short messages, and participate in a public chat room with other participants.

Cornejo et al. [2] developed Tlatoque, a situated display aimed to seamlessly integrate older adults into the social networking services used by their relatives. The system was evaluated in Mexico where some elderly family members live abroad. According to the authors, the device provides the means to ease the integration of older adults to their social networks, enhancing the asymmetric relations with their younger family members. The system is a lightweight Facebook client application running on an all-in-one PC with multi-touch screen capability. To start using the tool, a user acting as administrator sends an invite to the participating family members from a Facebook account created for the older adult. Using such information and the services provided by the Facebook API, the system retrieves the last ten uploaded photographs of the members in the social network of the elder. Over the time, complementary services aimed to provide ambient awareness to family members were considered, such as: comments on photos, context of the photo owner, weather, newspaper news, music, and Facebook likes.

Barbosa et al. [1] developed InTouch, an accessible software application running on Android-based tablets, targeted to older adults aged 80 and more under risk of social isolation and loneliness. The system was evaluated with five residents of a long-term care facility. The application has a non-language specific user interface based on icons, and it supports asynchronous communication. Given that accessibility concerns were extensively addressed during design, no typing is required for interacting with the system.

While the reviewed systems range from enhancing a sense of community among older adults, to facilitating intergenerational exchanges with family members, the novelty of our followed approach is that we explicitly involve the entire family network in the process. Furthermore, SocialConnector addresses cultural factors that enhance the perceived value and increase the technology appropriation of older adults interacting with such systems in collectivistic families. These design decisions, which are addressed differently with regard to the nature of cooperative work in informal elderly caregiving in other Western countries [7], provide an alternative view on how to design domestic technology to explicitly mediate intergenerational exchanges involving older adults.

3 SocialConnector

The SocialConnector system is a computer-supported intergenerational family communication mediator that uses cloud services to allow older adults to interact with their family networks using touch-based and voice commands [17]. The system mediates the communication between two parties, so that each participant could interact using their preferred media. The communication media currently supported are: synchronous and asynchronous voice messaging, synchronous video messaging, text messaging, and multimedia messaging. SocialConnector runs in a Tablet PC, physically installed in the older adult's house in one of two possible arrangements: fixed to a wall (Fig. 1a) or over a piece of furniture (Fig. 1b).

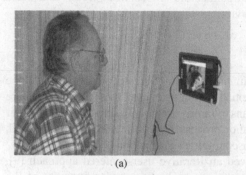 

(a)   (b)

Fig. 1. Possible home arrangements of SocialConnector

Older adults interact with the system using their voice and selecting very simple options by touching the screen. The design of its user interface was initially informed by guidelines supported by the research community [13, 24], and later redefined with participatory iterative prototyping involving a sample of users in the target population. In terms of functionality, the application also monitors the interactions carried from and to older adults, and processes ambient data to infer details about the social health of older adults through embedded sensors in the Tablet PC, particularly the front camera.

3.1 System Description

This system was designed to facilitate the technology adoption and appropriation by older adults who are first-time computer users through seamless and simple user interfaces. The main interaction paradigm involves providing bidirectional synchronous and asynchronous communication services, exposing social media services to older adults without the burden of having to manage user accounts and passwords, and allowing family members to interact with their older adults using the communication media they prefer. Therefore, SocialConnector internally acts as a communication hub and as a mediator for enabling, facilitating, and rendering easier the social interaction process within a family network across multiple generations.

As a communication mediator, SocialConnector consumes and processes public social media data retrieved from the accounts of an older adult's family members, particularly email, Instagram photos, and Facebook posts. Then, it renders this content in an intuitive and accessible way for older adults, hiding behind a usable interface the inherent complexity of retrieving, processing, and transmitting social interaction data from the cloud [17]. Therefore, this system helps address the asymmetry of media preference among family members. Although currently SocialConnector supports Skype, email services, and Instagram, its modular design allows that interacting with any other service provider—such as WhatsApp, Telegram, or even new social media applications—could be possible in the future. The main restriction in accessing these services is that the owner provides access to them through regular Application Programming Interfaces (APIs), which are used for matching the dedicated connectors of SocialConnector with those provided by the third-party social media services.

3.2 Design Rationale

Acknowledging that intergenerational communication is asymmetrical [2, 6, 15], and the preferences of each party might not be negotiable, it turns evident that one major feature of any mediator has to be providing the means to family members to interact through their preferred means. Otherwise, the communication process may not be effectively completed, thus negatively impacting older adults by discouraging socialization [17].

The design of SocialConnector followed an iterative user-centered approach [9], involving multiple cycles of design, prototyping, evaluation, and refinement of the proposed services. Following an empirical approach, we worked directly with different samples of older adults who interacted with the system and tested it through successive stages of prototyping, until reaching a mature and robust product that could be evaluated in a real-life scenario. In particular, we followed the recommendations suggested by Barbosa Neves et al. [1] on design considerations for facilitating the adoption of communication technology by older adults.

3.3 Mediating Intergenerational Family Communication

The interaction services provided by SocialConnector have been conceived and iteratively refined based on the definition of intergenerational communication and caregiving roles, as well as the attitudes, expectations, viewpoints, and concerns of family members regarding computer-supported communication mediators, as defined by Gutierrez and Ochoa [7]. Therefore, the current version of the system implements five communication channels (upper menu in Fig. 2), through which older adults can interact with their family members using regular social media services. Next we briefly explain each channel.

- **Video calls.** This service provides access to audio/video calls mediated through Skype. Once the older adult selects this option in the menu, SocialConnector displays a list of contacts presented as an interactive carousel, where the names and profile pictures of his/her family members are displayed. The user just needs to select the target contact for initiating the call, without having to require a username or password. In fact,

SocialConnector internally manages the user authentication process using the credentials stored in the system. Then, it gives the session token to Skype for making the call. Once both parties end up the videoconference session, the system regains the session token and the user interface is redirected to home, leaving the user at the same starting point, ready for a new interaction.

- **Outgoing messages.** The older adult using SocialConnector can send a message to a family member of his/her choice through email. In order to simplify the process of composing a new message, the older adult uses a speech-to-text service in which he/she dictates the message he desires to send to his family member, and SocialConnector internally manages the user authentication and sends the email.
- **Incoming messages.** Through this service, the system displays the ten most recent messages received in the social media accounts of the older adult. In particular, this component translates the message structure from the original source, and uniformizes it in a format that can be understood by the older adult interacting with the system. In order to prevent misuse and spamming from external sources, this service filters the incoming messages to those belonging to the list of contacts—family members—that was defined during setup.
- **Incoming photos.** Similar to the previous service, in this module SocialConnector organizes the incoming photos and other multimedia content, rendering it in an accessible and uniform way to older adult. Although this service was originally conceived as an output channel of content, i.e., not providing the means for a direct interaction between the family member publishing the contact and the older adult, through conducting pilot field studies of SocialConnector we realized that this service could be used as a mechanism to trigger interactions between the involved parties.
- **Photo album.** This is a collection of the most recent media content sent to the older adult by his/her contacts. The photos displayed in this album are organized as an interactive carousel where the older adult can navigate through them. During the last stages of prototyping with end users, we learned that older adults found a hidden value in this service by augment the stored photos with short messages, hence acting as a sort of shared memory between the older adult and his/her contacts.

In addition to the presented services, SocialConnector manages notification mechanisms. On the one hand, they serve to alert the older adult of new content within the system (i.e., notification badges, as shown in Fig. 2). On the other hand, they can act as social awareness triggers to alert family members, such as in the case of new content created by the older adult, or as reminders for engaging them in social interaction. Finally, given that SocialConnector runs on a Tablet PC, it uses the embedded sensors in the hardware to assist in monitoring the activities of the older adult in a non-invasive way.

Fig. 2. Interaction services provided to older adults (main user interface)

4 Study Design

Through an empirical in-the-wild study, we evaluated the effect of introducing the SocialConnector system at the home of a sample of older adults, and mediating their interaction with their family network using social awareness mechanisms (i.e., reminders and notifications). In particular, we gathered quantitative data regarding system usage by older adults through automatically generated system usage logfiles, which were then aggregated for conducting the data analysis.

4.1 Participants

Through online notices, email lists, and convenience and snowball sampling, we recruited nine middle-class adults acting as informal caregivers for their parents. Following the characterization on intergenerational communication and elderly caregiving family roles proposed by Gutierrez and Ochoa [7], these participants assumed at the time of the study either the role of *assistant* or *monitor* within their families.

We centered our sampling strategy on these recruited caregivers, extending then to their wider family network. In particular, we approached the informal caregivers' parents (who were the main targets of the proposed intervention) as well as their siblings, children, and nephews. In all cases, participants had to be over the age of 14 and explicitly express their intention of being part of the study. Furthermore, we restricted the study sample to cover at least one older adult, one assistant, one monitor, one helper, and one outsider in each participating family. Table 1 summarizes the structure of the participant family networks. In each family network, gender and age of each participant are provided.

Table 1. Structure of participating family networks

Family	Older adults	Assistants	Monitors	Helpers	Outsiders
1	1M (81)	1F (71)	0F	1F (36)	3F (21, 17, 14)
		0M	2M (48, 39)	1M (19)	0M
2	1M (78)	1F (54)	1F (49)	1F (23)	0F
		0M	0M	1M (51)	2M (18, 21)
3	1F (69)	0F	1F (33)	2F (39, 37)	0F
		1M (31)	1M (38)	0M	1M (16)
4	1F (73)	1F (44)	1F (37)	0M	1F (19)
		1M (41)	0M	1M (25)	0M
5	1F (75)	0F	0F	2F (48, 41)	0F
		1M (42)	2M (49, 25)	0M	2M (25, 23)
6	1M (72)	1F (39)	1F (44)	0F	2F (21, 19)
		0M	1M (42)	1M (41)	0M
7	1F (79)	1F (34)	1F (38)	0F	0F
		1M (29)	0M	1M (31)	1M (29)
8	1M (71)	1F (68)	1F (66)	0F	1F (38)
		1M (69)	0M	1M (34)	0M
9	1F (80)	1F (59)	1F (36)	1F (39)	1F (16)
		1M (30)	1M (37)	0M	1M (15)

The final study sample was composed of 64 people across 9 family networks (n = 9, 7, 7, 6, 8, 7, 6, 6, 8, respectively in each family). All families were based in Santiago, Chile, and were spread across several households within the urban area of the city.

4.2 Materials

Each older adult participating in the study was provided with a tablet PC equipped with the latest version of the prototype system. The evaluated version of SocialConnector runs on a 9.6-inches Samsung Galaxy Tab E tablet under Android 4.4 as operative system.

In order to control the effect of Internet bandwidth in the perceived user experience, we equipped each tablet with a SIM card providing mobile access to Internet over 3G. Participants in each family interact with the older adult using their own terminals over Skype (for instant messaging) and email (for direct messages and photo albums).

4.3 Procedure

We structured the study design in three stages, spanning over a time period of nine weeks.

- **Setup.** We recruited a sample of informal family caregivers, who acted as seeds for recruiting the family networks participating in the study and will assume the role of coordinator during the study. Being a family coordinator involves setting up the device by collecting and managing the social network data of family members within the system, and assisting the older adult on using the system in case of need. After conducting a short interview with the candidate caregivers, we screened their family networks against the stated sample requirements. Once defined and confirmed the participant family networks, we asked all members for their explicit, free, and informed consent to participate in the study. Finally, we organized an informal meeting at the home of the participating older adult with the assistance of the coordinator, where we installed the system at a location chosen by the older adult, performed a demonstration on its usage, and asked the informal caregiver acting as coordinator to setup the initial data of the involved family members. All participants were aware that the system would track their interactions with the older adult and were left with information sheets on the proposed services and contact information of both the caregiver acting as coordinator and the research team.

- **System usage.** A daily log of the system usage by the older adult was automatically generated and reviewed by the research team every day. In such a log, we kept the following data: (1) incoming Skype calls, (2) outgoing Skype calls, (3) incoming email messages, (4) outgoing messages, and (5) incoming photos. The system usage was tracked for a period of nine weeks. During the first three (i.e., *pre-intervention*), we did not integrate any method for mediating the interaction with other family members. During the following three weeks (i.e., *intervention*), we introduced a social awareness mechanism informing the family members on the effect of their interaction with the older adult (e.g., we send an informal message once the older adult has read an email sent by them), and we explicitly send periodic messages to family members to invite them to interact with the older adult. In order to contrast the effect of this intervention with the baseline measure obtained on the setup stage of the study and on the pre-intervention stage of system usage (i.e., *post-intervention*), we removed these awareness mechanisms during the last three weeks of the trial.

- **Closure.** After the nine weeks of the deployment, we organized a second informal meeting with each family at the home of the older adult. In these meetings, the first author moderated in each family a focus group contrasting the viewpoints of all participants regarding their perceptions on system usefulness, family connection, privacy issues, motivation, reasons to use/not use the system, and articulation with the informal elderly caregiving process. By the end of the family meeting, we removed the device from the home of the older adult.

4.4 Data Collection and Analysis

By studying the generated log files reporting the interaction activity with the Social-Connector system, we aim to study whether the system encourages a sustainable increase in the frequency of social interaction exchanges from/to the family older adults. This can be formulated in the following two work hypotheses:

- (H1) The social awareness mediation increases the frequency of exchanges with older adults; and

- (H2) After removing the mediation prompts, such frequency of exchanges does not decrease.

We studied the main effect of the intervention following a one-way repeated measures ANOVA. In those cases where the collected data violated the assumption of sphericity, we corrected accordingly the degrees of freedom for the effect following the Greenhouse-Geisser procedure. In order to study both contrasts, we performed post-hoc tests whenever the main effect was deemed significant. In such a case, we adjusted accordingly the significance level following the Bonferroni correction for multiple comparisons.

All statistical analyses were conducted using SPSS 21. The calculation of Cohen's d effect size value was performed following the method proposed by Morris and DeShon [16] for within-subjects studies. We considered $\alpha = 0.05$ as significance cut-off.

5   Results

In order to study the effect of mediating the interaction within the family network through contextualized social triggers, we ran a one-way repeated measures ANOVA to compare the volume of incoming calls, messages, and photos in three times: pre-intervention (weeks 1 to 3), during the intervention (weeks 4 to 6), and post-intervention (weeks 7 to 9). Figure 3 shows the volume of incoming interaction along the study.

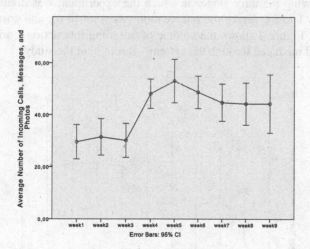

Fig. 3. Volume of incoming interaction through SocialConnector

Mauchly's test indicated that the assumption of sphericity had not been violated, $\chi^2(2) = 0.031$, $p = 0.985$; therefore, degrees of freedom were not corrected. The results show that there was a significant effect of mediating the interaction with social awareness notifications: $F(2, 16) = 28.83$, $p < 0.001$, partial $\eta^2 = 0.783$.

Three paired-samples t-tests were used to make post hoc comparisons between conditions with p-values and significance levels adjusted following the Bonferroni correction. A first paired-samples t-test indicated that there was a significant difference in the scores for pre-intervention ($M = 91.1$, $SD = 19.1$) and intervention ($M = 149.8$, $SD = 25.3$) conditions; $t(8) = -7.223$, $p < 0.001$, $95\%CI = [-83.182, -34.172]$, $d = -2.466$. A second paired-samples t-test indicated that there was a significant difference in the scores for pre-intervention ($M = 91.1$, $SD = 19.1$) and post-intervention ($M = 133.1$, $SD = 31.1$) conditions; $t(8) = -5.458$, $p = 0.002$, $95\%CI = [-65.208, -18.792]$, $d = -2.063$. Finally, running a third paired-samples t-test indicated that there was not a significant difference in the scores for intervention ($M = 149.8$, $SD = 25.3$) and post-intervention ($M = 133.1$, $SD = 31.1$) conditions; $t(8) = 2.067$, $p = 0.218$, $95\%CI = [-7.647, 40.981]$, $d = 0.705$.

These results suggest that *mediating the interaction of family members with notification triggers does have an effect on the volume of calls, messages, and photos sent to the older adults participating in the study.* More specifically, our results suggest that during and after sending contextualized social awareness reminders to family members, they tend to increase their volume of interactions with their older adult. However, further research needs to be conducted in order to verify if the effect of intervening the social interaction space of the involved family members lasts longer than the observed period in the study.

Similarly, aiming to understand how older adults interacted with the system as a way to communicate with their fellow family members throughout the observed period, we ran a one-way repeated measures ANOVA to compare the volume of outgoing calls and messages following the three stages in which the experiment was divided: pre-intervention (weeks 1 to 3), during the intervention (weeks 4 to 6), and post-intervention (weeks 7 to 9). Figure 4 shows the volume of outgoing interaction—originated from older adults and mediated through the system—throughout the study.

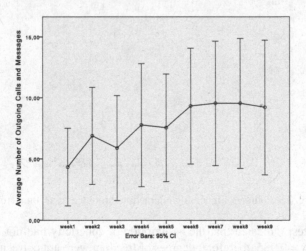

Fig. 4. Volume of outgoing interaction through SocialConnector

Mauchly's test indicated that the assumption of sphericity was violated, $\chi^2(2) = 6.152$, $p = 0.046$; therefore, degrees of freedom were corrected using

Greenhouse-Geisser estimates of sphericity ($\varepsilon = 0.631$). The results show that there was a significant effect of time on the volume of outgoing interactions generated from the older adults participating in the study: $F(1.26, 10.09) = 6.367$, $p = 0.025$, partial $\eta^2 = 0.443$.

Three paired-samples t-tests were used to make post hoc comparisons between conditions: pre-intervention ($M = 17.1, SD = 13.5$), intervention ($M = 24.7, SD = 16.4$), and post-intervention ($M = 28.3, SD = 19.9$). None of the pairwise comparisons were seen as significant, when adjusting the p-values and significance levels with the Bonferroni correction: pre-intervention vs. intervention: $t(8) = -2.630$, $p = 0.091$, $95\%CI = [-16.219, 1.108]$, $d = -0.928$; pre vs. post: $t(8) = -2.654$, $p = 0.087$, $95\%CI = [-23.975, 1.531]$, $d = -1.007$; and intervention vs. post: $t(8) = -1.687$, $p = 0.390$, $95\%CI = [-10.220, 2.887]$, $d = -0.666$.

These results suggest that *there is a slight tendency in time to increase the frequency of outgoing interactions, although not statistically significant between experimental conditions*. Therefore, we cannot generalize that this situation will be sustained in time. We hypothesize that this tendency can be attributed to either: (1) a learning effect and/or (2) a positive moderation on the frequency of outgoing interaction due to the increasing volume of interaction produced by family members (i.e., given that family members contact the older adult more frequently, s/he will contact them back more frequently).

6   Discussion

The aggregated results for the variables measured through SocialConnector (i.e., incoming calls, messages, and photos, and outgoing calls and messages) show that there was a significant main effect on the interaction mediated by the system before and after the introduction of social awareness messages; this supports H1. Furthermore, this effect was not affected after the messages were removed from the system (H2), although we can only argue for the validity of this effect on the studied period.

Following the study results, notification messages are an effective way to mediate the social interaction between family members and older adults. However, this effect has not been necessarily reciprocated by older adults, who did not show increasing levels on their participation as a result of this mediation. Nevertheless, they did show increasing values on their engagement with the SocialConnector system, either by a learning effect or by an indirect positive feedback on their activity production (i.e., outgoing calls and messages) due to an increasing number of incoming calls, messages, and photos.

Similarly, this observation was also suggested by the results of outgoing interaction; however, we cannot attribute the mediation of social awareness messages as a cause to the slight increase on older adults' mediated calls and photos through SocialConnector, given that post hoc test results were not statistically significant. In that respect, we hypothesize that this variation could be due either to a learning effect or to an indirect feedback on the behavior of older adults triggered by a positive increase on incoming calls, messages, and photos sent by other members in the family network. In any case, replicating this study with a larger sample of older adults could possibly increase the statistical power of tests, and therefore provide more ground for validating or not the stated hypotheses.

6.1 Implications to Design

As broader design concepts, we identified in the exit focus groups that the design of computer-supported intergenerational communication mediators needs to account for the opposed views on ageism and technology design. These views particularly contrast the perceived independence assumed by older adults and the views on decline and technology reluctance raised by their family members. In particular, that of the family members who are more closely involved in assuming caregiving tasks.

While prior literature acknowledges the existence of a vicious circle on technology adoption, particularly that expressed by older adults in collectivistic families [Guti16], the study results go a step further in this line of research. In particular, the study results imply that socio-domestic computing systems aiming to mediate intergenerational family communication need to account for the diversity of views and involvement of different stakeholders within the family network.

The perceived effects of mediating the social interaction space with SocialConnector are also in line with the claims of Grönvall and Verdezoto [5], which state that supporting systems should move away from passive monitoring and surveillance, to solutions that assess and assist the individual enforcing active information seeking. In that respect, the design of SocialConnector as a mediator, while uses as input monitoring data retrieved from ambient sensors, the main intervention in the social interaction space is pushed toward family members in the supporting network. Therefore, design considerations, such as personalization and adaptation in persuasive and social awareness triggers, will be addressed in future research.

6.2 Study Limitations

While valuable, the reported results are only applicable to the studied participants as the sample size is not big enough for yielding high statistical power, which would warrant generalization for a broader population. Regarding the qualitative analysis grounded on the mediation effect of SocialConnector in the studied nine families, the implications of the study findings are applicable only to the particular socio-cultural scenario.

7 Conclusions and Future Work

In this paper we presented the main findings of a mixed-methods in-home study, understanding the mediation effect of SocialConnector in a sample of intergenerational families. On the one hand, we measured how older adults and their family members interacted through the system. On the other hand, we explored the implications of the mediation of SocialConnector across the studied family networks through a focus group session with each family at the end of the trial.

The obtained results suggest that older adults using SocialConnector did show increased social engagement, particularly with family members, when exposed to interacting with the system over a period of nine weeks. In particular, regarding the mediation with family members in the surrounding network, social awareness notification messages to encourage user participation are an effective way to mediate the social interaction space of the involved parties. Although subtle, the study results also show there was an increase in the produced outgoing interaction of older adults with their family members, which can be attributed either to a learning effect or an indirect positive feedback due to an increased volume of incoming messages, calls, and photos.

In terms of design, we inferred implications that can be used to inform the development of further software applications or functionality to better impact the social interaction space of family members. In particular, the study results suggest that older adults liked interacting with SocialConnector, as it offered them an alternative way for engaging in social interaction with fellow family members. However, participating older adults also reflected on a major concern involving privacy matters and information disclosure across the family network. The reason behind this concern can be attributed to an intention to not worry or burden the family members caring for them, and because there is still a reticence on trusting an external agent—such as SocialConnector—for mediating intergenerational communication about personal matters.

As future work we will explore the relationship between system usage and discriminant factors, such as: gender, prior experience of older adults using computer-based technology, whether they share or not their household, and their social engagement. Similarly, we plan to extend our qualitative analysis on system usage and perceived value, by conducting individual semi-structured interviews with the participating family members in this study.

Acknowledgments. This work has been partially supported by the Fondecyt Project (Chile), grant: 1150252. The work of Francisco J. Gutierrez has been supported by the Ph.D. Scholarship Program of Conicyt Chile (CONICYT-PCHA/Doctorado Nacional/2013-21130075).

References

1. Barbosa Neves, B., Franz, R.L., Munteanu, C., Baecker, R., Ngo, M.: My hand doesn't listen to me!: adoption and evaluation of a communication technology for the 'Oldest Old'. In: Proceedings of the ACM SIGCHI Conference on Human Factors in Computing Systems, CHI 2015, pp. 1593–1602. ACM Press, New York (2015)
2. Cornejo, R., Tentori, M., Favela, J.: Enriching in-person encounters through social media: a study on family connectedness for the elderly. Int. J. Hum Comput Stud. **71**(9), 889–899 (2013)
3. Dean, A., Kolody, B., Wood, P., Matt, G.E.: The influence of living alone on depression in elderly persons. J. Aging Health **4**(1), 3–18 (1992)
4. Garattini, C., Wherton, J., Prendergast, D.: Linking the lonely: an exploration of a communication technology designed to support social interaction among older adults. Univ. Access Inf. Soc. **11**(2), 211–222 (2012)

5. Grönvall, E., Verdezoto, N.: Beyond self-monitoring: understanding non-functional aspects of home-based healthcare technology. In: Proceedings of the ACM International Joint Conference on Pervasive and Ubiquitous Computing, UbiComp 2013, pp. 587–596. ACM Press, New York (2013)

6. Gutierrez, F.J., Ochoa, S.F.: Mom, i do have a family!: attitudes, agreements, and expectations on the interaction with chilean older adults. In: Proceedings of the ACM Conference on Computer-Supported Cooperative Work and Social Computing, CSCW 2016, pp. 1400–1409. ACM Press, New York (2016)

7. Gutierrez, F.J., Ochoa, S.F.: It takes at least two to tango: understanding the cooperative nature of elderly caregiving in Latin America. In: Proceedings of the ACM Conference on Computer-Supported Cooperative Work and Social Computing, CSCW 2017, pp. 1618–1630. ACM Press, New York (2017)

8. Harley, D., Fitzpatrick, G.: YouTube and intergenerational communication: the case of Geriatric 1927. Univ. Access Inf. Soc. 8(1), 5–20 (2009)

9. Harper, R., Rodden, T., Rogers, Y., Sellen, A.: Being Human: Human-Computer Interaction in the Year 2020. Microsoft Research, Cambridge (2008)

10. Hawkley, L.C., Masi, C.M., Berry, J.D., Cacioppo, J.T.: Loneliness is a unique predictor of age-related differences in systolic blood pressure. Psychol. Aging 21(1), 152–164 (2006)

11. Kaye, H.S., Harrington, C., Laplante, M.P.: Long-term care: who gets it, who provides it, who pays, and how much? Health Aff. 29(1), 11–21 (2010)

12. Kochera, A., Straight, A., Guterbock, T.: Beyond 50.05 – a report to the nation on livable communities: creating environments for successful aging (2005). https://assets.aarp.org/rgcenter/il/beyond_50_communities.pdf. Accessed 27 Jun 2017

13. Kurniawan, S., Zaphiris, P.: Research-derived web design guidelines for older people. In: Proceedings of the International ACM SIGACCESS Conference on Computers and Accessibility, ASSETS 2005, pp. 129–135. ACM Press, New York (2005)

14. Lewin, D., Adshead, S., Glennon, B., Williamson, B., Moore, T., Damodaran, L., Hansell, P.: Assisted Living Technologies for Older and Disabled People in 2030: A Final Report to Ofcom. Plum Consulting, United Kingdom (2010)

15. Lindley, S.E., Harper, R., Sellen, A.: Designing for elders: exploring the complexity of relationships in later life. In: Proceedings of the British HCI Group Annual Conference on HCI, BCS-HCI 2008, pp. 77–86. ACM Press, New York (2008)

16. Morris, S.B., Deshon, R.P.: Combining effect size estimates in meta-analysis with repeated measures and independent-groups designs. Psychol. Methods 7(1), 105–125 (2002)

17. Muñoz, D., Cornejo, R., Gutierrez, F.J., Favela, J., Ochoa, S.F., Tentori, M.: A social cloud-based tool to deal with time and media mismatch of intergenerational family communication. Fut. Gener. Comput. Syst. 53, 140–151 (2015)

18. Mynatt, E.D., Melenhorst, A.-S., Frisk, A.D., Rogers, W.A.: Aware technologies for aging in place: understanding user needs and attitudes. IEEE Pervasive Comput. 3(2), 36–41 (2004)

19. Osorio-Parraguez, P., Seguel, A.G.: Social construction of dependence in elderly men in Chile. Health 6, 998–1003 (2014)

20. Östlund, B.: Design paradigms and misunderstood technology: the case of older adults. In: Östlund, B. (ed.) Young Technologies in Old Hands: An International View on Senior Citizen's Utilization of ICT. DJOF Publishing, Copenhagen (2005)

21. Roberts, C., Mort, M., Milligan, C.: Calling for care: 'Disembodied' work, teleoperators, and older people living at home. Sociology 46(3), 490–506 (2012)

22. Siibak, A., Tamme, V.: 'Who introduced granny to Facebook?': an exploration of everyday family interactions in web-based communication environments. Northern Lights Film Media Stud. Yearb. 11(1), 71–89 (2013)

23. Sun, Y., Ding, X., Lindtner, S., Lu, T., Gu, N.: Being senior and ICT: a study of seniors using ICT in China. In: Proceedings of the ACM SIGCHI Conference on Human Factors in Computing Systems, CHI 2014, pp. 3933–3942. ACM Press, New York (2014)
24. World Wide Web Consortium: Web Content Accessibility Guidelines (WCAG) 2.0. http://www.w3.org/TR/WCAG20/. Accessed 30 Mar 2017

Speakers' Empowerment with Keywords: The Speaking Competency Development for Multilingual to Contribute in a Real-Time Interaction

Hiromi Hanawa[1(✉)], Xiaoyu Song[1(✉)], Mengyuan Tang[1(✉)], and Tomoo Inoue[2]

[1] Graduate School of Library, Information and Media Studies, University of Tsukuba, 1-2, Kasuga, Tsukuba, Ibaraki 305-8550, Japan
{hanawa, songxy}@slis.tsukuba.ac.jp
[2] Faculty of Library, Information and Media Science, University of Tsukuba, 1-2, Kasuga, Tsukuba, Ibaraki 305-8550, Japan
inoue@slis.tsukuba.ac.jp

Abstract. Multilingual communication often causes difficulty when speakers have different language proficiency. Real-time keywords potentially demonstrated positive effects when they are provided in cross-cultural communication. Previously it was found that keywords enhanced mutual understanding and knowledge in conversation, and it was beneficial when it was shown with the latency of 3 s of all matched utterance. However participants' speech have not ever been investigated to reveal how speakers improved utterance in multilingual discussion with the textual support. In this paper speakers' interaction were examined from the data set collected through the experiment as well as the use of keywords. It was found that dyad contribution to conversation was facilitated in mean length of utterance with the use of keywords, which was consistent with the data that speakers increased episodic utterance to refashion and expand own prior speech. Consequently speakers extended speech length by keywords, which was supported by speakers' large number of sequence completion with repair sequence. These findings indicated real-time keywords boosted speakers' utterance and progressed intercultural discussion via keywords.

Keywords: Intercultural communication · Keyword typing · Non-native speaker · Text-enhanced audio conference

1 Introduction

Intercultural communication has increased on a daily basis. This communication often causes difficulty when speakers using common language. Native speaker (NS) who naturally acquire it from early childhood and Non-native speaker (NNS) study and learn it after development stage are mutually incapable of understanding each other in conversation due to different language skills. It has been reported audio conference is difficult for NNS because it is dependent on audio signal and participants' language skills [6].

© Springer International Publishing AG 2017
C. Gutwin et al. (Eds.): CRIWG 2017, LNCS 10391, pp. 148–163, 2017.
DOI: 10.1007/978-3-319-63874-4_12

Text support in real-time conversation is advantageous resolution of the issue. Multilingual party has worked together to achieve collaborative tasks with text support [1, 2]. There are multiple approaches of presenting textual information such as hand writing, typing, and speech. Handwriting is the slowest and transition of messages during a task is limited [3]. Automated speech recognition (ASR) was examined whether and how the use of it affected real-time communication. Speed and quality of transcription generation varies with its methods [1]. Keyword highlighting was conducted since generated transcripts by machine translation (MT) were not as good as texts written in one's native language. Comparing no highlighting, random highlighting, with keyword highlighting, participants rated clarity of messages significantly higher when keywords were highlighted [2]. Textual information varied in its effect depending on its usage.

Previous study investigated effects of keywords and stated that keywords enhanced NNS comprehension of a conversation [2, 5]. We have investigated effects of speakers' keyword generation from essential and incomprehensible portion of a conversation of the speech that NS typed for NNS to comprehend during talking. Experiments tested the method that NS typed down keywords, and reported it enhanced mutual understanding and knowledge between NNS and NS [10, 11]. As the previous works indicated, speakers' keyword generation demonstrate positive effects on multilingual conversation.

However no research has examined speakers' course of utterance that was caused by the use of keywords. It is thus unclear that how speakers enhanced communication during tasks that resulted in positive effects on conversation. Previous research has indicated real-time transcript partly supports participants to take part in interactive discussion [8]. Hence we posed the first research question that is about how NNS and NS participated in discussion with the use of keywords. As for the supporting evidence, this study also focused on noun phrases expressed in conversation. Proper noun, pronoun, and noun phrases (NP) have become the core of natural language processing, therefore the second research question is about NP referring to speakers' utterance. Throughout the conversation tasks participants are involved in a collaborative activity to perform the social process, thereby we explored speakers' forms of utterance for the third research question. This paper investigates how speakers facilitated multilingual discussion through the observation of speakers' utterance with speakers' keyword generation. We conducted data analysis of speakers' utterance that was changed by the use of keyword to investigate these research questions.

2 Related Work

2.1 Text-Enhanced Audio Conference

Conference is an important situation to perform actual and social processes. Previous research has reported audio conference was harder than face-to-face (FTF) communication because audio conference was dependent on audio signal and participants' language skills [6]. Besides, conference often engaged with terminologies that were hard to understand when they were presented in a fast paced spoken language.

Previous works investigated effects of keywords and stated that keywords enhanced NNS comprehension of a conversation [2, 5, 10]. As automated keyword detection from spoken language has reported its algorithm and is technically developing [13], researchers have conducted manual highlighting on keywords. Keyword highlighting was investigated to overlook erroneous translation in machine translation (MT) mediated text-based discussion. MT generated transcripts were not as good as texts written in one's native language. We proposed the method that NS typed essential and incomprehensible portion as keywords. Speed of NS typing was mean latency of 3 s by averaging the latency of all matched utterance. Latency of NS input was not too long, although most of all typists were not skilled typists and they looked at the keyboard when they typed [21]. It was found presentation of keywords enhanced mutual understanding and knowledge among NNS and NS. This approach utilized human resource and natural language to generate keywords, which is feasible to conduct in any other languages [10, 11]. When speakers communicated in text chat, textual feature reflected on them as to polish, selected information, and considered interpersonal relationship [4]. As previous studies have shown, real-time keyword generation has demonstrated positive effects on real-time interaction.

However speakers' utterance have not been investigated in the earlier studies. Speakers' behavior is supposed to change as they generate and look at keywords during talking in a real-time conversation. No research has found how speakers performed audio conversation with the use of keywords. This study investigated speakers' utterance that was transformed by the use of keywords through the data observation of experiments that tested the effects of keywords in real-time conversation. We posed research questions about participants' speech to explore behavioral change that was caused by the use of keywords. Although real-time keywords demonstrated positive effects, it is unclear how speakers improved their utterance in multilingual audio conversation. The purpose of this paper is to conduct research about speakers' utterance.

2.2 Conversation Using Second Language

Audio communication is difficult for NNS because it is dependent on audio signals and language skills more than face-to-face communication. It imposes an extra burden on NNS that process the second language to understand as well as organize own expression [6]. Even though participants are appeared to be proficient and successful in language assessment tests, standardized tests only examine the target language comprehension to provide scores of reading and listening ability. The exam score hardly assure the test taker's fluency in spoken language [17]. It is important to support both of NNS and NS to achieve mutual understanding and to contribute to a real-time conversation.

Real-time captioning enables hearing-impaired people to keep up with class lectures with less than 5 s delay, but not consistently participate in interactive class discussion [8]. In this paper NS typed down essential and incomprehensible portion of a conversation by keyboards in real-time conversation. Speed of NS typing provided keywords with mean latency of 3 s, which had reasonable latencies of less than 5 s. This appeared to be helpful for speakers to participate in a conversation. Therefore we pose a research question about how NNS and NS participate in discussion.

- RQ1: How much did speakers increase utterance in real-time conversation due to keywords?

As known as proper noun and pronoun, noun phrases (NP) present a substantial role in a discourse. NP captures the main points when speakers refer to it in a conversation. The previous research provided 6 distinct types of NP in accordance with speaker's reference as a collaborative process. In the collaborative process of a conversation, the participants repair, expand, and replace NP until mutually accepted. Speakers are mutually responsible for their joint effort toward understanding [12]. Concerning conversation task as a collaborative process, we posed the second research question about NP. This question explores speakers' forms of NP to investigate speakers' changed course of utterance as well as speakers' effort toward understanding with the use of keywords.

- RQ2: How were noun phrases expressed in a conversation with the use of keywords?

Collaborative dialogue is knowledge-building dialogue that constructs linguistic knowledge where language use and language learning can co-occur according to the collaborative dialogue scenario. It allows speakers to perform cognitive activity of verbalization and produce something in the target language. Participants outstrip own linguistic competence in an activity through problem-solving, negotiation, and other to carry out social processes [7]. Conventionally understood as being tied to classroom or instructional setting, the sequence closing third is a unit that complete a conversational sequence with a recognizable form sustained by co-participants [18]. In this paper NNS are involved in this activity with NS, and such activity implemented the setting NNS and NS constructed linguistic knowledge. Thus we posed the third research question to investigate whether there were more factual information to propose sequence closing in conversation with keywords, compared to one without keywords.

- RQ3: Did speakers construct more number of forms embodied sequence closure with the use of keywords?

3 Experiment

Experiment tested the use of keywords that NS types essential or incomprehensible portion of a conversation with a computer keyboard to support NNS comprehension of the content. This research conducted user behavior observation to investigate research questions about speakers' utterance and keyword generation. Figure 1 shows Experiment environment.

3.1 Participants

Participants were 16 people of native Japanese speakers and the same number of non-native speakers. NNS were international students from China whose Japanese Language Proficiency Test N1 average score were 118.9 [14]. NS were all Japanese

Fig. 1. Experiment environment.

who were born and grew up in Japan. Both of NNS and NS were college students and mutually met for the first time at experiment. Gender distribution was 17 male and 15 female, and their mean age was 25.3.

3.2 Experiment Design

Conversations in two different conditions were compared. NS typed an essential and incomprehensible portion of speech on a computer keyboard while NS was speaking, which was "Keyword condition". Nobody typed on a computer keyboard and participants performed audio conversation, which was "Control condition". A within-subject was adapted. Participants were randomly assigned to pairs, and each pair participated in two conditions within a day. The combination of conversation tasks and experiment conditions were balanced to cancel out an order effect. Two conversation tasks were combined alternately with two conversation methods across pairs. Eight pairs performed a debate in the Keyword condition first, and eight pairs conducted in the Control condition first.

3.3 Conversation Tasks

The conversation task was a debate of nuclear energy and death penalty system. Task-oriented information was provided in advance to both sides of pros. and cons. to acknowledge definition of terminologies, major issues and representative opinions as for a self-guide. Participants modified the task-oriented information on PC according to own opinion and it was not mandatory. There was no judge for the debate.

3.4 Software and Equipment

All experimental process was conducted on computers, the pair seated at the PC tables back to back in the laboratory, which was a simulation environment of an audio conference. Participants utilized Lenovo B590 15.6 in laptop PC with an external monitor. Participants wore a microphone to record their voice, and each pair listened and spoke directly from the co-participants while seating back to back. PC connected to the intramural local area network. Monitors were synchronized with the co-participants' PC via Skype that hardly caused delay by Skype screen-sharing option [15]. Figure 2 shows participants' PC monitor. Skype is a commonly used software application for voice and video call. Each PC launched Skype and started a voice call. PC kept Skype sounds turned off and disabled a video call. Opening task-oriented information on the right hand side of the monitor, participants did not share the task information with the co-participant.

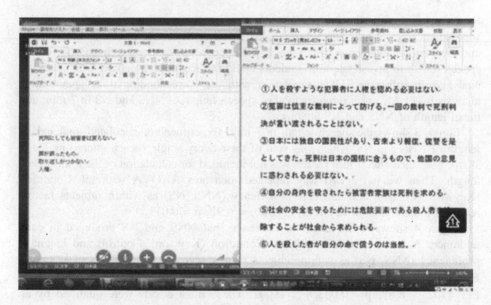

Fig. 2. Software and equipment.

3.5 Procedure

Experiment was conducted in the laboratory. Participants filled out the consent forms and demographic surveys before experiment. International students also received instruction in Chinese unless s/he understood instruction in Japanese. Experimenters provided the written experimental procedures and oral instruction before experiment. There were two rounds of each 7 min debate, and 14 min of conversation as a whole. Experimenters instructed participants, NS to type down essential and incomprehensible portion as keywords during talking, but not to type a whole sentence. All the experiments were conducted in compliance with the protocol reviewed by the ethics committee and approved by the University of Tsukuba.

4 Result

Collected data was combined in EUDICO Linguistic Annotator (ELAN) for an integrative analysis of each pair's utterance and typing. ELAN is a text annotation application to create an embedded text annotation for the media files. Annotated texts in every single timelines are saved with the time corresponding to the annotation [16]. Utterance was described with inter pausal unit (IPU). IPU is a pause-free unit of speech from a single speaker separated by a pause at least 50 ms, marked out with pose [20]. Typing was annotated from the moment when typed characters were shown on a screen to the moment of finishing typing. Video data was 224 min as a whole. Results show objective evidence based on quantitative data analysis.

4.1 Speakers' Contribution to a Conversation

Real-time transcript allows students to participate in class lectures when it has reasonable latencies of less than 5 s. It also partly supports to take part in class questions and answers, or interactive discussion [8]. Hence we pose a research question about speech length to investigate how students could participate in a debate. Utterance was analyzed according to ELAN annotation with the corresponding time. Quantitative analysis by ELAN result provides total of speech length of NNS and NS in 7 min, and mean length of NNS and NS utterance.

Figure 3 shows the speech length in 7 min. Experimenters calculated total speech length of NNS and NS, which was sum of their every single speech uttered in 7 min sharp. Utterance after 7 min passed was not included for calculation of the total speech length. Then we ran a two way repeated measures ANOVA with the Condition (Keyword, Control) and language proficiency (NNS, NS) as within subjects factors revealed main effects of keyword, $F(1, 60) = 6.92$, $p = 0.011$.

Figure 4 shows mean length of utterance that NNS and NS produced in each utterance. A 2×2 ANOVA with the Condition (Keyword, Control) and language proficiency (NNS, NS) as within subjects factors revealed main effects of keyword, $F(1, 4102) = 119$, $p < 0.001$, $\eta_P^2 = 0.028$, and speakers' language proficiency $F(1, 4102) = 8.97$, $p = 0.003$, $\eta_p^2 = 0.002$. These main effects were qualified by an interaction between keyword and language proficiency, $F(1, 4102) = 15.5$, $p < 0.001$, $\eta_p^2 = 0.004$. A Bonferonni post hoc test indicated that mean length of utterance differ significantly between the Keyword and the Control condition ($p < 0.001$), and NNS and NS in the Keyword condition ($p < 0.001$).

Figure 3 showed speakers extended total speech length in 7 min with the use of keyword. It indicated speakers increased their speech length as well as reduced awkward silence during conversation. Figure 4 presented mean length of speech of both of NNS and NS became longer due to keywords. This declared that speakers stretched their utterance in each times with the use of keywords. These results indicated keywords encouraged speakers to take part in a conversation. RQ 1 asked about speakers' contribution to a conversation when they utilized keywords. As the previous study noted, texts facilitated communication for both of NNS and NS. NS typed characters as

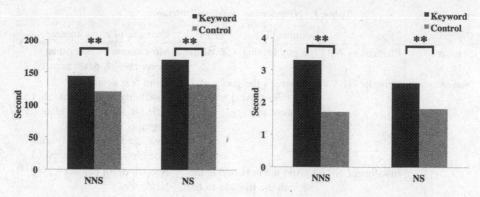

Fig. 3. Total speech length in 7 min.   **Fig. 4.** Mean length of utterance.

keyboard, and NNS looked them during talking in the Keyword condition, such behavioral difference affected mean length of NNS and NS utterance.

4.2   NP Referring to Speakers' Utterance

As earlier studies have shown NP has become the core of natural language processing, this study regards keywords as NP referring to speakers' utterance. Table 1 shows NP classifications of the previous work referring speakers' utterance with examples. The detailed definition of each NP is as follows: Elementary NP are uttered in a single tone group, presumed the next speaker get it accepted, speaker's most preferable standard type utterance, accurate and typically uttered quickly and shorter. Episodic NP are uttered in two or more easily distinguished episodes or tone groups, judged to be insufficient and added the restrictive phrase. Installment NP are uttered in episodes but gets explicit acceptance or midcourse response of each installment before going on, paused and invited addressees to affirm understanding. Episodic and Installment NP are expansion and repair of speaker's prior utterance although it is non-standard type. Other NP types are Provisional, Dummy and Proxy NP come with inadequate phrase and least found NP in an actual conversation [12].

In accordance with Table 1 classification, experimenters marked explanatory NP on conversation transcript. Explanatory NP is meaningful information expressed in comprehensible manner, which was to say definition, statement, explanation, description, knowledge, and the rest. Then NP were divided into 6 types and counted the number of cases of each NP type.

Two experimenters worked independently and inter-rater agreement amongst the two was high (k = 0.65). Figure 5 shows NP with the use of keywords, and Fig. 6 shows NP without the use of keywords. We ran a Friedman test to see if the NP types varied across all 6 types. Result indicated that the difference in NP with the use of keywords was significant ($X^2[5] = 57.5$, p < 0.001). Post hoc tests (A Wilcoxon Signed-ranks test with Bonferroni correction) indicated that the difference between Elementary and Episodic type NP was significant (p<0.01), and Episodic and Installment type (p<0.001).

Table 1. NP referring speakers' utterance.

Category	Type	Example [12]	Example of experiment
Standard	Elementary NP	The guy leaning against the tree	Most countries other than Japan abolish death penalty
Non-standard	Episodic NP	Number 7's the goofy guy that's falling over, with his leg kicked up	From fear against (.) possibility of risk, that, ah: (.) little bit ah: in an accident (.) Umm. is a problem to continue to operate (2) until the safety can be ensured (.)
	Installment NP	A. And the next one is the one with the triangle to the right... B. Okay A. With the square connected to it	NS: Uh:death penalty NNS: Yes NS: Is decided, then NNS: Yes NS: It's ah: said a miscarriage
Inadequate	Provisional NP	And the next one is also the one that doesn't look like anything. It's kind of like the tree?	But eh: well, yes (.) that when earthquake occurs, this, earthquake, isn't it
	Dummy NP	The whatchamacallit	The: ah (.) few (.)
	Proxy NP	A. And number 12 is, uh, ... B. Chair A. With the chair, right B. Got it	NNS: Um:the convicted man (.) is ire: irevoc: a: irevoca:ah: NS: Irrevocable? NNS:Irrevocable

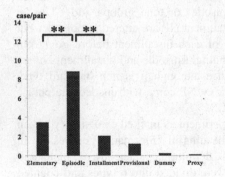

Fig. 5. NP with the use of keywords.   **Fig. 6.** NP without the use of keywords.

A Friedman test indicated that difference across 6 types NP without the use of keywords was significant ($X^2[5] = 55.8$, $p < 0.001$). Post hoc tests (A Wilcoxon Signed-ranks test with Bonferroni correction) indicated that the difference was significant between Elementary and Episodic type NP ($p < 0.01$), and Episodic and Installment type NP ($p < 0.001$).

Whereby it was found that the Keyword condition had episodic utterances to refashion and expanded own prior speech. It was consistent with the data in the previous section that mean length of NNS and NS utterance was significantly longer in the Keyword condition than the Control condition.

Elementary and Episodic NP had large number of occurrences, but Installment, Provisional, Dummy and Proxy are few. There were few numbers of inadequate phrases in the Keyword condition, hence keywords added information and explanation to standard type utterance. This indicated keywords encouraged speakers to utter and get interlocutors acceptance. RQ2 asked about utterance type in a conversation with and without keywords. The data shows both of speakers had episodic utterances to refashion and expanded own prior speech in the Keyword condition. NNS and NS often uttered briefly and shorter in standard manner in the Control condition, and went to the next move. Previous study tested keyword highlighting, no highlighting and random highlighting in order to investigate clarity of messages and collaboration via text-based discussion. Clarity and collaboration were significantly higher in the Keyword condition, and they had significantly positive correlation in-between [2]. It indicated speakers increased repetition of prior speech in the Keyword condition, thus participants enhanced clarity of the message as well as collaboration amongst the two in a dialogue with the use of keywords.

4.3   Speakers' Exchange Structure

NNS and NS were involved in collaborative dialogue. Collaborative dialogue scenario was defined as an occasion where speakers constructed linguistic knowledge through the language use [7]. Thus we investigated speakers' exchange structure with a close look at the collaborative dialogue scenario. Exchange structure embodies teacher's initiation, pupil's response, and teacher's follow-up as the normal form inside the classroom. A teacher always closes down sequence by using the last word and has two turns to speak for every pupil turn, identically the teacher talk for two-thirds of talking [22]. Sequence closing third is post expansion of adjacency pairs, a structure to inform closure of a sequence, implemented by assessments or evaluations as they are referred to in the literature on classroom setting. Table 2 shows examples of the Sequence closing third in the previous and current study.

"Oh" and "OK" (Information receipt) are to mark or claim acceptance, deployed to register a responsive action, as producing a change in its recipient from non-knowing to now-knowing. "How are you" and "Repeat" (Assessment) articulate personal state inquiry, sequence closed by having responses, and in the other turn types "Repeat" serves to close the repair sequence, called the test question or more suitably known-answer question, assessments or evaluations that are understood as being tied to classroom or instructional setting. "Oh", "OK", "Good" and "Telling" (Composite) are combined sequence closure of common composites "oh" plus "okay" or "Good" in that order, in other turn types "Telling" is undertaken to convey information or to carry the material with rejection of dispreferred preceding part, serves to close the repair sequence, it is confronting troubles in hearing, understanding, and speaking the talk, forms for other-initiated repair are largely questions. Postmortems (Mute) is nothing

Table 2. Sequence closing third.

Category	Type	Example [18]	Example of experiment
Informing	Oh, OK	A: You want me to bring something? B: No: no: nothing A: O:kay	(x)
Assessment	How are you	A: hHow uh you:? B: Oka:::y?hh A: Good	(x)
	Repeat	A: Oh I have one class in the evening B: On Monday? A: Yuh:Wednesday B: Uh-Wednesday	NS: Well, after used nuclear fuel (.) e: this is not to burn-up but to react NNS: React NS: Uranium is used as fuel for a nuclear reactor
Composites	Oh, OK, Good	A: I don't think I ever sent Marcia a birthday presentr her baby did I? B: Yeah I think we di:d A: Oh:, good	(x)
	Telling	A: They didn' have all the colors, the orange is really nice but they only had it in these bowls. B: Which is orange? A: The reddy orange. This one B: Oh	NNS: To be legal:is e:legal: (.) well (.) law.i: (.) e:illegal one shouldn't be pro (.) protected. NS: Is it penalty against illegal act? Or punishment? NNS: It's punishment NS: Punishment (.) has lots of options, I dun' think it has to be capital punishment.
Postmortems	Mute	A: What do you doing with that big bow-puh-tank? B: (0.5) (cough) Uh-h-h (1.0)	(x)

being said, which is subject to interpretation by recipient [18]. "Oh" and "OK" (Information receipt) are hardly found in institutional task conversation and few in hospital, court, and school [19]. Debate tasks in this paper had neither of "Oh" and "OK" (Information receipt), nor "How are you" (Assessment). Mute (Postmortems) is negative observation that is absence of occurrence or activities, hence it is at risk of the principals [18], then we did not mark it.

Conversation was transcribed for the purpose of coding. Two experimenters coded conversation line by line based on the Table 1 examples. Experimenters counted the number of cases per pair of "Repeat" and "Telling". Experimenters worked independently and inter-coder agreement was high (k = 0.86). Coding result shows number of cases per pair in Fig. 7. Sequence closing third in Keyword (M = 3.06, SD = 3.34) was significantly larger than the Control (M = 0.81, SD = 1.36) using Wilcoxon signed-rank test, Z = 3.09, p = 0.002.

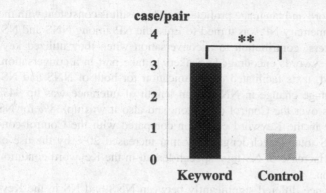

Fig. 7. Sequence closing third coding result.

Result showed speakers constituted sequence completion in the Keyword condition. RQ3 asked about sequence closure in the Keyword condition. The data showed conversation with keywords completed large number of sequence with the sequence closing third. It indicated speakers added the third part to address problems in conversation with the use of keywords. It was consistent with the data that NNS and NS increased speech length within 7 min in the Keyword condition.

Speakers produced large number of sequence completion by repeat and telling in the Keyword condition. Those prototypes of a sequence are called known-answer questions, evaluation, and repair sequence to address problems in conversation, which are commonly seen in classroom or instructional setting. Anything in the talk would be treated as in need of repair if troubles unaddressed. Speakers produced large number of repair sequence that was an effort to solve problems in speaking, hearing and understanding [18]. Despite conversation without keywords had few of repair sequence and left incomprehensible part alone, conversation with keywords facilitated speakers to make efforts to collaborate with interlocutor. It indicated collaborative tasks implemented a meaningful site of interaction commonly seen in classroom, as well as NNS and NS had fruitful discussion in the Keyword condition.

5 Discussion

5.1 Speakers' Contribution to a Conversation

Preceding study reported real-time transcript allows students to participate in class lectures when it has reasonable latencies of less than 5 s [8]. This research investigated how much speakers increased their utterance in conversation with the use of keywords. Figure 3 shows speakers' total speech length in 7 min debate. Data found that NNS and NS extended their speech in the Keyword condition. This was supported by the evidence that speakers constructed the sequence completion after adjacency pairs though the use of keywords. Figure 4 shows the mean length of speakers' utterance. Result indicates mean length of speech of both of NNS and NS became longer in the Keyword condition. Main effects on mean speech length were qualified by an interaction between keyword and language proficiency. The result is consistent with the type of utterance that Elementary NP was turned to Episodic NP among NNS and NS. RQ 1 asked about speakers' contribution to a conversation when they utilized keywords. Data found that keywords encouraged speakers to take part in a conversation. As previous studies noted, texts facilitated communication for both of NNS and NS. Data showed that percentage change in NNS mean length of utterance was up 94% with the use of keywords over the Control condition, and also it was up 38% for NS mean length of utterance in the Keyword condition compared with the Control condition. Besides that, NNS total speech length in 7 min increased 20% by the use of keywords, and also 31% increase of NS total speech length in the Keyword condition over the Control condition.

Mean length of utterance differed significantly between NNS and NS in the Keyword condition. NNS increased mean length of speech, although NNS did not type down keywords. Previous work has reported presentation of keywords enhanced mutual understanding and knowledge [10]. It indicated NNS and NS had large number of shared information in the Keyword condition. NNS obtained audio and literal cues from NS in the Keyword condition, thus NNS extended mean length of utterance due to such abundant shared knowledge. Keywords facilitated communication for both of NNS and NS. NS typed characters using keyboard, and NNS looked them during talking in the Keyword condition, such behavioral difference affected NNS and NS speech.

5.2   NP Referring to Speakers' Utterance

NP represent the main points in conversation when speakers refer to it [12]. Concerning conversation task as a collaborative process, we investigated NP referring to speakers' utterance. Figures 5 and 6 show speakers had episodic utterances to refashion and expanded own prior speech in the Keyword condition. On the other hand the Control condition provided elementary type utterance among NNS and NS, which was uttered briefly and shorter in standard manner, and went to the next move. RQ2 asked about utterance type in a conversation with and without keywords. Result showed uses of keywords encouraged speakers to utter and get interlocutors acceptance. NNS and NS repetitively uttered their prior speech in the Keyword condition, thus keywords enabled speakers to clarify their messages as well as collaborate in a conversation tasks. Mean number of typed characters per minute (CPM) was 12.7 (SD = 5.8), mean number of typed words (WPM) was 6.7 (SD = 3.2), and keywords showed 80% of main points of conversation matched in transcript of conversation. Speakers altered the course of utterance from elementary to episodic with the use of keywords, which was consistent with the data shown in the previous section that speakers extended their mean length of speech in the Keyword condition.

5.3   Speakers' Exchange Structure

In this paper NNS are involved in collaborative dialogue that constructs linguistic knowledge through language use with NS [7]. Speakers performed cognitive activity of verbalization and produced something in the target language. We examined speakers' exchange structure by coding the Sequence closing third. Sequence closing third is a form of the post expansion that involves the addition of one turn to a sequence after its second pair part. Figure 7 shows that speakers produced significantly large number of the sequence completion in the Keyword condition. The data was consistent with that NNS and NS stretched their total speech length in 7 min of conversation with the use of keywords. It indicated NNS and NS had repair sequence not to leave incomprehensible part alone and transformed discussion from ordinary into rewarding one by keywords.

6 Limitation and Future Directions

In this paper conversation task was a debate in the experiment. Participants equally uttered and exchanged their opinions. In advance of the experiment NS were instructed to type essential and incomprehensible part as keywords. NS considered to generate keywords hence NS input NNS utterance in some cases. The data analysis thereby split up the result into NNS and NS in this regard. It indicated analyses only showed experiment results. Methodology that argues how to produce effective keywords is to be discussed in the successive research, which leads contribution to the future work of keyword generation represented by human approach.

7 Conclusion

Previously real-time keywords demonstrated positive effects on conversation. It was unclear how speakers enhanced multilingual discussion between NNS and NS with the use of keywords. In this paper we analyze the data set that NS typed keywords in intercultural audio conference. RQ1 was how much speakers increased utterance in conversation due to keywords. Data showed that percentage change of NNS utterance was 57% increase on average by the use of keywords, and also NS utterance was up 36% over the conversation without the use of keywords. RQ2 was how speakers expressed noun phrases in conversation with the use of keywords. NP referring to speakers' utterance showed that speakers' repeated and expanded prior own speech with the use of keywords, which resulted in collaboration and enhanced clarity of messages in conversation. RQ3 asked whether speakers constructed large number of sequence closure with the use of keywords. Conversation analysis indicated speakers produced sequence completion with repair sequences. These findings indicated conversation between NNS and NS implemented a productive site often seen in classroom, which means they transformed discussion from standard into rewarding one with the use of keywords.

Acknowledgements. This research was partially supported by the JSPS Grants-in-Aid for Scientific Research No. 26330218.

References

1. Gao, G., Yamashita, N., Hautasaari, A., Echenique, A., Fussell, S.R.: Effects of public vs. private automated transcripts on multiparty communication between native and non-native English speakers. In: Proceedings of the SIGCHI Conference on Human Factors in Computing Systems, pp. 843–852, April 2014
2. Gao, G., Wang, H., Cosley, D., Fussell, S.R.: Same translation but different experience: the effects of highlighting on machine-translated conversation. In: Proceedings of the SIGCHI Conference on Human Factors in Computing Systems, pp. 449–458, May 2013
3. Chapanis, A.: Human factors in teleconferencing systems. Final report, vol. 53, p. 30, John Hopkins University, Department of Psychology (1976)
4. Kuramoto, I., Munemori, J., Yuizono, T., Sudo, M.: Effects of text -based communication on a groupware for a new-idea generation support system. J. Inf. Process. Soc. Jpn. **39**(10), 2778–2787 (1998)
5. Echenique, A., Yamashita, N., Kuzuoka, H., Hautasaari, A.: Effects of video and text support on grounding in multilingual multiparty audio conferencing. In: Proceedings of the 5th ACM International Conference on Collaboration Across Boundaries: Culture, Distance and Technology, pp. 73–81, August 2014
6. Yamashita, N., Echenique, A., Ishida, T., Hautasaari, A.: Lost in transmittance: how transmission lag enhances and deteriorates multilingual collaboration. In: Proceedings of the Conference on Computer Supported Cooperative Work, pp. 923–934, February 2013
7. Swain, M.: The output hypothesis and beyond: mediating acquisition through collaborative dialogue. In: Sociocultural Theory and Second Language Learning, pp. 97–114 (2000)
8. Kushalnagar, R.S., Lasecki, W.S., Bigham, J.P.: Accessibility evaluation of classroom captions. J. ACM Trans. Accessible Comput. **5**(3) (2014). Article 7
9. Imai, T., Oku, T., Kobayashi, A.: Advances in real-time closed-captioning for live broadcast by speech recognition, IPSJ SIG Technical report, vol. 2011, SLP-88, No. 4, pp. 1–6, October 2011
10. Hanawa, H., Song, X., Inoue, T.: Key-typing on teleconference: collaborative effort on cross-cultural discussion. In: Proceedings of the 8th International Conference on Collaboration Technologies and Social Computing. Communications in Computer and Information Science, vol. 647, pp. 74–88, September 2016
11. Inoue, T., Hanawa, H., Song, X.: With a little help from my native friends: a method to boost non-native's language use in collaborative work. In: Proceedings of the 9th International Workshop on Informatics, pp. 223–226, September 2015
12. Clark, H.H., Wilkes-Gibbs, D.: Referring as a collaborative process. Cognition **22**(1), 1–39 (1986)
13. Jothilakshmi, S.: Spoken keyword detection using autoassociative neural networks. Int. J. Speech Technol. **17**(1), 83–89 (2014)
14. Japanese Language Proficiency Test. http://www.jlpt.jp/e/about/levelsummary.html
15. Sirintrapun, S.J., Adela, C.: Dynamic nonrobotic telemicroscopy via skype: a cost effective solution to teleconsultation. J. Pathol. Inform. **3**(1), 28 (2012)
16. Rosenfelder, I.: A short introduction to transcribing with elan, Technical report, University of Pennsylvania, January 2011
17. Hautasaari, A., Yamashita, N.: Do automated transcripts help non-native speakers catch up on missed conversation in audio conferences? Proceedings of the 5th ACM International Conference on Collaboration Across Boundaries, pp. 65–72 (2014)
18. Schegloff, E.A.: Sequence Organization in Interaction: A Primer in Conversation Analysis, vol. 1, pp. 115–127. Cambridge University Press, Cambridge (2007)

19. Heritage, J.C., Roth, A.L.: Grammar and institution: questions and questioning in the broadcast news interview. Res. Lang. Soc. Interact. **28**(1), 1–60 (1995)
20. Levitan, R., Hirschberg, J.: Measuring acoustic-prosodic entrainment with respect to multiple levels and dimensions. In: Interspeech (2011)
21. Hanawa, H., Song, X., Inoue, T.: Keyword generation by native speaker is quick and useful in conversation between native and non-native speaker. In: IEEE 21st International Conference on Computer Supported Cooperative Work in Design, April 2017
22. Coulthard, M.: An Introduction to Discourse Analysis. Longman, London (1985)

Worth the Wait?: The Effect of Responsiveness on Interpersonal Attraction Among Known Acquaintances

Matthew Heston[✉] and Jeremy Birnholtz

Department of Communication Studies, Northwestern University, Evanston, USA
heston@u.northestern.edu, jeremyb@northwestern.edu

Abstract. As users adopt new communication technologies, they also develop new norms and expectations about responsiveness: the time it takes an interaction partner to respond to a message. Prior work suggests violation of responsiveness expectations can lead to negative evaluations, but this has not been studied within the modern communication ecosystem, where ubiquitous mobile devices and connectivity enable constant contact with friends and colleagues. We present results from a lab-based experiment examining how violation of such expectations can affect interpersonal attraction. In studying pairs of known acquaintances, we find that low-responsive partners are rated lower in social attraction than high-responsive partners. We also provide an exploratory analysis of chat logs from the experiment which indicates that responsiveness behavior is part of an interactive process where parties involved negotiate for each other's attention over time.

Keywords: Responsiveness · Interpersonal communication · Messaging

1 Introduction

More than ever before, people use a wide range of communication media to facilitate nearly continuous contact with others [26]. These include mobile-specific media such as texting (SMS) [30], as well as platforms like Facebook Messenger, Google Hangouts, and iMessage, which can be used seamlessly across many devices [2]. This capacity for communication across many contexts and devices can make people feel they are constantly online [22]. For those who communicate regularly, this can mean people develop an "ambient" awareness of how and when to talk to others, and have adopted a variety of strategies to signal their own availability as well as assess the availability of their contacts [37].

Moreover, this capacity for constant connection with others has arguably changed people's expectations in communication relative to a time when much mediated communication was available only on desktop computers. For example, people often expect their contacts to be online and available to respond to messages more or less constantly [27]. Expectations around responsiveness can affect our impressions of others in text-based interaction. Kalman and Rafaeli [18],

© Springer International Publishing AG 2017
C. Gutwin et al. (Eds.): CRIWG 2017, LNCS 10391, pp. 164–179, 2017.
DOI: 10.1007/978-3-319-63874-4_13

for example, showed how job candidates' delayed response to email led some managers to view the candidates as unprofessional. This finding provides a useful starting point for considering how responsiveness can impact impressions of others in online interaction. In particular, Expectancy Violation Theory (EVT) [6] allows us to consider how users develop expectations around responsiveness and how violations of these expectations can have relational consequences. This has important implications for the design of communication platforms, as designers of these systems may wish to understand how different features can change expectations, and therefore can affect interpersonal relationships in different ways.

Questions about the effects of responsiveness are particularly salient now due to the constant contact and near-instant response people often expect using today's communication media in both work and social settings. As researchers attempt to exploit contextual information to better design for pervasive computing [25, 28], it is important to empirically evaluate how cues such as response time are interpreted and can affect our impressions of one another. Empirical work in this area has tended to focus primarily on response in work communication contexts. While this has important implications, we argue that responsiveness can have consequences in social contexts as well. For example, while we know that failure to respond to workplace emails can affect perception of workers, we know less about how failure to respond to a text message can affect perception of a close friend. In particular, failure to respond could cause frustration or potentially affect friends' desire to be around each other and remain friends, also known as interpersonal attraction [24]. Some researchers have begun to propose novel methods to seem attentive to others' responsiveness needs in messaging platforms, such as using machine learning to predict the likely time frame for response [13, 27], but this work has not considered the potential relational consequences of response time and other social nuances. If, for example, expectation violations are found to decrease positive feelings among close friends, we may need to think carefully about how we display predicted response times that can affect expectation formation. More empirical work is needed to understand how expectations around responsiveness form and what their effects are.

While expectancy violation theory allows us to gain insights on how a message sender evaluates a partner based on the timeliness of a response to their message, this perspective does not fully capture the interactive dynamics of the situation. As people are often in contact with many others and may also be engaged in face-to-face conversations or other activities, any given incoming message can be seen as one item among many that are competing for the receivers finite and scarce attention [1, 3]. It then becomes important to consider what strategies people use to attract attention when faced with an unresponsive partner. Some recent work [37] has conceptualized attention management as a negotiation process analogous to the grounding process described by Clark [8]. Viewing responsiveness as part of a joint attention management process allows us to begin to explore the dynamics of responsiveness and attention. Furthermore, understanding this process can guide the design of systems that attempt to predict responsive time or attentiveness [1, 13, 27] by providing insight into how responsiveness behavior changes during an interaction.

In this paper we present results from a lab experiment designed to explore the relationship between responsiveness and interpersonal attraction between known acquaintances. By manipulating responsiveness in online interaction, we found evidence that delayed responsiveness is associated with lower levels of social attraction, the feeling of friendship and wanting to spend time with another person. In addition to these results, we present a qualitative analysis of chat logs to understand how individuals negotiate for attention when faced with delayed responsiveness.

2 Background

2.1 Responsiveness and Impressions

Participants in text-based interaction often interpret cues such as word choice [16] or emoticons [11,21] in forming impressions of others [35]. These cues can affect relational outcomes such as trust and liking between communication partners [23,29,32,36]. It has also been shown that chronemics, or the use of time, in online conversation can be interpreted as a cue that reveals social information [19]. Response time has been shown to affect impressions of others, as in Tyler and Tang's [33] finding that workers have expectations about appropriate email response times and that workers have anxiety about when to expect a response from new contacts. Delay in response has also been identified as a serious problem for geographically dispersed virtual teams, as workers often misinterpret the meaning of silence [10].

It is clear that, like explicit cues such as word choice and emoticon use, responsiveness can affect our impressions of others. However, as the studies above demonstrate, the effect of responsiveness on impressions has primarily focused on either email or instant messaging in the workplace. As people increasingly use messaging platforms such as Facebook Messenger and Google Hangouts to communicate with friends [2] and develop expectations for immediate response at virtually all times [27], we need to understand how responsiveness can affect perceptions among known acquaintances and account for these expectations when designing communication platforms for their use.

We know that participants in online interaction interpret various cues in forming impressions of others [15,23]. We also know that response time can be interpreted in forming impressions of others and have evidence that delayed responsiveness can lead to negative impressions in the workplace [10,18]. Given that friends and acquaintances increasingly use text-based platforms to communicate with one another [2,22,30] we would expect them to also interpret response time in evaluating others, and we would expect them to evaluate the same types of partner attributes as they do when interpreting other cues, such as liking, warmth, and trustworthiness [20,29,32]. A good overall measure to capture these attributes is interpersonal attraction: judgments about how much a person likes someone else [24], it is useful to think about responsiveness in terms of the message sender's expectation, and how violation of this expectation can lead to changes in evaluation of others.

Responsiveness and Expectations. A useful theoretical framework for exploring these questions is Expectancy Violation Theory (EVT) [6], which suggests that violation of an expectation results in heightened attention to the behavior, which is then interpreted and evaluated. In our case, we assume people expect a quick response and that delayed response violates that expectation which may lead to a negative evaluation. In this paper, one of our goals is to understand how expectations of responsiveness are affected by behavior, i.e., if delayed responsiveness causes changes in expectations, and whether or not this has an effect on impressions of others. Doing so will allow us to better understand the effects of the "always on" nature of modern communication platforms on relationships. Below, we use EVT to derive a series of hypotheses we test in a lab experiment. While previous studies applying EVT have focused on the moderating effect of communicator reward valence in EVT, this is often applied when forming impressions of strangers [18]. Given that our participants already knew each other, our hypotheses focus on the other elements of EVT, namely the formation of expectations and the valence and magnitude of expectancy violations.

Hypotheses. EVT suggests that the outcome of a violation depends in part on the magnitude of deviation from an expectation. The theory also suggests that violations are psychologically arousing, or in other words, a violation draws attention to itself. Given that we are focusing on responsiveness among known acquaintances, we expect that these individuals have some pre-existing expectations about responsiveness. In order for a response delay to have an effect on interpersonal attraction, the expectation violation must be perceptible and cross some threshold such that it is psychologically arousing. While we expect known acquaintances to have general expectations about each others response behavior that may not change as the result of one interaction, we also know that individuals form context specific expectations within an interaction [5]. We therefore also expect them to make contextual adjustments to their expectations within a particular conversation. A useful way to know whether or not a violation occurred, then, is to assess someones expectations immediately following an episode. We expect that communicators adjust their expectations following a violation, such that when a delayed response is sufficiently long to attract attention as considered a violation, an individual will set a lower bar for expectations about responsiveness and expect longer delays. We refer to individuals with longer delays as "low-responsive" and individuals who respond quickly as "high-responsive."

H1: Individuals will have lower responsiveness expectations for a low-responsive partner than for a high-responsive partner.

Violations of these responsiveness expectations should draw attention and evaluation. To assess impressions, we focus on attraction as a multifactor construct as defined by McCroskey and McCain [24]. In particular, we study the effect of responsiveness on both social attraction, the feeling of friendship and wanting to spend time with another person, as well as task attraction, or respect for another person and belief in their ability to complete tasks. We expect slow response to lead to a decrease in both social and task attraction.

H2a: Low-responsive partners will be rated lower in social attraction.

H2b: Low-responsive partners will be rated lower in task attraction.

A violation occurs only when a threshold is crossed such that the violating behavior leads to psychological arousal. In the case where an individual is unable to respond quickly, he may be distracted from the conversation such that he does not notice delayed responsiveness from his partner. In this case, we would not expect a change in expectations following an interaction, because attention to the violating behavior was not heightened. In other words, an individual's own ability to respond will affect their expectations of responsiveness.

H3: Low-responsive and high-responsive individuals will have different expectations of their partners.

Furthermore, we would expect that, because violations will be less frequent for people with lower expectations, those with lower expectations will be less likely to form negative impressions of their low-responsive partners:

H4: Compared to low-responsive individuals, high-responsive individuals will have a larger decrease in attraction towards low-responsive partners.

2.2   Responsiveness and Attention

Studies of workplace email use have shown workers adapt to others' expectations of quick responses to email by using a variety of strategies, such as sending short messages signaling their intent to reply more thoroughly later [4,33]. Such practices suggest that responsiveness is one part of a process in which people strategically manage their attention through negotiation over time. This is to say, in the examples cited above there is a normative expectation to respond quickly which may interfere with the ability to focus on the task at hand, leading individuals to respond quickly but in such a way as to manage expectations about a longer, in-depth response.

This perspective has been adopted in some recent studies of attention management. For example, Wohn and Birnholtz [37] found that mobile device users develop various strategies to both display their own availability for interaction and assess the availability of others. Drawing on Clark's [8] grounding process, this perspective emphasizes that individuals in an interaction adjust their behavior based on evidence of each others mutual attention (or lack thereof). Responsiveness can be viewed as one type of evidence of attention, and likely has an effect on how participants in a conversation interact with one another.

With regard to responsiveness, this perspective raises questions about how people attempt to get attention from a partner who is not responding. We therefore asked the following research question:

RQ1: What strategies are used by individuals seeking higher attention from their conversation partners?

3   Method

We ran a between-participants lab experiment in which pairs of participants located in separate rooms completed a task together that required coordination via text chat. Pairs were randomly assigned to one of three conditions, in which individuals responsiveness was manipulated via the presence of a separate distractor task that slowed response: (1) high-responsive/high-responsive (i.e., no distractor for either partner), (2) high-responsive/low-responsive (distractor task for only one participant) and (3) low-responsive/low-responsive (distractor task for both). Since our analysis treats individual condition and partner condition as main effects, in order to have a balanced design, we doubled the number of participants assigned to condition 2 (i.e., to account for both low/high and high/low).

3.1   Participants

Participants included 48 undergraduate students (24 pairs) from a Midwestern U.S. university (age 18–26). Participants were recruited in pairs, and required to have known each other for at least three months. Fifty-four percent of pairs were female-female (40% mixed, 6% male-male). Recruitment was done via flyering on campus, social media posts, and in-class announcements. Participants were guaranteed $5 for participation, with a possible $3 bonus that incentivized different behaviors across conditions.

3.2   Task

Collaborative Task. The collaborative task assigned to all pairs was a "desert island" task (derived from Gottman [14]), in which the pair reads a scenario about being stranded on a desert island. They are given a list of many available items (e.g., first aid kit, matches, compass) and are told that they both must decide on the top 5 most important items for their survival. Each individual had to first construct their own list of the top 5 items to submit using a web-based tool, which also included a chat interface to coordinate with their partner. This type of task is commonly used in studies of this nature (e.g., [31]) and is appropriate here in that it replicates real-world scenarios in which people use text to coordinate in an environment with competing priorities [3].

We used a point system to incentivize participants to complete their respective tasks and manipulate their priorities. Each person could earn a total of 300 points, resulting in up to $3.00 extra compensation. Low-responsive participants earned 50 points for completing the collaborative task, while high-responsive participants earned 150.

We encouraged participants to discuss their choices carefully by telling them (falsely) that a survival expert had compiled a list of the "correct" top 5 items. High-responsive participants were told they could earn an additional 150 points for matching this list, and low-responsive participants were told they could earn an additional 50 points. As there was no actual "correct" list, participants always earned these points as long as they both submitted identical lists.

Distractor Task. As mentioned earlier, responsiveness was manipulated through a distractor task consisting of a series of web-based jigsaw puzzles. Focus on these puzzles was motivated by the possibility of 50 points per completed puzzle. To ensure that the tasks were done at the same time (such that the distractor would impact response time), each puzzle expired after 2 min. After each puzzle was completed, there was also a 10 s break before the next puzzle appeared, providing time to respond to their partner without having another puzzle to focus on.

3.3 Procedure

Participants arrived at the lab together and were seated in separate experiment rooms, intended to simulate separate locations. After consenting, participants filled out a questionnaire containing demographic questions, as well as items related to their initial attraction to their partner and their expectations about their partner's responsiveness.

Next, participants completed the tasks described above. They were given up to 8 min to complete their tasks, with no late completions accepted. This time limit is based on pilot studies showing this was enough time to complete the tasks with a sense of urgency. Finally, participants again rated their partner's attractiveness and responsiveness.

3.4 Measures

Responsiveness expectation was measured with a 5-point, 3-item scale asking whether or not they expected their partner to respond in a timely manner ($\alpha = .71$). High values indicate expecting a person to be attentive and respond quickly.

Task attraction ($\alpha = .79$) and social attraction ($\alpha = .79$) were measured using 5-point, 10-item scales from McCroskey and McCain [24].

Responsiveness was measured as the number of seconds it took for an individual to respond to the first in a set of messages from their partner. This means that if an individual began a conversation, "Hey," and after several seconds said, "You there?," before their partner responded, we counted the number of seconds between the initial message ("Hey") and the response.

Completion time was measured as the number of seconds it took from beginning the task to both partners submitting their lists for the collaborative task.

3.5 Analysis

Responsiveness and Attraction. To verify that our manipulation worked, individual mean response times were calculated and compared using a one-tailed t-test. On average, low-responsive participants took 10 s longer to respond than high-responsiveness participants ($M = 24.5$ s, $SD = 13.3$ s vs. $M = 14.6$ s, $SD = 5.2$ s), a statistically significant difference ($t(46) = 3.37$, $p < .01$).

To test for differences in responsiveness expectations and attraction, we fit three separate mixed-effect linear models, with responsiveness expectations, task attraction, and social attraction as the dependent variables. Given that our design involved pre- and post-task data, we used post-task values as the dependent variable while including pre-task values as a covariate [12]. The DV can be interpreted as post-task values that control for pre-task values.

To test our hypotheses, each model follows a 2×2 factorial analysis, in which we include the following independent variables: individual condition (high-responsive vs. low-responsive), partner condition (high-responsive vs. low-responsive) and an interaction term for these two variables (to test H3 and H4). To account for interdependence between observations, pair is included as a random effect in the model. We used an alpha level of .05 for all statistical tests.

Responsiveness and Attention Negotiation. In order to understand different strategies taken to negotiate attention across conditions, the author and two research assistants carefully read through chat logs of all participants across conditions, which includes messages sent as well as timestamps. These analyses were guided by turn-taking strategies in conversation analysis [17] with special attention paid to situations in which participants seemed to react to delayed responsiveness and get their partners attention. Each researcher made detailed notes on their transcripts and themes were identified through discussion among the researchers.

4   Results

4.1   Differences in Expectations

H1 predicted individuals will have lower expectations about responsiveness after interacting with a low-responsive partner. The data support *H1*. Partner condition did have a significant effect on expectations of responsiveness $(F(1,\ 42.72) = 4.72,\ p < .05)$, and those with low-responsive partners did have lower responsiveness expectations. In comparing the least-squares means across partner conditions, we found the average expectations score among those with high-responsive partners $(M = 3.49,\ SE = 0.08)$ to be higher than those with low-responsive partners $(M = 3.23,\ SE = 0.08)$. A higher score on this scale indicates that a participant felt his partner was attentive and responded in a timely manner.

We found no significant effect of an individual's own responsiveness condition $(F(1,\ 39.37) = 0.02,\ p = 0.88)$, or the interaction term $(F(1,\ 21.98) = 0.30,\ p = .59)$.

4.2   Differences in Attraction

Given support for *H1*, it seems that individuals did notice response latency in forming their expectations, and we can now turn to the question of whether or not this leads to changes in attraction. We found evidence for *H2a*, which predicted lower social attraction for low-responsive partners. We did not, however, find evidence for *H2b*, which predicted a change in task attraction.

As predicted by *H2a*, partner responsiveness condition was found to have a significant effect on social attraction $(F(1, 43) = 5.18, p < .05)$, and social attraction was higher for responsive partners $(M = 4.13, SE = 0.06)$ than those with delayed responsiveness $(M = 3.95, SE = 0.06)$. Consistent with the results for H1, the effect of an individuals own responsiveness condition $(F(1, 43) = 0.26, p = .61)$ and the interaction term $(F(1, 43) = 0.00, p = .99)$ were not statistically significant.

We found no evidence for *H2b*, as no significant results were found for levels of task attraction. The effect of partner responsiveness was not significant $(F(1, 43) = 2.97, p = .092)$, and, similar to the other models, no significant results were found for an individuals responsiveness condition $(F(1, 43) = 1.23, p = .27)$ or the interaction term $(F(1, 43) = 0.98, p = .328)$.

Given the lack of a significant interaction effect in any of our models, we did not see evidence for *H3* or *H4*. In other words, expectations of responsiveness and the effect of partner responsiveness on attraction did not vary depending on an individuals own responsiveness. These results are summarized in Fig. 1.

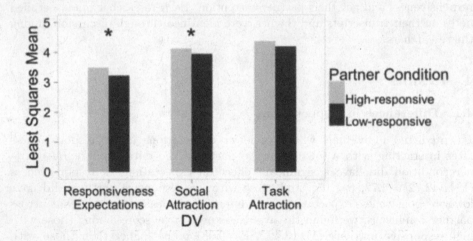

Fig. 1. Least squares means of DVs across conditions. Note: *indicates p < .05

4.3   Completion Time and Interaction

While we found evidence supporting our hypotheses, it is possible that this effect is due to the distractor task, which could plausibly have influenced pair performance or the amount of communication between participants. We tested for this possibility, but found no significant effect of condition on task completion time (see Table 1), $(F(2, 21) = 3.32, p = .06)$. We also compared the mean number of messages sent by participants in the low-responsive $(M = 17.67, SD = 7.49)$

Table 1. Average completion time across conditions

Responsiveness types in pair	Mean completion time (seconds)	SD
High-high	380.5	52.4
Low-low	443.5	40.2
High-low	423.0	33.8

and high-responsive ($M = 20.92$, $SD = 9.12$) conditions but found no significant difference ($t(46) = 1.34$, $p = .186$).

4.4 Responsiveness and Attention

Our research question asked what strategies are used to heighten attention from a low-responsive partner. High-responsive participants attempting to get their partners attention did so in several ways and in varying levels of politeness.

Question asking was one way participants attempted to elicit responses from their partners. We noticed differences, however, in the types of questions asked and how they were addressed.

For example, participants sometimes asked questions about the collaborative task. This is to say, rather than directly inquire about their partner's status, participants would attempt to elicit a response by eliciting input about their joint task. One high-responsive participant, for example, after not receiving a response from their low-responsive partner to their greeting for 20 s, followed up by asking "which 5 r u thinking," which elicited a quick response.

In other cases questions are also used, but more directly to assess partner availability and whether or not they see the messages at all. For example, after not receiving a response to their greeting after 35 s, a high-responsive individual followed up with "do you see this?" and after another 57 s with "testing 123" which then elicited a response from their partner. Following this exchange, the low-responsive partner tended to answer subsequent questions within 15 s.

In one case a high-responsive partner initiated with a question related to the task ("ok deserts get cold so blankets?"), and followed up with a question about availability after not receiving a response ("you there?").

In our ANOVA models, we did not find evidence that a user's own responsiveness condition affected his expectations or evaluation of partner responsiveness. We also saw evidence in the chat logs that participants in the low-responsive condition occasionally took breaks to speak with their partner, and also used similar strategies when not receiving a response. One low-responsive participant, for example, after not receiving any response from their partner after one minute, started sending a series of question marks (e.g., "????????") to their partner, rather forcefully and explicitly attempting to elicit a response.

However, participants did not always use questions to explicitly signal the desire for a response. In some cases, participants would initiate a conversation with a greeting or other phrase they likely felt would yield a response. After enough time had elapsed that it was clear the expected turn taking would not occur, the participant would move on. After 93 s and no response from a low-responsive partner, one high-responsive participant followed up with "So, on my list, I have: matches, compass, water, peanuts, and pocketknife" and then with "We def don't want the soda, pretzels, or pillows."

5   Discussion

As users increasingly use communication platforms that span multiple devices and develop new expectations about availability of their contacts, it is important to understand how these new expectations affect how we communicate and how responsiveness may affect interpersonal relationships. Our results suggest that responsiveness can impact impressions among known acquaintances and that individuals use different strategies to get attention from an unresponsive partner.

5.1   Responsiveness and Impressions

Our study extends prior work such as Tyler and Tang [33] and Kalman and Rafaeli [18], which found that long delays in email response in the workplace resulted in negative evaluation of workers. Our experiment was designed to test for these effects in synchronous text-based interfaces among known acquaintances who have competing demands for their attention. We believe this experiment design closely resembles the attributes of contemporary communication platforms [2,3]. Furthermore, while recent work has noted the new expectations about immediate response in these types of messaging platforms [7,27], our study provides evidence of what can happen when these expectations are violated even with relatively small delays. Our finding that response time can affect social attraction has implications for the design of new communication platforms.

The main finding in our experiment was that participants who took, on average, just 10 s longer to respond were evaluated lower in social attraction. The fact that participants' impressions of one another could be altered by an average response delay of 10 s suggests that they are acutely aware of response delay when engaged in online conversation. In the context of our experiment, message senders were aware that they had limited time to complete a task that they needed their partner's attention to complete. This suggests that in some scenarios communicators have contextual expectations about partner responsiveness, and from an EVT perspective, deviation from such contextual expectations will trigger psychological arousal and negative evaluations. While recent work has explored contextual information in notification management [25,28], our results indicate system designers should also be aware of how implementation of such features affect response time, as this can affect relationships.

Importantly, we note that, as Fig. 1 shows, social attraction ratings across all partner conditions were still high, even when they varied: close to 4 on a 5-point Likert scale. Nevertheless, the effect seems important given that the pairs we recruited were people who had an existing relationship. Given that we were able to see a difference in social attraction among friends, this finding raises questions about how such effects may play out over a longer period of time and across different types of relationships.

As participants worked on a collaborative task during the experiment, it is interesting that while we saw a significant difference in social attraction, we did not find a significant difference in task attraction. It is possible that since we recruited friends, who likely had a primarily social relationship, these pairs may not have had much experience working together which could result in a larger amount of variance in evaluating each other's task attractiveness. This suggests that type of relationship may be important to consider in thinking about responsiveness and its effects.

Also of interest is the lack of evidence we found for Hypotheses 3 and 4, which suggested that the effect of lower expectations and lower attraction would be moderated by an individual's own responsiveness condition. In particular, we assumed that individuals in the low-responsive condition would fail to notice their partners response latency, and therefore not change their expectations or their attraction towards their partner. We did not find evidence that this was the case. One possible explanation for this may be the fundamental attribution error, in which people attribute behavior of others to internal characteristics and attribute their own behavior to external characteristics. In other words, a participant may be more likely to rationalize his own failure to respond immediately by noticing the competing demands for his attention, while simultaneously blaming his partner's slow response time on some personal characteristic of his partner. Such attribution errors have previously been noted in text-based interaction [9,34]. While we cannot be certain why partner attraction ratings did not vary depending on an individual's condition, this question merits further research, as it suggests that an individuals own ability to respond is not necessarily a reliable indicator of his expectations of others' responsiveness. If attribution errors do drive such behavior, this may have important implications for the design of systems that attempt to predict responsiveness [1,13,27], as we must think carefully about how users will interpret such predictions.

5.2   Responsiveness and Attention

Our chat log analysis helps us further understand responsiveness as one part of a joint process between actors in negotiating attention. This negotiation process also has important implications as we consider how communication is changing with new media platforms. Individuals may choose not to respond to chat requests when they have another task to focus on [1], and even if they do want to respond in a conversation, their attention is likely divided as users split their attention across many different conversations occurring at the same time [3].

We saw evidence that people react to delayed response in various ways when heightened attention is needed from a partner. Users of messaging platforms are often strategic when they have an urgent message to communicate, for example by switching to a more synchronous medium in attempting to contact someone [37]. Our chat logs indicate that users also rely on different types of linguistic strategies in obtaining partner attention when limited to a text-based messaging platform. These may include explicit strategies of asking about availability ("are you there?") or other indicators of frustration at lack of response (simply typing "???" over and over). However, they also include other strategies such as simply moving forward in a conversation, as we saw with the participant who shared his desert island list after not receiving a response to his greeting for 93 s.

Recent work has explored systems that predict when a user is available [1,28]. Our chat log analysis indicates that, in some cases, users who are distracted or otherwise busy may still alter their responsiveness behavior in response to different types of strategies used by those seeking their attention. If this is the case, predictive systems may want to categorize message recipients not in categories of available or not available, but rather more broadly consider attention as existing on a spectrum and offering various levels of attention seeking behavior.

6   Limitations and Future Work

We attempted to design for ecological validity by choosing tasks that mimicked the competing attention demands in the real world. However, as with any lab experiment, our study necessarily made tradeoffs between experimental control and external validity. We believe this study provides the basis for interesting avenues of future research.

We found that users adjusted their expectations of responsiveness as a result of partner response time after a brief 8 min interaction. Observational studies of existing messaging logs or longitudinal study designs could help us better understand patterns of responsiveness as they play out across the multitude of new communication platforms and how expectations about responsiveness shift over an extended period of time. While our lab study showed a difference in social attraction based on responsiveness, such studies could provide further evidence on how relational variables are affected by responsiveness over time.

Mobile devices no doubt play an important part in new communication media. Many of the services used on these devices also extends to laptop or desktop use, contributing to the pervasive nature of many of these platforms. Our lab study relied on participants using desktop computers in our lab allowing for greater experimental control. Nevertheless, future work should study these dynamics on mobile devices as well.

7   Conclusion

We have presented results from a lab experiment designed to understand the effect of responsiveness on attraction among known acquaintances as well as a qualitative analysis of chat logs to understand how individuals strategically attempt to get attention from an unresponsive partner. Our experimental results indicate that individuals who are slower to respond are rated lower in social attraction. Our analysis of chat logs showed that individuals use different strategies to get attention from an unresponsive partner, including asking questions about their partners availability as well as skipping their partners turn in conversation. These results indicate the importance of understanding responsiveness behavior and its effects in new communication platforms where people are constantly online and expect their contacts to be online and available to respond.

Acknowledgements. This research was funded by the National Science Foundation award IIS–217143. The authors would like to acknowledge undergraduate research assistants Ada Jing and Sarah Shi for their assistance with this project.

References

1. Avrahami, D., Fussell, S.R., Hudson, S.E.: Im waiting: timing and responsiveness in semi-synchronous communication. In: Proceedings of the Conference on Computer Supported Cooperative Work, pp. 285–294. ACM (2008)
2. Bailey, S.K.T., Schroeder, B.L., Whitmer, D.E., Sims, V.K.: Perceptions of mobile instant messaging apps are comparable to texting for young adults in the United States. In: Proceedings of the Human Factors and Ergonomics Society Annual Meeting, vol. 60, no. 1, pp. 1235–1239 (2016)
3. Battestini, A., Setlur, V., Sohn, T.: A large scale study of text-messaging use. In: Proceedings of the International Conference on Human-Computer Interaction with Mobile Devices and Services, pp. 229–238 (2010)
4. Birnholtz, J., Dixon, G., Hancock, J.: Distance, ambiguity and appropriation: structures affording impression management in a collocated organization. Comput. Hum. Behav. **28**(3), 1028–1035 (2012)
5. Burgoon, J.K.: Interpersonal expectations, expectancy violations, and emotional communication. J. Lang. Soc. Psychol. **12**(1–2), 30–48 (1993)
6. Burgoon, J.K.: Expectancy violations theory. In: Littlejohn, S.W., Foss, K.A. (eds.) Encyclopedia of Communication Theory. SAGE Publications Inc., Thousand Oaks (2009)
7. Church, K., de Oliveira, R.: What's up with whatsapp? In: Proceedings of the International Conference on Human-Computer Interaction with Mobile Devices and Services, pp. 352–361. ACM (2013)
8. Clark, H.H.: Using Language. Cambridge University Press, Cambridge (1996)
9. Cramton, C.D.: Attribution in distributed work groups. In: Distributed Work, pp. 191–212 (2002)
10. Cramton, C.D.: The mutual knowledge problem and its consequences for dispersed collaboration. Organ. Sci. **12**(3), 346–371 (2001)
11. Derks, D., Bos, A.E.R., Grumbkow, J.V.: Emoticons and social interaction on the Internet: the importance of social context. Comput. Hum. Behav. **23**(1), 842–849 (2007)
12. Dimitrov, D.M., Rumrill Jr., P.D.: Pretest-posttest designs and measurement of change. Work **20**(2), 159–165 (2003)
13. Dingler, T., Pielot, M.: I'll be there for you: quantifying attentiveness towards mobile messaging. In: Proceedings of the International Conference on Human-Computer Interaction with Mobile Devices and Services, pp. 1–5. ACM (2015)
14. Gottman, J.M.: The Marriage Clinic. A Scientifically-Based Marital Therapy. W.W. Norton & Company, New York (1999)

15. Hancock, J., Birnholtz, J., Bazarova, N., Guillory, J., Perlin, J., Amos, B.: Butler lies: awareness, deception and design. In: Proceedings of the ACM SIGCHI Conference on Human Factors in Computing Systems, pp. 517–526 (2009)

16. Hancock, J.T., Landrigan, C., Silver, C.: Expressing emotion in text-based communication. In: Proceedings of the ACM SIGCHI Conference on Human Factors in Computing Systems, pp. 929–932 (2007)

17. Hayashi, M.: Turn Allocation and Turn Sharing. Sidnell/The Handbook of Conversation Analysis. Wiley, Chichester (2013)

18. Kalman, Y.M., Rafaeli, S.: Online pauses and silence: chronemic expectancy violations in written computer-mediated communication. Commun. Res. **38**(1), 54–69 (2010)

19. Kalman, Y.M., Scissors, L.E., Gill, A.J., Gergle, D.: Online chronemics convey social information. Comput. Hum. Behav. **29**(3), 1260–1269 (2013)

20. Lea, M., Spears, R.: Paralanguage and social perception in computer-mediated communication. J. Organ. Comput. Electron. Commer. **2**(3–4), 321–341 (2009)

21. Lee, J.Y., Hong, N., Kim, S., Oh, J., Lee, J.: Smiley face: why we use emoticon stickers in mobile messaging. In: Proceedings of the International Conference on Human-Computer Interaction with Mobile Devices and Services, pp. 760–766. ACM (2016)

22. Lenhart, A.: Teens, Social Media & Technology Overview 2015. Pew Research Center, Washington (2015)

23. Liebman, N., Gergle, D.: It's (not) simply a matter of time: the relationship between CMC cues and interpersonal affinity. In: Proceedings of the ACM Conference on Computer-Supported Cooperative Work and Social Computing, pp. 570–581. ACM (2016)

24. McCroskey, J.C., McCain, T.A.: The measurement of interpersonal attraction. Speech Monogr. **41**(3), 261–266 (1974)

25. Pejovic, V., Musolesi, M.: Interruptme: designing intelligent prompting mechanisms for pervasive applications. In: Proceedings of the International Joint Conference on Pervasive and Ubiquitous Computing, pp. 897–908. ACM (2014)

26. Pettegrew, L.S., Day, C.: Smart phones and mediated relationships: the changing face of relational communication. Rev. Commun. **15**(2), 122–139 (2015)

27. Pielot, M., de Oliveira, R., Oliver, N., Kwak, H.: Didn't you see my message?: Predicting attentiveness to mobile instant messages. In: Proceedings of the ACM SIGCHI Conference on Human Factors in Computing Systems, pp. 3319–3328. ACM (2014)

28. Schulze, F., Groh, G.: Conversational context helps improve mobile notification management. In: Proceedings of the International Conference on Human-Computer Interaction with Mobile Devices and Services, pp. 518–528. ACM (2016)

29. Scissors, L.E., Gill, A.J., Geraghty, K., Gergle, D.: In CMC we trust: the role of similarity. In: Proceedings of the ACM SIGCHI Conference on Human Factors in Computing Systems, pp. 527–536. ACM (2009)

30. Smith, A.: Americans and Text Messaging. Pew Research Center, Washington (2011)

31. Tang, A., Pahud, M., Inkpen, K., Benko, H., Tang, J.C., Buxton, B.: Three's company: understanding communication channels in three-way distributed collaboration. In: Proceedings of the ACM Conference on Computer Supported Cooperative Work, pp. 271–280. ACM (2010)

32. Toma, C.L.: Perceptions of trustworthiness online: the role of visual and textual information. In: Proceedings of the 2010 ACM Conference on Computer Supported Cooperative Work, pp. 13–22. ACM (2010)

33. Tyler, J.R., Tang, J.C.: When can I expect an email response? A study of rhythms in email usage. In: Proceedings of ECSCW, pp. 239–258 (2003)

34. Vignovic, J.A., Thompson, L.F.: Computer-mediated cross-cultural collaboration: attributing communication errors to the person versus the situation. J. Appl. Psychol. **95**(2), 265–276 (2010)

35. Walther, J.B.: Social Information Processing Theory (CMC). Wiley, Hoboken (2016)

36. Walther, J.B., Bunz, U.: The rules of virtual groups: trust, liking, and performance in computer-mediated communication. J. Commun. **55**(4), 828–846 (2005)

37. Wohn, D.Y., Birnholtz, J.P.: From ambient to adaptation: interpersonal attention management among young adults. In: Proceedings of the International Conference on Human-Computer Interaction with Mobile Devices and Services, pp. 26–35 (2015)

An Approach Using the Design Science Research for the Development of a Collaborative Assistive System

Daniel Maniglia Amancio da Silva[1]([⊠]), Gian Ricardo Berkenbrock[2], and Carla Diacui Medeiros Berkenbrock[1]

[1] Universidade do Estado de Santa Catarina (UDESC), Joinville, SC, Brazil
danielmanilha@hotmail.com, carla.berkenbrock@udesc.br
[2] Centro Tecnológico de Joinville, Universidade Federal de Santa Catarina (UFSC), Joinville, SC, Brazil
gian.rb@ufsc.br

Abstract. Advances in technology, as well as society's evolution have been going toward social inclusion of people with disabilities. They have motivated the development of tools to support people with cognitive problems. This paper aims to create communication artifacts, in smartphones, for the development of a collaborative geographic monitoring system, called Collabtrack. The system enables the communication among people with intellectual disabilities and their caregivers in daily displacements. This research was guided by the Design Science Research (DSR) methodology and it was divided into steps of discovery of knowledge. The first step uses the User Centered Design (UCD) approach to identify the system requirements and it results in prototypes of augmentative communication screens. The second step uses the Participatory Design (PD) approach which allows users to choose the screens images and evaluate the system usability. As a result, the benefits of using the Design Science Research as methodology, measured in a qualitative way, in a collaborative and assistive context are highlighted. The evaluation of Collabtrack indicates the potential to provide the users with intellectual disabilities autonomy, as well as increased the safety for their caregivers.

Keywords: Design Science Research · Communication · Collaborative Assistive System

1 Introduction

Intellectual disability is a term that is used when a person presents certain limitations in their mental functioning. Is an abnormality that has enormous social effects. It not only affects the people who suffer from it but also the family and the society [19].

Networking computing systems are provoking transformations in all sectors of contemporary life [7]. However, there are challenges in developing assistive

© Springer International Publishing AG 2017
C. Gutwin et al. (Eds.): CRIWG 2017, LNCS 10391, pp. 180–195, 2017.
DOI: 10.1007/978-3-319-63874-4_14

technologies and collaborative systems. The characteristics of multidisciplinarity, the particularities, limitations and different needs of users make it complex the development of these systems focused on "special users". Developing systems are always challenging tasks and the challenges are even greater in developing systems for people with special needs. The combination of reduced communication skills and additional stakeholders, such as parents, teachers, or caregivers, results in a rather complex situation. According to Grudin [10], in systems development, considering people with intellectual disabilities as "vulnerable users" only reveals the lack of adequate design methods, difficulty in communication or in understanding the reality of these users.

Communication is one of the pillars of collaborative systems. Communication is also a need for social relationships and a difficulty for people with intellectual disabilities. This work aims to facilitate the communication of people with intellectual disabilities and their caregivers. In this context, the Augmentative and Alternative Communication (AAC) emerges as a possibility of collaboration. This paper presents an approach to support the development of a monitoring and communication system for people with intellectual disabilities and their caregivers. The approach uses the Design Science Research (DSR) methodology to define two research cycles that allow the exploration of knowledge to understand the users and build the computational components for interaction.

2 Application of the Research Methodology

Design Science Research is a research method centered on the evolution of a "design science". According to its author [3], the knowledge needed to conduct research in information systems involves the paradigms of "behavioral science" and "design science". The behavioral science is addressed by developing theories that explain phenomena related to the identified business needs. Design science approaches is addressed by developing and evaluating artifacts designed to reach the identified business needs.

In the context of the present research, the behavioral science will guide the developers to understand the limits of users with intellectual disabilities in communication as well as the users to understand the software. The design science will guide the development of interfaces adapted to these users.

2.1 Problem Relevance

People with intellectual disabilities daily go to bakeries, supermarkets or to the companies where they work. Most of the time, due to their deficiencies, these people depend on the personal supervision of their caregivers during the track.

In some cases, the person with intellectual disability has capacity to do these movements without the presence of caregivers, but caregivers may not be sure if the person would be safe doing it alone. This insecurity is justified by the possibility of problems in the course, which the person with intellectual disability may have difficulties to solve by themselves. For instance, getting on the wrong bus, having a nervous breakdown during the displacement, feeling scared or lost, and so on. According to Glat [9], the care of people with intellectual disabilities imposes daily adaptations, which can make many families get social isolation and consequently lead them to reinforce mechanisms of overprotection. Glat also emphasizes that in such cases, the difficulties of a person with a disability may be oversized in detriment of their abilities and the extreme care may damage their independence and autonomy. Then, Glat carried out studies with family members of adults with intellectual disabilities that demonstrate overprotection, evidencing the need to construct a resocializing space. Overprotection is also evidenced by Rosa and Denari [18], which encourages families to offer to the person increased independence and integration into society.

In this context, this work aims to support the therapeutic work with the objective of increasing the autonomy of people with intellectual disabilities through the development of a collaborative system of care and location. Thus, a system was created so that people with intellectual disabilities and their caregivers can collaborate and thus provide confidence to caregivers and increase the autonomy of people with intellectual disabilities in their daily displacements.

Therefore, the use of a monitoring system, where collaboration is used as a care tool for patients using mobile devices, may allow some autonomy for the patients. By conducting monitoring in a collaborative way (with coordination, cooperation and mainly communication), the aim is to reduce the risks during displacements, to provide confidence to the caregivers and to ensure safety to the patients.

2.2 Artifact

This paper focuses on the definition of communication software artifacts understandable for people with intellectual disabilities in order to enable the collaboration between the user and his/her caregiver. Basically, communication is the process of transferring information and involves the transmission and reception of messages (thoughts, ideas, desires and feelings) from one person to another [21]. Communicative capacities are important in the development and maintenance of social relations. However, people with intellectual disabilities frequently have communication difficulties. Then, we aim to develop an Augmentative and Alternative Communication (AAC), where the user can collaborate with their caregivers using communication artifacts adapted on the user's smartphone screen.

2.3 Solution Search Process

The development of the research was divided into two design cycles. The first cycle is entitled "Knowing the User" and the second cycle is called "Collaboration Features". Both cycles are detailed as following.

Design Cycle 1: Knowing the User. The first step in building the communication artifacts was to know the users who would communicate and collaborate.

People with intellectual disabilities who have difficulties to communicate will use the system and artifacts to provide communication. Understanding their limitations is important in order to design artifacts tailored to their needs.

The User Centered Design (UCD) approach was used in this design cycle to identify the users and their needs. The first technique applied was "Open Interview". The open interview obtains greater detail of a given subject, according to the interviewer's view. It is also used in the description of individual cases, in the understanding of certain groups and for the comparability of various cases [13].

- **Understanding needs:** The open interview was conducted by the system's development team and was attended by a health professional of an institution for people with intellectual disabilities. This professional is an occupational therapist, who carries out therapeutic work with the patients in order to promote socialization and increase their autonomy in their daily life. Such work often requires the involvement of family members in order to guide them about how to care or keep the follow-up of the therapeutic activity outside the institution. Therefore, the interview was applied to a person who can visualize the use of the system by the interested parties, as well as to verify the gain of autonomy and safety.

  The interview aligned expectations regarding the purposes of the system with the development team. This step identified the macro-scope of the system, the functionalities contained in the systems and the intensity of use. Table 1 describes the main features of the system.

  Table 1 shows the system modules and their main features. The monitoring module allows sending the location of the monitored user, and the graphic monitoring with the use of maps. The collaboration module allows exchange texts, send images and voice messages between user and caregivers, besides making emergency telephone calls.
- **User Identification:** Based on the macro-scope definition and system functionalities, one can identify two major classes of users in the system: monitor users and monitored users. The monitor users are parents, friends, relatives or medical team responsible for caring the person with intellectual deficiency.

Table 1. Macro-scope of system features

Functionality	Description	Module
Maps	Graphical identification of the position of the monitored person	Monitoring
Location	Geographical position submission	Monitoring
Chat	Collaborative environment for exchanging voice, text messages and images	Collaboration
Voice messaging	Caregivers send questions by voice messages and users answer by images	Collaboration
Telephone call	Emergency call	Collaboration

Monitored users are patients with intellectual disabilities. The system aims to provide collaboration mechanisms where users can interact. Monitor users may interact with other monitors, but the focus of the research, reported in this paper, is to enable the inclusion of monitored users (with intellectual disabilities) in the collaboration process.

The activities of sending text and voice messages are allowed only to monitor users. The monitors are people without disabilities, who read, write and use mobile devices. Sharing location and status are activities of monitored users. Sending the location is performed automatically by the device and status information through images representing feelings.

– **Usage scenario identification:** According to Luckasson and others [5], intellectual disability has been identified as an individual condition, inherent, restricted to the person. Historically, intelligence quotient (IQ) was used to classify and measure the degree of severity of intellectual disability in people. The American Association of Mental Deficiency (AAMD), for example, has used the concept of IQ to identify intellectual disability for many years. However, intelligence tests are criticized when used for classification or diagnosis of intellectual disability. According to Belo et al. [2] IQ tests are questionable because they disregard the social concepts, verbal or academic abilities of individuals. Since 1933 the American Association on Mental Retardation (AAMR) has been leading the field of study on intellectual disability, defining concepts, classifications and theoretical models. The most current model proposed by AAMR is called "2002 System". It consists of a multidimensional, functional and bioecological conception of mental deficiency [5]. There are other models such as DSM-IV and ICD-10. The DSM-IV was published by the American Psychiatric Association in 1994. It is considered a manual for diagnosis and statistics of mental disorders. The ICD-10 is the international classification of diseases, which presents the characteristics of classification of intellectual disability.

Personas technique [17] was used to identify the characteristics, limitations and capacities of the system users. Personas is a technique for collecting user data in order to provide designers with a clear view of the user profiles that would be dealing with the developed product and the context of use.

The activities of each person according to this research are:

– Fabiana is a 40-year-old woman with intellectual disability and attends the institution for therapeutic activities such as supervised theater, painting and walking, as well as psychological medical follow-up. In the institution, her treatment focuses on increasing her autonomy. Fabiana is not literate and has no ability to understand numbers and therefore does not make phone calls. She identifies and knows the colors, communicates verbally with difficulties and presents cognitive capacity for identification of images. Currently, Fabiana does not use smartphones to communicate. She can talk on the phone but cannot dial because she does not recognize the numbers. Her main caregivers are her mother, her sisters and the professionals who attend her in the institution.

- Maria is a health professional. She is an occupational therapist that works with the intellectual disabled persons. She knows the difficulties, limitations and opportunities of each one of her patients. She maintains direct contact with the patients caregivers. Carrying out activities involving caregivers, believing that those responsible are key to the development of patients' autonomy.
- Ana is Fabiana's mother. Ana has no intellectual disability. She is literate and uses mobile devices to communicate and for leisure. Ana accompanies Fabiana in her daily displacements. She is concerned about the safety and well-being of her daughter.

With the identification of users and the definition of their limitations and needs, it was possible to identify the collaboration among them and the system. The Collaborative 3C Model (Communication, Coordination and Cooperation) [6] can be used to classify collaborative systems [14].

According to Preece [16], prototype is a limited representation of a design that allows users to interact with it and exploit its conveniences. Preece also mention that low fidelity prototyping suggests a product still in development, allowing and encouraging suggestions for improvements or adaptations to the use when presented to users. In order to visualize the system, prototypes of the main screens of the system were created.

Figure 1 shows the system prototypes. Figure 1(a) presents the route configuration screen, where the caregiver user defines the route that will be traversed by monitored user. This is the definition of the safety area route. Figure 1(b) represents the chat screen in the view of caregivers. This screen shows the text-to-text conversation between users, automatic system messages, sending voice messages to the monitor, and monitored user interactions, such as responses (by icons) to inquiries, status of the route. Figure 1(c) illustrates how the monitored user communicates. With the difficulty of speaking and writing, Fabiana can communicate by sending information of his feelings, using the symbols on the screen. Figure 1(d) shows the prototype of the warning communication screen informing that the monitored user is out of the safety area route predefined by the caregiver user.

Design Cycle 2: Collaboration Features. The second development cycle is based on Participatory Design (PD) approaches to define the images in the screens of users with intellectual disability. The purpose of this cycle is to identify and evaluate the use of the most representative images for these users. The prototype of the screen where the person with intellectual disability can communicate is shown in Fig. 1(c). This screen allows user interaction with three system features: (1) Emergency telephone connection; (2) Answer the voice message; (3) Displacement status submission. After analyzing the characteristics of users with intellectual disabilities and taking into account the inability to read, we chose to use images to represent the functionalities of the communication screen.

One of the PD techniques that includes the end user in the process of designing and evaluating systems is the "Cooperative Workshops for Requirements

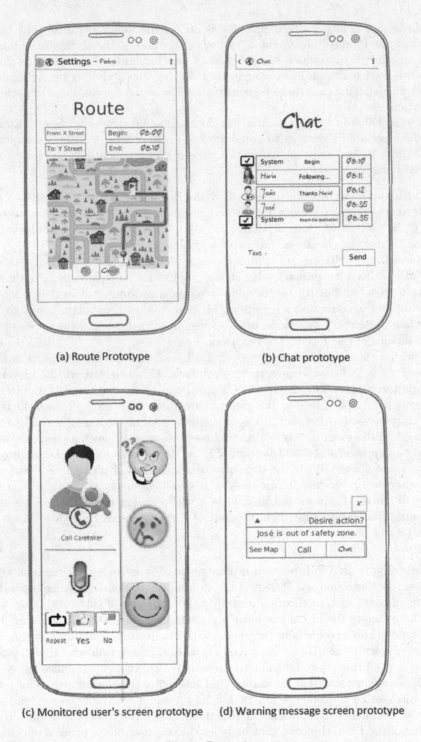

(a) Route Prototype   (b) Chat prototype

(c) Monitored user's screen prototype   (d) Warning message screen prototype

Fig. 1. Prototypes

Definition", which according to Macaulay [12] is a technique that aims to support communication among people in a diversity of backgrounds and difference of understanding.

Communication attributes were defined for the communication screen of the user with intellectual disability, however it was necessary to eliminate the subjectivities around the understanding of the screens and usability by these users. This section uses the seven steps defined in the Cooperative Workshops for Requirements Definition technique to describe the activities carried out, with the participation of all interested parties, in the validation of the functionalities and definition of the screen images.

The Cooperative Workshops for Requirements Definition, as a practice of PD approach, is composed of seven steps being three with direct participation of users [12]. The steps are: (1) Identify the stakeholders; (2) Identify the business problem that needs to be addressed; (3) Formulating the team; (4) Definition of the scope of Workshops; (5) Validation of the user environment; (6) Validation of Workshop; and (7) Validation of scope with stakeholders. The following is described as each of these steps was contemplated in the present work.

1. Stakeholders
   According to Macaulay [12], stakeholders are those responsible for the development of the artifact, people with financial interest, responsible for keeping the system functioning and others interested in using it. Basically, for the context of the research described in this work, two types of users were identified as "Monitors" and "Monitored". Monitors are responsible for monitoring the intellectual disabled during their displacements. They can be caregivers (legal guardians, family, close friends) or the team of professionals who perform work as occupational therapists, psychologists, teachers. More than one monitor can use the system simultaneously for monitoring. Monitored are the end users. They are the patients with intellectual disabilities that use Collab-Track to communicate with the monitors users during their displacements.

2. Problem identification
   According to Tomasello [21], communication is the process of transferring information and involves the transmission of messages (thoughts, ideas, desires and feelings) from one person to another. Communication skills are important in the development and maintenance of social relationships. People with intellectual disabilities often have communication difficulties. Therefore, in order to develop a collaborative system that enables collaboration (communication, coordination and cooperation) where there are users with communication difficulties, it is necessary to know the users and their limitations, as well as to provide technological mechanisms (understandable software attributes) in order to the communication be established.

3. Team
   According to Helander [11], the work carried out in the execution of the practice called Cooperative Workshops involves a series of workshops, with users and stakeholders, to define and evaluate the system requirements.

The Workshop was held with the participation of stakeholders' representatives. The development and research team was responsible for preparing, guiding and monitoring the execution of the activities. The monitored representative was a forty-year-old woman with slight intellectual disability and no written ability. This one had the function of executing the activities by the use of the system. The monitors were represented by the mother of the monitored user and an occupational therapist that is part of the treatment team. They participated in the elaboration of the activities, observation and in tool use training.

4. Scope definition

The Workshop aimed to validate the functionalities presented in the screen prototype and to assist the development team in choosing representative images for end users. Two activities were defined for the workshop: Evaluate the response capacity of the monitored to question by audio message and identify the most representative images for normality, apprehension (worry, fear) and danger (risk, need for help).

5. Workshop

According to Gittins [8], icons are graphical representations of data or processes within a computer system, which are used to support a dialogue between computer and the end user. The use of emoticons has been found in the literature since the late 1980s, as Asteroff [1] which has defined it as "relational icons". For the context of the present work the "drawing" is understood as a software object whose processing generates an image that is presented to the user and which user can interact with [4].

Therefore, emoticons, icons or drawings can represent a user's feeling and the purpose of this Workshop was identify the images that best represent feelings of danger, apprehension or normality of the user with intellectual disability. Four images were presented for each type of image (emoticons, icons and drawings). These images were first presented printed on paper and later, in the same sequence, presented on the screen of a smartphone.

The activity was based on the recording of the choices of the images by the user with intellectual disability when presented contextualized. The contexts were: In a situation of normality, in a situation where the user is in apprehension and in a dangerous situation. For each of the contexts were presented sixteen images divided into emoticons, icons and drawings.

The images were printed and also presented on the smartphone screen with the same layout and sequence. The images were grouped by type (emoticons, icons and drawings). For this activity, the user should choose only one of the four images that best represented the previously presented context. Each image was identified with a number and the choices on both paper and mobile device were recorded and can be seen in the Table 2.

Table 2 shows the result of the images choose by the user. The "Situation" column describes which situation the image should represent. The "Image Type" column identifies the type of the rendered image. The "Chosen on smartphone" column shows the number of image chosen by the user through the smartphone screen. The "Chosen on paper" column represents the number of the image chosen by the printed presentation of the image. Finally, the "Equality" column has an "X" when the same image has been chosen to represent the same context, both in smartphone and in the print version. This activity sought to identify which images are more representative for the user in a given context.

6. Validation of workshop

Both the activity of verifying the responsiveness of the monitored and the activity of identifying the representative images were evaluated by two systems evaluation techniques, "User Observation" and "Usage Record". According to Prates and Barbosa [15], observing the user's utilization of the system allows the evaluator to have a view not only of the problems being experienced by the users but also the positive aspects of the use. Prates and Barbosa also mention that collecting information about how users use the system can be done by records. This can be done by logs, which stores in a file the actions performed on a system, by recording the user's interaction with the system, or even by video recording of the user experience.

This activity seeks to identify which images are most representative for the user in a given context. Table 2 shows the choices of the images by the user. Where the "Equality" column indicates whether the user chose the same image in printed and smartshone version. During execution of the activity using the smartphone, the system recorded the choices. During the activity that presented the printed images, the chosen images were manually recorded. The activity was recorded on video and could be analyzed later. The forms of images presentation can be visualized in the Fig. 2, which is a photograph that registered the material used for this activity.

7. Validation of scope and presentation of results

Based on activity records, performed both by the system and manually, one can identify which images are most representative for the end user, as well as the types of images. The video recording of the activities and their subsequent analysis did not identify doubts or errors in the choice of the images made by the smartphone screen. There were no indications that the user would have clicked on an image by mistake.

For each round of execution of the activity, in total, thirty-six images were presented, and the user chose nine images. Then, for each type of image and context the user chose an image among four. Analyzing the same choices in different environments, the user chose six times the same images on paper or via the system. That is, in 66.66% of the time the user chose the same image on the screen and in the printed version.

Analyzing the intersections between the set of images chosen via smartphone and the set of images chosen through the printed version, we can identify that:

1. Only the image representing apprehension in drawing type was chosen using smartphone and also when presented in paper version.

Table 2. Result of user choice of images

Situation	Image type	Chosen on smartphone	Chosen on paper	Equality
Normality	Drawing	4	3	
Apprehension	Drawing	4	4	X
Danger	Drawing	4	3	
Normality	Emoticon	1	1	X
Apprehension	Emoticon	4	4	X
Danger	Emoticon	3	1	
Normality	Icon	2	2	X
Apprehension	Icon	2	2	X
Danger	Icon	2	2	X

Fig. 2. Photographic record of material used for activity

2. The same emoticons in the context of normality and apprehension were chosen via smartphone and in paper version.
3. The icons had the same choices via smartphone and in paper version.

Therefore, it is concluded that, for this end user, the graphic representations are better identified by the icons, because in 100% of the cases, the situations represented by the icons were chosen in both environments.

2.4 Search Rigor

According to Thomas and Hatchuel [20], for a research to be reliable, it must be concerned not only with the relevance but also with the rigor that must be present from its conduction to the presentation of its results. In order to present the rigor in the research, the evaluation methods will be described for the two solution search cycles in Sect. 2.5.

The first cycle of search of the solution of this research resulted in the construction of prototypes of the communication screens of the system based on the concepts of the UCD approach. The validation of the artifact generated in this cycle was an analytical evaluation method called "Expert Opinion Collection". According to Prates and Barbosa [15], analytical evaluation methods are those in which evaluators inspect or examine aspects of a user interface related to usability. Still in the first cycle, two evaluation techniques were used, "User Observation" and "Usage Record".

The second search cycle considered the users participation in the evaluation, but based on the system usage and its functionalities and no longer based on prototyping. The activity of verifying respondent's responsiveness to voice messages, identifying representative images and the usability of the telephone activity were evaluated by observation and recording. Observation of user system usage allows the evaluator to have a view not only of the problems being experienced by the users, but also the positive aspects of the use [15].

2.5   Search Evaluation

The artifacts resulting from the design cycles were the prototypes of the system screens. The evaluation consisted of evaluating the use of the "Monitored" screens by people with intellectual disabilities. Firstly, the technique called "Expert Opinion Collection" was used by specialists to inspect the prototypes in order to analyze the use of the software by users with intellectual disabilities, based on the knowledge and experience of these specialists.

According to Prates and Barbosa [15], in the use of this technique the experts examine the interface and identify possible difficulties that users may have when using the software. In this context, it was used the opinion of an occupational therapy professional with a wide knowledge of the end users and their limitations. This professional evaluated the prototype screen and expressed her opinion about usability based on the known characteristics of the intellectual deficient. The main data collected in the expert's evaluation were:

- The screen should be simple, with few features;
- Give preference to images and not to texts;
- It is required an evaluation with end users to ensure understanding of the meaning of the images and usability.

The need for validation of screen functionalities with the end user identified in the Expert Opinion Collection motivated the second evaluation of the prototype. Therefore, the communication attributes defined for the communication screen of the user with intellectual disability were evaluated with the objective of eliminating the subjectivities around the understanding of the screens and usability by that user. User observation and logs were techniques used to carry out this evaluation.

The use of the evaluation techniques sought to identify the capacity of understanding of the screens by the users with intellectual disability, as well as the capacity of interaction with the system. In this stage, the user's ability to respond, in a computational environment, to questions provided by audio messages was evaluated in a controlled environment. Ten questions were predefined recorded in audio file and made available to the user. For each question the answer possibilities were "yes" or "no". In a non-computational environment, the user would be able to answer each of the questions easily because the questions were based on the user's personal and day-to-day information. The construction of the questions had participation of two representatives of the monitors user, the mother and an occupational therapist. This participation was used to elaborate and validate the questions. The execution of the question rounds happened after a contextualization of the activity and a quick training with the monitored user. After a training run, three executions of each of the ten questions were performed. For registration, the end-user's use of the software was filmed and a log with all responses was recorded.

The interface of the mobile device used in this activity is shown in Fig. 3.

Three buttons are displayed on the screen. The first button allows to repeat the voice message, the second to answer "no" and the third to answer "yes". A previous training and an execution of the questions were carried out as a form of training, where the user was able to question and to clear his doubts during the use. This execution was discarded from the results.

Fig. 3. Response capability screen

The analyzes were performed based on the logs of the responses and in the subsequent analysis of the video recording of the activity. These analyzes allowed some conclusions about the interface, the functionalities and the usability of the system by the user.

The majority of responses (27 of 30) were answered correctly. Analyzing the video and the context where the user answered in the wrong way, one can identify that verbally he hit the answer, but chose the wrong icon to answer.

Some common characteristics among the wrong answers have been identified. By evaluating the graphs of the Figs. 4 and 5 one can identify that: (1) Related to the three wrong answers, two were the first question and one was the second question; (2) The user missed the first question in two runs; (3) It can also be verified that the second question was answered incorrectly in the second execution of the test, moments after the user also missed the first question.

The error hypothesis for the complexity of the question was discarded because the user answered correctly orally before choosing the wrong icon of the answer. Then there is the assumption that at the beginning of the usage the user is not totally comfortable with the use of the system yet, and tends to miss the first questions even knowing the answer. Another conclusion that can be reached is that in the third execution, the user hit all the answers, which indicates a evolution of learning of use of the system by the user.

It can also be considered that the screen components are meeting the usability needs of the end user, since the average score was 90%. The final execution with 100% accuracy reinforces this indicator.

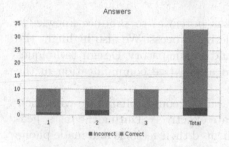

Fig. 4. Total errors and correct answers during the three executions

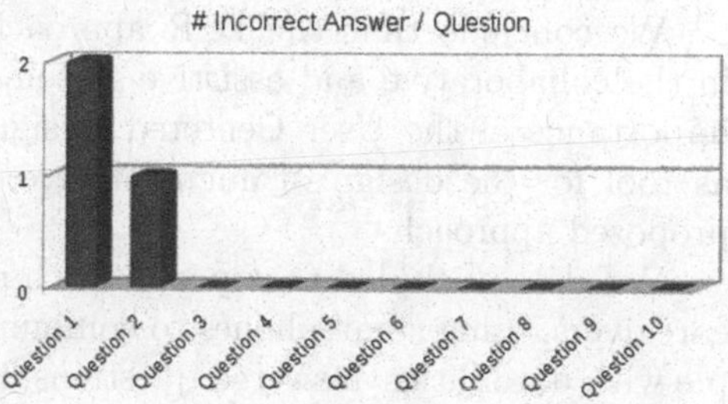

Fig. 5. Total errors and correct answers per questions

2.6   Search Contributions

In the present research, regarding "Design Science" functionalities and screens were generated for communication by smartphones, adapted to the use of people with intellectual disabilities. Usability assessments demonstrate the quality of the adaptations that have resulted in a screen where a user with intellectual disability can participate collaboratively in her monitoring and personal care.

Related to "Behavioral Science", the research contributed to a greater understanding of the limits and possibilities of people with intellectual disabilities in the use of computer systems to communicate. In addition to strengthening the use of HCI approach in the development of collaborative and assistive systems.

There are several types of intellectual disability, just as there are a lot of factors that aggravate this deficiency in people. The involvement of a small population of users with intellectual disabilities can be highlighted as one of the limitations of this research.

3   Conclusion and Future Work

This paper presents an approach to support the design of communication in a collaborative system for monitoring people with intellectual disabilities, producing artifacts that allow the communication of people with intellectual disabilities with their caregivers. This approach intends to provide confidence to the caregivers and increase the autonomy of people with intellectual disabilities in their daily displacements. The approach uses Design Science Research (DSR) methodology and is divided into two cycles of discovery of knowledge.

In the first cycle a prototype of low fidelity was generated as artifact of the "design science". The "behavioral science" of the first cycle is defined by the users' knowledge needs, which are users with reduced cognitive abilities. The first cycle was characterized by the use of the User-Centered Design approach.

The second cycle has the objective of validation and adjustments in the prototype obtained in the first cycle. The artifacts of the second cycle are the communication screen components used by users with intellectual disabilities, as well as defined with the support of these users and based on the Participatory Design approaches.

We conclude that the DSR approach has potential to produce knowledge in the collaborative and assistive systems design process. We also highlight the importance of the User Centered Design and Participatory Design techniques as tool for the design of augmentative and alternative communication in the proposed approach.

We also concluded that people with disabilities could collaborate with their caregivers, using smartphones to communicate effectively. During the tests, people with disabilities answered questions, indicated their feelings and made phone calls using Collabtrack.

As future work, we intend to deal with the gaps identified in the communication interface of the tool. We also plan to study the usability of Collabtrack by the monitors users, as well as running experiments with a more extended group of users and focus on more complex scenarios of communication and coordination.

Acknowledgments. We would like to thank the *Núcleo de Assistência Integral ao Paciente Especial* (NAIPE), in special Luciana Hang Correia, Tatiane Dominoni Rodrigues and Juliane Cristine Koerber Reis, for all your support.

References

1. Asteroff, J.F.: Paralanguage in electronic mail: a case study. Ph.D. thesis, Columbia University New York (1987)
2. Belo, C., Caridade, H., Cabral, L., Sousa, R.: Deficiência intelectual: terminologia e conceptualização. Revista Diversidades **22**, 4–9 (2008)
3. Alan, H.R.: A three cycle view of design science research. Scand. J. Inf. Syst. **19**(2), 4 (2007)
4. Cybis, W., Holtz, A., Faust, R.: Novatec, Ergonomia e usabilidade. São Paulo (2010)
5. Luckasson, R., et al.: Mental retardation: definition, classification, and systems of supports. American Association on Mental Retardation (2002)
6. Clarence, A.E., Simon, J.G., Rein, G.: Groupware: some issues and experiences. Commun. ACM **34**(1), 39–58 (1991)

7. Fuks, H.: Sistemas Colaborativos. Elsevier, São Paulo (2011)
8. Gittins, D.: Icon-based human-computer interaction. Int. J. Man-Mach. Stud. **24**(6), 519–543 (1986)
9. Glat, R.: Uma família presente e participativa: o papel da família no desenvolvimento e inclusão social da pessoa com necessidades especiais. In: Anais do 9° Congresso Estadual das APAEs de Minas Gerais, pp. 1–7 (2004)
10. Grudin, J.: Computer-supported cooperative work: history and focus. Computer **5**, 19–26 (1994)
11. Helander, M.G.: Handbook of Human-Computer Interaction. Elsevier, Amsterdam (2014)
12. Macaulay, L.: Cooperation in understanding user needs and requirements. Comput. Integr. Manuf. Syst. **8**(2), 155–165 (1995)
13. de Souza Minayo, M.C.: Challenge of the Knowledge: Researches Qualitative in Health, pp. 1–10. Hucitec-Abrasco, São Paulo/Rio de Janeiro (1993)
14. Pimentel, M., Gerosa, M.A., Filippo, D., Raposo, A., Fuks, H., Lucena, C.J.P.: Modelo 3c de colaboração para o desenvolvimento de sistemas colaborativos. Anais do III Simpósio Brasileiro de Sistemas Colaborativos, pp. 58–67 (2006)
15. Prates, R.O., de Souza, C.S., Barbosa, S.D.J.: Methods and tools: a method for evaluating the communicability of user interfaces. ACM Interact. J. **7**(1), 31–38 (2000)
16. Preece, J., Sharp, H., Rogers, Y.: Interaction Design: Beyond Human Computer Interaction. Wiley, New York (2002)
17. Pruitt, J., Adlin, T.: The Persona Lifecycle: Keeping People in Mind Throughout Product Design. Morgan Kaufmann, San Francisco (2010)
18. Rosa, F.D., Denari, F.E.: Trabalho, educação e família: perspectivas para a pessoa com deficiência intelectual. Revista Educação Especial **26**(45), 73–90 (2012)
19. Schalock, R.L., Borthwick-Duffy, A.: Intellectual disability: definition, classification, and systems of supports. In: ERIC 2012
20. Thomas, H., Hatchuel, A.: A foundationalist perspective for management research: a European trend and experience. Manage. Decis. **47**(9), 1458–1475 (2009)
21. Tomasello, M.: Origins of Human Communication. MIT press, Cambridge (2010)
22. Ugulino, W., Nunes, R.R., Oliveira, C.L., Pimentel, M., Santoro, F.M.: Dos processos de colaboração para as ferramentas: A abordagem de desenvolvimento do projeto communicatec. In: Companion Proceedings of the XIV Brazilian Symposium on Multimedia and the Web, WebMedia 2008, pp. 233–240. ACM, New York (2008)

Case Studies of Industry-Academia Research Collaborations for Software Development with Agile

Isabelle Guillot[1(✉)], Geetha Paulmani[2], Vivekanandan Kumar[1], and Shawn N. Fraser[1]

[1] Athabasca University, Athabasca, Canada
{iguillot,vivek,shawnf}@athabascau.ca
[2] University of Eastern Finland, Joensuu, Finland
paulmani.geetha@gmail.com

Abstract. Successful industry-academia research collaborations (IARCs) in the software development area can be challenging. The literature identifies best practices in IARCs along with process frameworks with the aim of ensuring successful outcomes for both industry and academia, namely: funding opportunities for universities, training and employment possibilities for students, new knowledge leading to innovative products for industry, and on-time delivery of software benefiting the economy, the institution, and the community. This paper shows ways in which core principles of the project management approach, Agile, and the Scrum framework have been applied and have led to the success of three IARCs. In addition to IARCs' common challenges, these case studies represented additional challenges as they were short-term software development projects accomplished by small geographically distributed teams. A report of the demographic, collaboration setting, and challenges, along with the lessons learned from the application of Agile and Scrum in these case studies will contribute to the body of knowledge in the field of IARCs. Using a qualitative and quantitative approach, five Agile/Scrum aspects for each project are assessed: product ownership, release, sprint, team, and technical health. Findings indicate several success factors directly linked to the application of the Agile principles and the Scrum framework. Specifically, early and frequent customer-centric software delivery, constant communications, responsiveness to change, and highly motivated individuals were key in terms of realizing the positive outcomes in spite of the obstacles inherent to IARCs. Cautions to this approach when applied in IARCs are reported along with solutions.

Keywords: Agile · Scrum · Research collaboration · Distributed research team

1 Introduction

The importance and value of industry and academia research collaborations (IARCs) have been well documented along with several benefits, challenges and pitfalls, as well as best practice recommendations [1–5]. Numerous process frameworks have also been proposed and tested [6–8], including the Agile/Scrum approach [6, 9].

A recent systematic literature review on IARCs in the domain of software engineering highlighted the need for more IARCs [2]. Yet major challenges can threaten the

© Springer International Publishing AG 2017
C. Gutwin et al. (Eds.): CRIWG 2017, LNCS 10391, pp. 196–212, 2017.
DOI: 10.1007/978-3-319-63874-4_15

success of IARCs. The most important challenge is the completely different mindset between industry and academia when it comes to anticipated research outcomes: industry looks for new products and sales, while academia targets new knowledge and fundraising [6]. However, these differing economic pressures on industry and academia can be conducive to the success of these collaborations, given that industry is keen to stay on top of the fast-changing technologies to remain competitive, while universities crave research funding [1]. Other common challenges are: (1) planning: industry wants clear goals with successful and useful industry-strength product within a short delay, while academia is more oriented towards addressing challenging research problems irrespective of the time required and of the result; (2) lack of resources or availability on both sides; (3) lack of interest and commitment; (4) communication, in terms of use and understanding of same terminology; (5) appropriate project management, development, and collaboration environments; and (6) intellectual property concerns [2, 10]. To address those challenges, the literature indicates several recommendations, including: (1) create good channels of communication; (2) demonstrate success early; (3) focus on an implementable outcome addressing a real-world problem in the funder's industry; (4) ensure the delivered product is sustainable, customizable, evolvable, simple, useful, and credible, with an elegant user interface design; (5) have a strong 'ambassador' or 'champion' within the industry believing in the project; and (6) manage the project in an Agile manner (iteration, flexibility, short-term objectives) [2].

Although the Agile principles and Scrum framework are mentioned in various degrees and under different angles in several IARCs' experience reports, it seems that none focused solely on reporting the applicability along with its benefits and cautions of Agile and Scrum, specifically in short-term IARCs (6 to 12 months) in software development [2, 6, 9, 10]. In fact, most reported IARCs are long-term collaborations [3, 5, 6, 8]. This paper intends to show through three case studies a practical linkage between the application of Agile and Scrum during the software development phase, and the key factors leading to the success. (RQ1: Are Agile principles and the Scrum framework applicable in short-term IARCs for software development, and how can they benefit and nurture the success of such collaborations?). Important observations on potential hurdles when applying Agile and Scrum in the context of such collaborations are also reported (RQ2: What challenges can be expected in applying Agile principles and the Scrum framework in IARCs and how can they be addressed?). These three case studies are short-term IARCs conducted by small distributed teams with varying computing skills, to study the software prototypes in completely novel area within the Learning Analytics domain, and were sponsored through research funding. By sharing these experiences, the authors hope to encourage academia research teams to apply the Agile principles and the Scrum framework in IARCs, specifically when software development is involved, while being aware of the subtleties entangled in the application of these principles and framework, such as the impact of the multiple-role phenomena for the product owner in the context of those collaborations.

2   Agile and Scrum

The Agile/Scrum approach is largely used in the software development area for nearly two decades, and have gained popularity in several other fields [11].

2.1   Agile Principles

The birth of the Agile Alliance occurred in 2001 in Utah when seventeen people, closely related to various approaches to software development, met in an informal way. Their goal was to put together principles that would help developers and organizations be free to act in the best interest of the customer with timely promised delivery, rather than to be constrained with unnecessary limitations and policies, known as bureaucracy. From their discussion, the Agile Manifesto emerged, which includes twelve principles including, satisfying "the customer through early and continuous delivery of valuable working software;" welcoming changes for "the customer's competitive advantage;" daily collaborative work between motivated business people and developers; face-to-face meetings between developers; measuring progress based on working software; sustainable development with regular pace; attention to technical excellence and good design; developing only what is necessary; self-organized teams produce the "best architectures, requirements, and designs;" and reflecting regularly for better effectiveness [12].

2.2   Scrum Framework

The Scrum framework creates an environment where the Agile principles can be integrated more naturally in the development process of a software. It includes specific artifacts, roles and responsibilities, as well as ceremonies (meetings) [13]. Figure 1 depicts the framework including the artifacts, roles, and ceremonies detailed in this section.

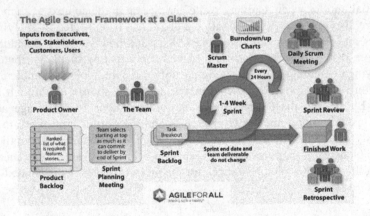

Fig. 1.   Scrum framework [14]

Scrum Artifacts. (1) Product Backlog (PB): List of all requirements (called stories) for the product. (2) Sprint Backlog: Set of stories from the PB selected to be accomplished in a Sprint and detailed in tasks, subtasks, and estimated size. Each developer pulls the stories they commit to accomplish. (3) Product Increment: Working software produced in each sprint as the sum of PBs completed in the current and previous sprints.

Scrum Roles and Responsibilities. (1) Stakeholders: Key provider of requirements and subject matter expertise. Recipient of project deliverables and associated benefits. (2) Product Owner (PO): Provide product direction and priority. Resolve product issues. Make final decisions and resolve conflicts or issues regarding product expectations across organizational and functional areas. Communicate directly with stakeholders or customers to obtain regular feedback on their priorities. (3) Scrum Master (SM): Coach the development team for highest performance, which involves removing impediments to progress, facilitating meetings, deciding on the process, ensuring the team abides by Agile/Scrum values and principles, and communicating closely with the PO to share issues, prioritize the PB, clarify PB items, and more. (4) Development Team (DT): Self-organize with the assistance of the SM. Analyze, design, develop, and test to deliver the highest value product. (5) Steering committee (this is not a typical Scrum role, but helpful): Monitor project progress and provide support to resolve the impediments blocking the important milestones that are beyond the PO's jurisdiction.

Scrum Ceremonies (Meetings). (1) Sprint planning: Finalize the stories to be accomplished for a product increment demonstrable after a two-week sprint. Commit to a set of tasks for the sprint. Frequency: First day of the sprint. Attendees: POs, SM, and DT. (2) Standup – also known as Daily Scrum: Share with other developers what has been done the previous day(s), what is planned to be accomplished the next day(s), and if there are any impediments to progress in the planned tasks or if any help is needed from other(s). Frequency: Every day. Attendees: POs, SM, and DT. (3) Sprint review: Inspect and adapt product. Show product increment as per the sprint goals established. Receive feedback from stakeholders. Allow product acceptance from the PO. Frequency: Last day of the sprint. Attendees: Stakeholders, POs, SM, and DT. (4) Retrospective: Inspect and adapt process. Team assessment of what went well, what needs improvement, and what actions need to be taken to improve the highlighted weaknesses. Frequency: Last day of the sprint. Attendees: POs, SM, and DT. (5) Backlog refinement: Refine, estimate, clarify the stories to be accomplished for the next sprint. Frequency: Middle of the sprint. Attendees: POs, SM, and DT. (6) Steering meetings: Obtain status update from POs and SM including issues and red flags. Discuss decisional items. Frequency: Once a sprint. Attendees: Stakeholders, POs, and SM.

3 Research Methodology

3.1 Scope of the Study

For the three cases reported here, the unit of analysis is the research collaboration itself. The following criteria were used to include or exclude the cases in the study: (1) Was there at least one higher education institution (HEI) and one industry partner involved in the collaboration? (2) Are the collaborators from at least two different legal entities? Joint research by more than one discipline from the same HEI is not considered as part of this study. (3) Is there some element of research as the intent of collaboration? Collaborations for other purposes than research are not included. (4) Is the collaboration in the field of "Computing"? (5) Are there at least three members from each of the participating organizations? (6) Are the research collaborations from 2015 to 2017? The setting of this study is purely observational with an intent to share learnings and not to prove causality.

3.2 Data Sources, Analysis, and Interpretation

This study gathered and organized the available quantitative and qualitative data for each project such as: demographic and collaboration setting; sprint data tracked in the JIRA backlog management tool (backlog items, their size in story points, progress, completed story points, and more), sprint goals, retrospective comments (anonymized), and observations of the main PO and SMs (in their private One Note). From the JIRA data, derived results are reported and analyzed for each project: the release burnup chart (ideal cumulative progress of work in story points towards project completion vs. reality), and the team's velocity (work completed in one sprint in terms of story points).

There are several models for assessing Agile adaption in teams, such as Sidky Agile Measurement Index [15], Agile Maturity Model [16], and Scaled Agile Framework (SAFe) Team Self-Assessment Grid [17]. Since a) this study is not about organizational level Agile maturity, and b) SAFe assessment tool assesses the Agile adaption, level of team collaboration, and predictable team outcomes, with ability to capture related challenges, and c) is easy to use by novice Agile practitioners, this tool was used in all three studies. There are five questions under each of the five aspects, namely (1) product ownership, (2) release, (3) sprint, (4) team, and (5) technical facets which are rated on a scale of 1 to 5 (0 - Never, 1 - Rarely 2 - Occasionally, 3 - Often, 4 - Very Often, 5 - Always). The tool produces a radar chart with the five aspects being axes. The team and the SM used all the data sources listed above as inputs during the self-assessment. Typical limitations of self-assessment have a tendency to manifest; however, since the usage of the tool is to understand the Agile applicability and related challenges and not to measure the accurate process adherence, impact of bias introduced by self-assessment is limited.

In addition, qualitative data from retrospective comments and SMs' personal notes have also been used to report linkage between Agile/Scrum and key success factors and challenges observed in these projects in the context of IARCs.

3.3 Ethical Considerations

Most authors were involved in at least one IARC in some capacity – either as an SM or as a PO. Though they had a strong stake in the project and wanted to make the collaboration effective to achieve the outcomes, they were not accountable for Agile adaption.

All the research participants were aware of, and had always access to, all the collected data. Exception is the SMs' notes, which were intentionally not shared to prevent any influence on their behavior. Team Retrospective comments were kept anonymous, in line with the principles of Agile. However, based on comments, those who were involved in the project may, in some cases, be able to trace back to the individual. None of the data was used for performance appraisals; they were strictly at the team level.

4   Case Study

Each case study involves common and distinctive characteristics that represent a challenge to how Agile intended a project to be conducted. Some challenges across projects were: POs playing multiple conflicting roles, team distributed worldwide resulting in few or no face-to-face meetings, and development of data heavy applications, usually considered non-conducive for Agile. Each project was handled with the Scrum ceremonies (sprint and release planning, backlog refinement, retrospective, review, standup meetings), two-week sprint cycles, and maintenance of: (a) the backlog and stories in JIRA, (b) the code in Git, and (c) the documents in a common document repository.

The three case studies are presented as follows: description of the demographic and collaboration setting of that specific IARC, description of five Agile/Scrum aspects based on the quantitative and qualitative data available for each project (see Fig. 2 for a quick overview of the self-assessment radar chart for each case study, which will be further detailed in this section), and description of observations and challenges in the applicability of the Agile/Scrum approach.

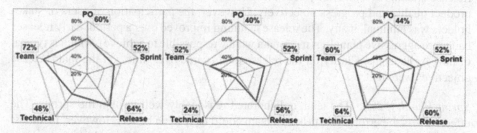

Fig. 2. Self-assessment chart showing health for case studies A, B, and C respectively

4.1   Case Study A

Demographic and Collaboration Setting. A group of computer science students in a Canadian university collaborated in a 6-month research project with a team of professional software developers from a renowned educational company in USA. The female SM aged 40+, located in Asia, thus in a significant different time zone, was an IT professional with 16 years of experience and with strong Agile skills. The PO for the academia DT was a male senior professor and lead researcher aged 50+, while the industry DT had a male senior administrator aged 50+ as PO. The academia team, all speaking fluently in English and beginners with Agile, included two very involved members and a few floating ones; undergraduate and graduate students, and one post-doc fellow; two women and men for the rest of the team aged 20–35. The English native speaking industry team, intermediates with Agile, included three stable members, one with a Master degree and two with PhDs having 2 to 10 years of professional software development experience; and two men and one woman all aged 30–45. Both teams met daily for online standups (same time zone for DTs) and most meetings were via video. There were a few face-to-face meetings during the project. Almost all members from both teams were partially allocated to this work, meaning they also worked in other projects.

Scores on Five Agile/Scrum Self-assessment. The total team score for that project is 59%, considering an average of the five-aspects score (see Fig. 2).

Product Ownership Health (60%). POs were quite good at facilitating story prioritiza-tion and negotiation. Their relationship with the steering committee was good and with users was reasonable. Story creation with acceptance criteria needed improvement. Moreover, not all stories were vertical, small, and independent. POs working with the team in refactoring the backlog improved over the sprints. Rigor to apply acceptance criteria and Definition of Done (DoD) while accepting stories needed improvement. Story acceptance was delayed as both POs were not available at the same time for joint decisions. Scheduled time for story acceptance in POs' calendars helped in getting the stories accepted on time. Overall, lack of availability of the POs affected the effective-ness of the team though the team tried to fill in for the POs on several occasions.

Release Health (64%). The system demos every two weeks helped understanding the product quality and progress objectively. However, the participation of users or stake-holders was minimal, if any. The release planning improved over a period; early releases had more aggressive planning (more than what was possible to achieve), which is typical of new Agile teams. Clarity on the release goals came over time, yet the main release objectives were met.

Sprint Health (52%). The team collaborated reasonably well to plan the sprints. The effectiveness to perform this task as a team could have been better. However, in almost all the sprints, the team over committed consistently in terms of number of stories as well as story points. In early sprints, sprint goals were not clear; this improved over the sprints. As shown in the graphs of Fig. 3 – where the x-axis shows the sprint ID, and the y-axis indicates the story points – the team's velocity was very irregular, and therefore unpredictable (data on stories planned for sprints 5 to 7 were not available, which explains incomplete lines for some graphs). Partial time allocation to work on this project from the industry team, and change in members on the academia side were contributing significantly to the predictability issue.

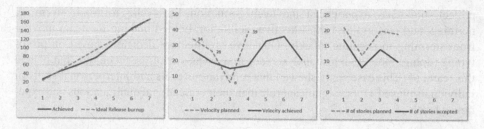

Fig. 3. Case study A: release burnup; story points planned/achieved; stories planned/accepted

Team Health (72%). Effective usage of tools for persistent chat, backlog management, and online meetings helped achieving goals. The daily standups helped collaboration greatly; time spent in standups was higher in the beginning, but improved significantly after the team became more disciplined with preparation for the meeting. The DT was self-organized, open enough to raise impediments and ask for help in the standups; yet, it could be observed that they functioned as two sub-teams often. It is interesting to note that impediment removal was left to the POs and DT, though the SM located in an entirely different time zone was tracking impediments.

Technical Health (48%). Architecture and technology decisions were planned and made at the beginning of the release. Prototyping and solving the architectural or technical problems practically instead of just conversations was a common approach appreciated by the POs and steering committee members. Such an approach helped when developers had strong preference for some technologies, and that the opinions were diverging more than converging. Most often the industry team was making independent decisions on architecture given their experience and knowledge in a greater variety of tools and technical infrastructure. It was also observed, that the academia team leaned towards more modern and user-friendly tools while the industry team had preference for tools known to them and already proven; their concern that novel tools could destabilize the technical architecture and affect the project timelines was observed in several occasions. Clean code practices such as code refactoring and active technical debt reduction were not practiced much; though certain types of testing were part of their DoD, rigorous unit testing or automated test coverage was a weak facet.

Observations and Challenges. (1) The POs had very different, but complementary knowledge and experience background as well as distinct perspectives in terms of outcome. The industry PO was mainly interested in seeing if the prototype will result in a marketable product, whereas the academia PO was looking for research advancement (observe if this prototype would be successful) and competence building of his students. In spite of these sharp differences, a combination of factors allowed both POs function efficiently. Their alignment on product vision, open-mindedness ability to adjust constantly, and regular interactions between them helped to a large extent. (2) It was also observed that the inherent quality to good professors to ask open-ended questions with an intent to understand or help others understand, was helpful in the role of a PO. This approach eased tensions during intense meetings. (3) Even in this short-term project, the team experienced the team formation life-cycle: forming, storming, norming, and performing [18]. Effective facilitation helped making the team moving from storming to norming quickly. Objective architecture decisions based on proto-typing (doing) more than just analysis (debating) was one of the technique that helped this team. (4) This case study showed that motivation levels and interpersonal skills of individuals played a more significant role than their educational qualifications and experience levels.

4.2   Case Study B

Demographic and Collaboration Setting. This project involved two small distributed DTs composed mainly of university students in computer science collaborating for the first time in a 6-month software prototype development intended for teachers' use. The female SM aged around 40, located in Canada, was undertaking that role for the first time without the presence of an Agile coach during the meetings, and was a well-known colleague for the industry DT. The academia team included three graduate students, all men aged 20–35, from a university in China with limited computing skills and without experience in research project development. Only one could communicate in English. They were beginners with Agile. The industry team comprised undergraduate highly skilled students employed by a start-up Canadian company also heavily involved in several other research projects. They were all speaking fluently in English with inter-mediate Agile skills; included two very involved members and two floating ones; all undergraduate students, two men and two women aged 20–35, with 1 to 4 years of experience in research project development. The male industry PO was a director of the start-up company, aged 50+. The PO for the Chinese development team was a female senior professor from their university, aged 45+. A 12-hour time zone separated both DTs; they never met face to face, and they only had one short video encounter due to the poor internet connectivity.

Scores on Five Agile/Scrum Self-assessment. The total team score for that project is 45%, considering an average of the five-aspects score (see Fig. 2).

Product Ownership Health (40%). Communications between POs was minimal due to the language barrier and the difference in computing skills' knowledge. POs' involve-ment with the DT at facilitating story prioritization and negotiation, as well as their relationship with users was also minimal. The academia PO was more involved when the development work assigned to her team was not progressing. The quality of the stories (vertical, small, well-estimated, and independent) was taken care of by the SM and one industry developer. Some comments in the retrospectives demonstrate that the team was struggling with this aspect: "was more than suspected. It will require more time and effort." In aspects to improve, one mentioned: "Better planning of tasks to accomplish and the time required also considering unexpected issues." The industry PO delegated the story acceptance to a developer in his team. Acceptance criteria were not developed for all stories. Backlog refinement was generally done by the DT at the same time than sprint planning without the presence of the POs.

Release Health (56%). The first three sprints focused on architectural and technical considerations, product intent, solution approach, and familiarizing the team in Agile practices; a structured release planning was carried out after that. Periodical demos to the POs were live or through recorded videos to address connectivity issues, which revealed the slow development progress on the academia side. Only two system demos were shown to larger audience of stakeholders. The release objectives were met with increased effort and workload on the industry side.

Sprint Health (52%). The planning of sprints was initiated by the industry team given they were more used with the Agile/Scrum approach. Close to the end of the release, the academia team expressed that the tasks were getting clearer. The application of acceptance criteria and DoD before accepting stories could have been better. Figure 4 shows (x-axis: sprint ID, y-axis: story points) that the team's velocity was very irregular; however, the distance between what was planned and achieved slightly improved as the release progressed. Sprint goals were generally achieved.

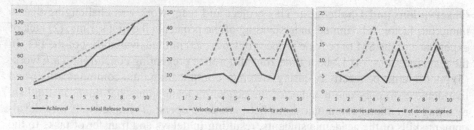

Fig. 4. Case study B: release burnup; story points planned/achieved; stories planned/accepted

Team Health (52%). The collaboration level between the industry and academia teams was poor given the language barrier, the significant programming skills difference, the difficulty to communicate online due to connectivity issues, and the opposite time zones. The limited level of entrepreneurship (wait-to-be-told mentality) and responsibility on the academia side resulting in lack of punctuality to standups and to update JIRA, in lack to take ownership of the success of the project, in attending meetings with a mobile rather than a computer (preventing efficient screen sharing) were additional impediments to an effective collaboration. The academia team slightly improved regarding the Agile process by the end of the Release. In the last sprints of the project, the academia team increased their effort and involvement to achieve their goals, but their skills level did not allow them to attain an industry-level result. The first graph in Fig. 5 displays that the team had to increase significantly their efforts from Sprint 8 to ensure to reach the release goal. Retrospectives were held after almost every sprint, generally by written, compiled by the SM, and shared to the team. The academia team recognized their scope for improvement and were working on them.

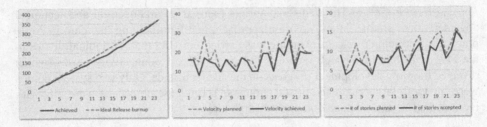

Fig. 5. Case study C: release burnup; story points planned/achieved; stories planned/accepted

Technical Health (24%). Aspects such as reducing the technical debt through clean code practices and automated testing as part of their DoD were not implemented. They resorted to manual testing techniques rather than Agile techniques. This explains this low score. Regarding the overall architecture, the team struggled in the first sprints to understand the product expected. This caused delays in the development process.

Observations and Challenges. This project and team work was challenging due to numerous factors: (1) limited understanding of the project in the first sprints; (2) lack of experience of the SM to provide proper guidance; (3) limited availability of the POs in the team meetings; (4) 12-hour time zone difference preventing concurrent team work; (5) poor internet connectivity during meetings complicating fluid communications and live demos; (6) only one member of the academia team somewhat fluent in English, resulting in minimal communications between developers; (7) limited software development skills of the academia students, resulting in delays and transfer of tasks to the industry team in the middle of the project; (8) adaptation to the Agile/Scrum practices; (9) different work mentality: initiative versus wait-to-be told; (10) server accessibility; (11) different technology preferences between teams; and (12) limited communications between developers due to delays at higher levels to authorize the transfer of tasks.

Though these challenges could have led to failure, the enactment of Agile principles such as frequent demos, motivated individuals, active communication (the SM communicated closely with the industry PO on issues encountered by the DT), and more, allowed the team to deliver the prototype software on time.

4.3 Case Study C

Demographic and Collaboration Setting. This one-year analytics software prototype project was a different IARC than the two previous ones. Several challenges known in the two case studies described above were absent here: (1) same country; (2) same culture; (3) no language barrier except for one developer; (4) one PO (male senior professor and lead researcher aged 50+); (5) almost same time zone (maximum of 3-hour difference between some members). Also, the DT was only on the academia side, while the industry partner, a start-up Canadian company, had the field knowledge (company owners; men aged 35–45). Both groups were beginners with Agile. For most of them, they were working together for the first time. Except for the SM, both teams met face to face several times throughout the project. The female SM aged around 40 was the same than in Case Study B; her second project in that role. The academia DT team included three men aged 30–40 (two for the first six months, and a third one joined for the last six months) with 1 to 3 years of experience in research project development; 2 undergraduates and 1 post-doc.

Scores on Five Agile/Scrum Self-assessment. The total team score for that project is 56%, considering an average of the five-aspects score (see Fig. 2).

Product Ownership Health (44%). The PO had a few extensive and productive meetings with the DT throughout the project, but not on a regular basis. This led developers to express half-way of the project, "hopefully the PO can continue to be more involved with this project in the future so that we can get his insights into the direction we should be taking", and at the end of the project, "I have found it to be somewhat poorly directed." The industry partner (also stakeholders of this project) had great trust in the PO, had several conversations with him during the project, and were reassured when he was present to Review meetings (PO attended two-thirds [16/24] of the Review meetings). Backlog refinement and the development of small, vertical, functional, and well-estimated stories with acceptance criteria were entirely done by the DT.

Release Health (60%). This project included 4 releases of 6 sprints each. Each release's goals had been established in the research proposal, and were slightly adjusted by the DT at each release planning. Developers expressed in their retrospective comments that a better definition of what was included in each release should have been laid out. A thorough backlog, well itemized and prioritized, guided by the PO would have helped. The team presented system demos at the end of each sprint, and the industry partner was highly satisfied as shown by this comment, "I was blown away with how well run all of the sessions were. The length of the meetings was pretty good, and I really liked how all the presentations had a visual component. The amount of work and attention to detail that went into each meeting was truly perfect." Most release goals were achieved to the entire satisfaction of the industry partner.

Sprint Health (52%). The team collaborated well to plan every sprint, with quite clear goals, though the level of engagement in planning was not similar across team members. Acceptance criteria were established by the developers, but not always detailed. The team established criteria within the DoD, which were more rigorously applied as the project progressed. As indicated in Fig. 5 (x-axis: sprint ID, y-axis: story points), the velocity of the team was not stabilized by the end of the project. However, the distance between what was planned and achieved is quite close, which is positive. Despite the novelty of the project and the new technologies the team had to learn 'on-the-fly', they always strived to deliver on their sprint goals. Still, they reflected that they "should have developed several small models one after the other with increasing functionality in each one" as intended for Agile projects. In other words, "more rapid prototyping."

Team Health (60%). The team members were respectful and prompt to help each other. They showed flexibility in adjusting with multiple simultaneous novelties and challenges: Agile processes, new technologies, limited direction, new team. Constant communication between them was a learning process until the end of the project. They started technical meetings in the second quarter of the project during which they discussed issues, integration, choices of technologies, and did code reviews to avoid mismatch in their development work. They all valued these meetings. Still, one developer felt the burden of the responsibility of the project was mainly on his shoulders, and would have liked others to take more ownership. Better facilitation by the SM could have prevented this. DT members attended meetings punctually. The SM was proactive in facilitating meetings and communications; however, she did not always discern communication gaps within the team until a problem occurred. Written comments were done for retrospectives individually followed by a discussion. A compilation of all anonymized comments was sent by the SM after the meetings.

Technical Health (64%). The DT did not discuss early on about coding standards, level of documentation, naming conventions, and so on; this resulted in difficulty in integration and technical debt. From Sprint 11, developers started to worry about the code, commenting: "code base is in danger of becoming unmanageable." The technical debt remained until the end of the project, though they dedicated one sprint at the end of each release to clean the code. Unit automated testing started in the third quarter of the project. They also experienced many challenges with the server. This aspect got stabilized only in the third quarter of the project. In retrospective, the team believed (1) they should have studied the technologies at the beginning of the project more closely before making decisions and starting the development process, (2) they should have done a better iterative development in order to build small increments with quality code; and they should have done automated testing from the start of the project.

Observations and Challenges. (1) The SM took some measures to ease the adaptation to the Agile/Scrum approach, such as (a) at the kickoff meeting, provide to the whole team clear written explanations on the Agile/Scrum ceremonies, their purposes, and estimated time; (b) schedule all Scrum meetings at the same time of different days (adapted if needed); (c) provide a meeting schedule plus send calendar invitations for all upcoming meetings; (d) prepare an agenda defining items, presenters, timebox in consultation with the DT and send it in advance to everyone for each review meeting; (e) send meeting notes after each review meeting; and (f) create a Skype group chat for continuous communications and persistent chat between the DT, SM, and PO. (2) The industry partner displayed a high motivation for making the project successful. When a matter involved their participation and decision, they were prompt to proceed. (3) Adjustments to the Scrum ceremonies were adopted such as holding standups twice a week rather than daily given the small size of the team. (4) The application of a 'technical' meeting every week among developers, as designed by Agile, to have in-depth discussions on technical issues and ensure all developers were technically in sync to deliver the expected increment at every sprint proved very helpful. (5) The PO filled several roles (multiple-role challenge) representing conflicting interests: PO (focus on customer interest for product and timeline), professor (keen to provide learning experiences to students irrespective of the time it takes or whether it brings or not immediate value to the product), and researcher (submit research proposals with appealing features securing funding approval). In this project, these conflicting roles were displayed in two specific occurrences: the DT worked hard on a feature included in the research proposal, but not really looked for by the industry partner. The PO wanted the developers to improve their expertise in that area. This task delayed the progress of the project. The PO decided to put it aside, but it caused some frustrations and additional pressure for the DT given the project deadline. A developer expressed "I don't want to simply drop all of that effort, but it seems like a solution searching for a problem right now." In the choice of the server infrastructure, the PO encouraged developers towards a complex platform as a learning experience, and suggested a simpler avenue only when the SM raised a red flag that the project was being delayed given this issue and that the industry partner was getting uneasy in seeing the instability of the system.

5   Summary

5.1   RQ1: Are Agile Principles and the Scrum Framework Applicable in Short-Term IARCs for Software Development, and How Can They Benefit and Nurture the Success of Such Collaborations?

The case studies described in the previous section showed that Agile and Scrum, though a challenge for new teams, still provided an ideal environment to conduct successful IARCs. Some Agile/Scrum practices that predominantly aided the success of the case studies presented were: (1) early and frequent delivery of working software (every sprint): the structure and transparency inherent to Scrum revealed weaknesses early on, and prevented derailments in all case studies; (2) the customer-centric principle helped to keep the focus on the right objectives, mainly for academia teams who tend to be research-oriented rather than result-oriented [6]; Cases A and C underlined that reality; (3) responding to change was an important facet in all projects, and helped to adjust quickly and move on towards the release goal; (4) the various meetings, creation of stories, acceptance criteria, DoD, specific roles, and more, contributed to encourage the teams to communicate and get organized; and (5) having highly motivated individuals who really wanted the project to succeed allowed to supersede the many challenges each team faced. The complexity of IARCs and related challenges oblige guiding principles and a framework aiding success, which Agile/Scrum does. This is especially true in short-term software development projects given less time is given to pinpoint discrepancies. In fact, most difficulties encountered in the Cases above can be linked to the breaching of one of Agile/Scrum principles. Therefore, according to the observations and results, it seems that applying Agile/Scrum principles and structure can help IARCs succeed, as show these comments:

Academia teams: "Definitely, Agile helps the growth of this project by conducting various meetings (each meeting with different objectives) and if there is any issue, we are updating/circumventing to find and get the solution for the team." On the contrary to the belief that collocated Agile teams are the best Agile teams, one of the team member felt, "Agile development is essentially required when the team members work remotely. It's the only way to keep people coordinated and on task. A remotely developed project of non-trivial scope is doomed to failure without such coordination."

Industry partners: "It creates an organized and structured environment of short and also long term goals that we believe absolutely helps the project grow in a productive and efficient manner." "Very happy with the overall structure of the project. I like how everything is delegated, and how all of the team members go about completing their tasks. Doesn't seem to be any wasted time, very happy with this." "I believe that Agile was a significant contributor to achievements of the project. More specifically it allowed for consistent communication, and organization within the entire timeline. I believe this ultimately allowed the passion, and effort of the team to continually rise to the surface. It also helped the team address and deal with obstacles and challenges in a productive and efficient manner."

5.2 RQ2: What Challenges Can Be Expected in Applying Agile Principles and the Scrum Framework in IARCs and How Can They Be Addressed?

Agile/Scrum brings also challenges when applied for short-term IARCs: (1) Agile encourages face-to-face meetings, which is almost impossible in the context of IARCs mainly composed of distributed teams. These collaborations can still be successful, as shown in the case studies presented in this paper, in taking alternate approaches, such as daily videocalls, audio calls, instant messaging, and emails. The role of the SM is crucial in constantly facilitating communication within the team. Short-term projects leave little margin for undetected error, and communications can clearly save projects in IARCs from failure. (2) Understanding the tricky multiple, conflicting-interest role phenomena, especially for the PO on the academia side (researcher, professor, and PO), can help the whole team (PO, SM, DT) avoid deviating from the core Agile principles where customer-centric frequent delivery need to occur. It is the SM's responsibility to ensure that the Scrum processes are applied and to coach the PO and the DT so that the focus and momentum remain on the right track. (3) In short-term projects with distributed teams as those described in this paper, the adaptation process to Agile/Scrum must occur as fast as possible. The SM plays an important role in facilitating this adaptation by providing in-meetings and off-meetings support to the team. Case C describes practical aspects that can be done by the SM to accelerate the adaptation process. (4) Having two POs in IARCs is very common, which increases the challenge for vision alignment. The DT absolutely needs to know the clear vision for the project for efficient development work. Case A shows two well-aligned POs, while Case B reveals the difficulty of two POs who have minimal communications, and thus, no clear common vision. The POs' alignment should ideally be looked at closely before engaging an IARC.

6 Conclusion

The observations from the case studies presented in this paper seem to indicate that with highly motivated and skilled individuals supported by the Agile/Scrum practices, short-term IARCs in software development can be successful irrespective of the many challenges inherent to such collaborations. The authors encourage researchers willing to conduct short-term IARCs to consider these recommendations: (1) select highly motivated students; (2) appoint a SM exhibiting leadership and organizing skills who will make sure the team applies the Agile/Scrum practices from day one and encourage good habits early on in the project (1st sprint should be dedicated to plan the release, establish the backlog, create communication channels [video-meetings are strongly encouraged], discuss standards for code, documentation, DoD [include code reviews], discuss strategies for technology selection, discuss automated testing, discuss openly the different mindsets of industry and academia; find out skill levels and strengths of team members to allocate tasks accordingly); (3) beware of the PO's multiple role phenomena; and (4) ensure POs, if the case, are well-aligned and can have a regular involvement with the team. In brief, short-term IARCs can be successful if motivated individuals apply Agile/Scrum from the start of the project, and thus get altitude as quickly as possible to successfully reach the destination, which is the delivery of the product.

References

1. Ankrah, S., Omar, A.T.: Universities–industry collaboration: a systematic review. Scandinavian J. Manag. **31**(3), 387–408 (2015). doi:10.1016/j.scaman.2015.02.003
2. Garousi, V., Petersen, K., Ozkan, B.: Challenges and best practices in industry-academia collaborations in software engineering: a systematic literature review. Inf. Softw. Technol. **79**, 106–127 (2016). doi:10.1016/j.infsof.2016.07.006
3. Grünbacher, P., Rabiser, R.: Success factors for empirical studies in industry-academia collaboration: a reflection. In: Proceedings of the 1st International Workshop on Conducting Empirical Studies in Industry, pp. 27–32. IEEE Press, May, 2013
4. Bekkers, R., Freitas, I.M.B.: Analysing knowledge transfer channels between universities and industry: to what degree do sectors also matter? Res. Policy **37**(10), 1837–1853 (2008). doi: 10.1016/j.respol.2008.07.007
5. Wohlin, C., Aurum, A., Angelis, L., Phillips, L., Dittrich, Y., Gorschek, T., Grahn, H., Henningsson, K., Kagstrom, S., Low, G., Rovegard, P., Tomaszewski, P., van Toorn, C., Winter, J.: The success factors powering industry-academia collaboration. IEEE Softw. **29**(2), 67–73 (2012). doi:10.1109/MS.2011.92
6. Sandberg, A., Pareto, L., Arts, T.: Agile collaborative research: Action principles for industry-academia collaboration. IEEE Softw. **28**(4), 74–83 (2011). doi:10.1109/MS.2011.49
7. Petersen, K., Gencel, C., Asghari, N., Baca, D., Betz, S.: Action research as a model for industry-academia collaboration in the software engineering context. In: Proceedings of the 2014 International Workshop on Long-term Industrial Collaboration on Software Engineering, pp. 55–62. ACM, September 2014. doi:10.1145/2647648.2647656
8. Martínez-Fernández, S., Marques, H.M.: Practical experiences in designing and conducting empirical studies in industry-academia collaboration. In: Proceedings of the 2nd International Workshop on Conducting Empirical Studies in Industry, pp. 15–20. ACM, June 2014. doi: 10.1145/2593690.2593696
9. Marchesi, M., Mannaro, K., Uras, S., Locci, M.: Distributed scrum in research project management. In: Concas, G., Damiani, E., Scotto, M., Succi, G. (eds.) XP 2007. LNCS, vol. 4536, pp. 240–244. Springer, Heidelberg (2007). doi:10.1007/978-3-540-73101-6_45
10. Jain, S., Babar, M.A., Fernandez, J.: Conducting empirical studies in industry: balancing rigor and relevance. In: Proceedings of the 1st International Workshop on Conducting Empirical Studies in Industry, pp. 9–14. IEEE Press, May, 2013

11. Scrum Alliance: The 2015 state of scrum report (2015). https://www.scrumalliance.org/why-scrum/state-of-scrum-report. Accessed 8 Apr 2017
12. Manifesto for Agile Software Development. http://agilemanifesto.org/
13. Scrum Alliance: The scrum guide. https://www.scrumalliance.org/why-scrum/scrum-guide
14. Introduction to Agile. http://agileforall.com/resources/introduction-to-agile/
15. Sidky, A., Arthur, J., Bohner, S.: A disciplined approach to adopting agile practices: the agile adoption framework. Innovations Syst. Softw. Eng. **3**(3), 203–216 (2007)
16. Humble, J., Russell, R.: The agile Maturity Model Applied to Building and Releasing Software. ThoughtWorks White Paper (2009)
17. Scaled Agile Framework (SAFe) Team Self-Assessment. http://www.scaledagileframework.com/metrics/#T4
18. Tuckman, B.W.: Developmental sequence in small groups. Psychol. Bull. **63**(6), 384–399 (1965). doi:10.1037/h0022100. PMID 14314073

Engineering Web Applications Using Real-Time Collaborative Modeling

Peter de Lange[1]([✉]), Petru Nicolaescu[1], Ralf Klamma[1], and Matthias Jarke[1,2]

[1] RWTH Aachen University, Lehrstuhl Informatik 5,
Ahornstr. 55, 52074 Aachen, Germany
{lange,nicolaescu,klamma,jarke}@dbis.rwth-aachen.de
[2] Fraunhofer FIT, Birlinghoven Castle, 53754 Sankt Augustin, Germany

Abstract. In agile practices, near real-time collaboration on the Web facilitates stakeholder activities, their communication and joint impact analysis. In providing an abstraction layer on the software development process, modeling enables participatory design and improves requirements negotiation by close involvement of end users. However, model-driven engineering is mostly used in classical software development to achieve standardization and mature processes. Little research in Model-Driven Web Engineering focuses on leveraging near real-time collaboration and collaborative modeling in order to support agile Web engineering processes. This paper proposes a new approach for Web-based collaborative near real-time modeling and generation of Web applications by tying together frontend components and microservices as key elements. This leads to well-defined service interfaces that facilitate inter-service and backend-frontend communication. Our evaluation results indicate increased productivity by better support for collaborative activities in Model-Driven Web Engineering.

Keywords: Model-Driven Web Engineering · Near real-time collaboration · Collaborative conceptual modeling · End user integration

1 Introduction

Model-driven development had a first peak already during the early 1980s, with the emergence of Computer-Aided Software Engineering (CASE) [22] tools. On the Web, model-driven approaches have increased in complexity [18], while simultaneously the mismatch between the large number of end users and the relatively small number of available developers increased. After the initial wave of Model-Driven Web Engineering (MDWE) approaches in the early '00s, the lack of standardization of Web applications, the rise of mobile applications and emerging mashups, the huge growth of social networking sites like Facebook and Twitter and the popularity of Content Management Systems (CMS) lead to a decrease in MDWE research. Among the core features of these technologies, CMS provide low-barrier means for Web users to author and publish online content, while mashups leverage the reuse of existing heterogeneous components to build Web

© Springer International Publishing AG 2017
C. Gutwin et al. (Eds.): CRIWG 2017, LNCS 10391, pp. 213–228, 2017.
DOI: 10.1007/978-3-319-63874-4_16

applications using data from various sources. However, CMS do not cope well with the heterogeneous needs of communities belonging to the long-tail [1] of the Web and mashups face a lack in commercial adoption and standardization (working with various service oriented architectures and cloud models), due to incompatibilities between interfaces.

In contrast, MDWE provides the ideal candidate to enforce a standardized Web application architecture engineering practice and its usage can help reducing the time needed to train new developers. Moreover, by employing modeling as a common discussion and work basis, all stakeholders can be involved into the development process. Because of their abstractive nature, dedicated models and views on certain components of a Web application can improve the integration of non-technical stakeholders. In MDWE this can be reflected using separate views where various stakeholders can focus together on application design and modeling only the backend, frontend, individual components, interfaces and interactions, according to their background, expertize and interest. For example, users without technical knowledge can contribute to design the elements that will be part of the frontend and express their opinion about the needed logic in collaboration with developers. As the application is automatically generated from the model and deployed on the fly, all participants involved in the collaboration process can see the outcome prototype, request and perform changes, regenerate, etc. Such a collaborative approach bears the potential to drastically improve the agility of the Web application development process.

With respect to the developed Web applications, the need for maintainability, flexibility in integration of new features or services, design for failure and scalability initiated a paradigm shift, moving away from monolithic systems. Agile practices and methodologies led to the development of emerging architectural styles such as microservice-based architectures [9,14], used by major Web players like Amazon, Netflix or Twitter. Microservice development tasks are executed on smaller pieces of code, functionality-centered and hence easier to understand without having the entire domain knowledge, making developer training faster and cheaper. Hence, in such new environments, support is needed to standardize the communication between microservices and ensure reusability. Concurrently, similar characteristics reflecting the microservice architecture are also desired on the frontend level. These can be achieved via componentization and by overcoming the challenges faced by mashup systems with the increasing adoption of HTML5 and its broad implementation on heterogeneous devices.

While methodologies with respect to Web applications [3,8,10,13,21], mashups [5,6,24] and human-computer interaction [13,20] are rather prominent in related literature, this paper describes a cyclic MDWE process that supports communities in collaboratively building and maintaining modular Web-based applications. Using previous work on Near Real-Time (NRT) view-based collaborative conceptual modeling [17], our approach covers the full Web application engineering process. To this purpose, we created an agile cyclic MDWE approach for the development and deployment of template-based community Web applications. The generated applications consist of a componentized architecture, with a backend consisting of microservices and frontend components realized as Web widgets. Furthermore, the applications are designed to be multi-user and multi-community. We realized our approach as a MDWE framework named Community Application Editor (CAE), which we used for the evaluation of our agile development lifecycle. The complete implementation is based on open standards and open source software. The current work answers the following questions:

1. How can a MDWE process be designed to support agility by combining NRT modeling together with code generation and deployment facilities?
2. Can NRT collaborative Web engineering improve developer training and integrate all stakeholders in the development of community Web applications?
3. How to engineer a NRT collaborative modeling approach to design, generate and automatically deploy Web applications?

In the rest of the paper, Sect. 2 presents the requirements and an example scenario for our collaborative MDWE approach. Section 3 describes the methodology and the proposed MDWE process. In Sect. 4 we introduce the metamodel used in our approach. Section 5 presents the architectural details of our implementation. Evaluation results are discussed in Sect. 6. Finally, Sect. 7 presents the related work and Sect. 8 concludes and provides an outlook for future research.

2   Community-Based MDWE Requirements

As our approach relies heavily on the collaborative aspects of MDWE, we base it on the CoP theory [23]. This theory defines a CoP as a group of people who share a common interest in a particular domain and solve similar tasks in a certain area. Via collaborative work and information sharing between the members, the group as a whole evolves. One characteristic of communities which are part of the long tail is that they rely on individual tool support. Most CoPs cannot develop the tools they need themselves.

As a *use-case scenario*, consider a professional community of medical doctors that uses videos and images as main study and documentation objects in their training practice, served by a collection of multiple existing services. Assuming that community members wish to integrate 3D objects in their activities (e.g. highly detailed digital representations of anatomical objects) and visualize metadata connecting existing digital artifacts, such features cannot be easily implemented without technical knowledge. Using the models as a NRT interaction medium, the microservices responsible for 3D objects and annotations, the frontends and the interactions between all these components are modeled. Existing models can be used in order to evolve the system architecture, or models can be authored from scratch. For each application component, the community instantiates dedicated views to specify the needed functionality. Doctors and (possible external) developers distribute according to their domain-specific knowledge to work on the corresponding views. Once the frontend and backend components have been modeled, the Web application is generated and can be automatically deployed on a custom infrastructure determined during the modeling phase.

In previous work [16], developer and user feedback was gathered during the development of a widgetizing methodology for community Web application reengineering. The study researched the use of mashup systems, composed of Web widgets as the frontend for RESTful Web services. Starting from the methodology's empirical study, we identified several main requirements, which we generalize further and which our framework and the generated applications are build to fulfill. The first is a *defined process and methodological support* for model-based Web application engineering in CoPs. For ensuring abstraction and interoperability, a *community Web application metamodel*, on which the modeling process builds upon, is required. A further requirement is the usage of *NRT collaborative modeling* to allow all members of a community to simultaneously work on the same application model. This supports the productivity, as modelers can easily present their ideas in NRT and it increases the learning (and thus evolution) effects in a CoP, since all stakeholders can follow and participate during the whole application development process. In this context, *awareness of user actions* is relevant, such that a modeler knows what other modelers are currently working on. Based on the models, the *code generation* of microservices, frontend components and complete applications should be possible at any time during the modeling process, provided that the current state of the application's model is valid. Another important requirement for the generated applications is the *support of community features* such as user and group management, synchronous and asynchronous communication, NRT collaboration and shared editing, etc. Since our methodology builds on a microservice architecture, *continuous and automatic deployment* of complete applications (or parts of it) is important to support rapid prototyping. By choosing a microservice architecture, the community can implement their services in a highly flexible way. This means support for *different programming styles and techniques*, *polyglot persistence* and the integration of other service functionalities via *well-defined communication channels*. Finally, the generated source code should be *publicly accessible* for all community members, should be easily extensible and modifiable in a way that all members can see these changes.

3   An Agile MDWE Process

To fulfill the requirements stated in the previous section, we developed an agile MDWE process that we describe in Fig. 1, depicted as the lifecycle of an application developed with our methodology. Since the target group of our approach is a whole CoP, users have various roles, of which we only depict the "community" symbolically for members of all professions being able to participate in this step and the "developer" role symbolically for (multiple) technical stakeholders working in this step, which for example also could include professions like "software architect". The basis for our modeling process is a predefined metamodel that is split up into three different views for frontend components, microservices and an application/communication view to allow for a componentized architecture that can be developed concurrently, also allowing the reuse of components for multiple applications.

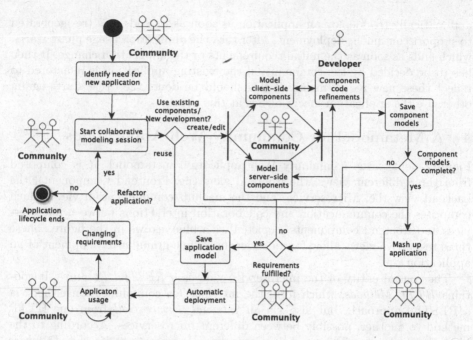

Fig. 1. Application lifecycle according to our process

The first step of our process is the CoP identifying the need for a new application and starting the collaborative modeling process. The first decision the community has to undertake is if they want to reuse existing components to mash up a new application or if there exists the need for developing or editing frontend components and/or microservices. If it was decided to not only reuse existing components, the modeling of the individual components starts. Here, all members of the CoP are able to bring in their ideas by collaboratively modeling the application components. During this phase, manual source code edits can be performed by community members experienced in the development of Web applications. These changes are then merged back into the model, allowing for a cyclic development with source code editing phases followed by modeling phases and vice versa. Both the modeling and the code editing phase are performed in a NRT collaboration setting on the Web, with all changes directly visible to all community members. At any time, the components can be persisted and the modeling process can be postponed and taken up again. Once the microservices and frontend components have been defined, the application mashup modeling phase starts. Members can choose at any point to mashup the Web application. If the current application's state does not meet all requirements yet, the application and its components have to undergo additional modeling/editing phases, until they match the requirements. Once the requirements are fulfilled, the mashup (e.g. full-fledged Web application model) can be persisted and the final application is generated. Finally, our approach features the possibility to automatically (re-)deploy an application as soon as its code was (re-)generated to support continuous deployment. After this, the application usage phase starts, which ends as soon as the initial requirements of the application change. It then has to be decided by the community if the existing application is refactored to reflect these new requirements. If this should be done, the cycle starts again, otherwise the application lifecycle ends at this point.

4   A Metamodel for Community Web Applications

Figure 2 depicts the community Web application metamodel. It is composed from three different views: the frontend view (i.e. Frontend Component), the backend view (i.e. Microservice) and the mashup/communication view, which comprises the communication and collaboration interactions between microservices and frontend components, depicted with blue arrows in the figure. These three respective views allow for an easier, more fine-granular development of an application.

The central entity of the microservice view is a *RESTful Resource*. It contains *HTTP Methods*, which form the interface for communication either via a RESTful approach, but also via an *Internal Service Call* from one HTTP method to another, possibly between different microservices. According to the idea of polyglot persistence, each microservice has access to its own *Database* instance.

The central entity of the frontend component view is a *Widget*. This widget consists of *Functions* and *HTML Elements*. HTML elements can either be *static*, meaning that they are not modified by any other element or functionality of the application, or *dynamic*, meaning that they either are created or updated by one of the frontend component's elements. Both static and dynamic HTML elements can trigger events, which can for example be a mouse click, that cause function calls. The second option to trigger a function call is via an *Inter Widget Communication (IWC) Response* object, that waits for an *IWC Call* to be triggered. These calls are again part of a function, which initiates them. A function is able to update or create a dynamic HTML element. The last part of the frontend component view are the communication and collaboration functionalities, which include the already mentioned IWC call - response mechanism, as well as microservice calls that are triggered by a function, and HTML elements instrumentalized with collaborative support, making it possible for elements to share the same state/content in the Web browser of all participating users, propagating changes in NRT.

The mashup/communication view on our metamodel builds the binding component between the client-side and server-side. It does not feature any new modeling objects, but provides a simplified view on the whole application, only depicting those objects directly involved in any communication processes. This includes microservice calls from frontend components to microservices, IWC call and response objects as well as collaborative HTML elements, since those, if they have the same id, are also collaborative across widgets. Finally, internal microservice calls are depicted here as well.

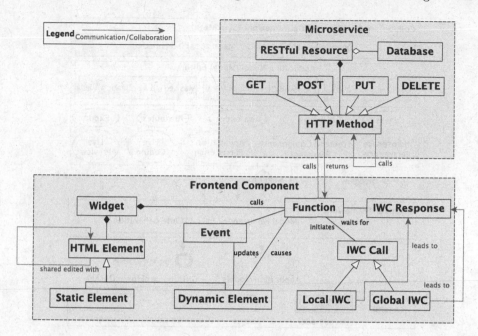

Fig. 2. Community Web application metamodel

5   Realization: Community Application Editor

Our conceptual approach presented in the previous sections is realized in a Web-based modeling and code generation framework called Community Application Editor (CAE). CAE uses the same concepts and technologies as its generated applications, relying on frontend components and microservices. Its early prototype implementation was presented within a demo [7] and a first introduction to its usage is available as a video[1]. CAE is based on SyncMeta [17], a framework which realizes NRT collaborative conceptual modeling in the Web browser. By using this framework, we achieve NRT collaboration in the modeling canvas, as well as awareness functionality, with each user being able to see what other collaborators are modeling in real-time. We extended this functionality to our live coding editor with the help of Yjs [15], a client-side framework that manages message propagation, shared editing and ensures that no conflicts occur during the collaboration. The architecture of CAE is depicted in Fig. 3. Since the focus of this contribution is laid on the conceptual aspects of our approach, we here only cover the basics of the technical implementation.

The backend consists of two microservices, which contain the logic for model storage and code generation. The microservices are implemented using las2peer [11], a Java-based open source framework for distributing community services in a peer-to-peer (P2P) infrastructure. Each P2P entity is called a node, which

---

[1] https://www.youtube.com/playlist?list=PLU6UMwJTlSlocffF26tPNVe3r75g-VPje.

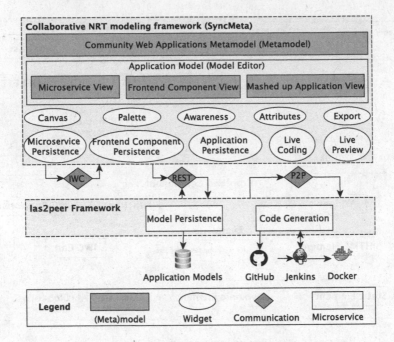

Fig. 3. CAE architecture overview

provides an arbitrary number of services in the network. las2peer offers a highly reliable and secure platform for hosting microservice backends, supporting end-to-end encrypted communication and storage facilities as well as load balancing across nodes. The microservices communicate with each other using this P2P network communication functionality. The models are stored in a dedicated database by the *Model Persistence Service*, whereas the *Code Generation Service* pushes the generated code into a GitHub organization. Frontend to backend communication is done via RESTful service calls, and we use *Inter Widget Communication* (IWC) on the frontend. To give a better overview on how the CAE's application modeling and code generation processes work in practice, we describe here an example setting of how a frontend component realizing user management functionality is modeled and generated (cf. Fig. 4).

The community uses the *Palette* widget to add nodes and edges to the modeling *Canvas* widget, according to the predefined frontend component metamodel, which prevents for example the insertion of wrong edges. Once the modeling process has finished, one of the community members uses the *Frontend Component Persistence Widget* to store the model. The store functionality of the widget invokes the *Model Persistence Service*, one of the two backend services. This service then parses the passed model and stores it into a relational database. Its second responsibility is to invoke the *Code Generation Service*, which is responsible for the model-to-code transformation. This process is based on pre-defined templates available on GitHub, that get modified via code injection according to

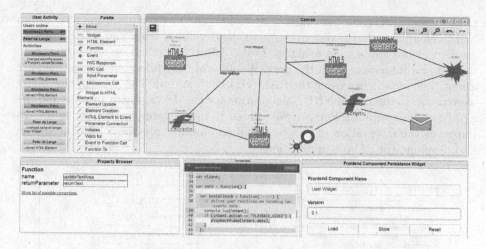

Fig. 4. Frontend component view screenshot of a user widget

the passed model. The generated code is then pushed to a newly created GitHub repository. From now on, it is also possible for developers participating in the modeling process to inject source code into the frontend component by using the *Live Code Editor* widget, which allows for code injection at certain parts whilst locking others (grayed out in the editor) that should only be modified by changing the corresponding parts of the model. These manual source code changes get synchronized with the model of the frontend component, thus allowing for cyclic modeling and code editing phases during the development process.

The deployment of a complete application is done in the mashup view (not depicted in the screenshot here). After all needed microservices and frontend components are added to the canvas, the complete application is build by a Jenkins CI server and put into a Docker container which both starts the backend microservice network as well as a server with the frontend components.

6   Evaluation

We evaluated our approach in two user evaluations, one in a simulated community setting with mixed teams of developers and non-technical members and one in a lab course of undergraduate computer science students.

6.1   Evaluation with Heterogeneous Teams

In our first evaluation, we considered groups of two to three people with various technical backgrounds. We carried out thirteen user evaluation sessions, with a total number of thirty-six participants. The groups consisted of at least one experienced Web developer and at least one community member without any technical experience in Web development who received a description of the application to be designed. During the evaluation session, the non-technical member group had to communicate the requirements to the developer team and collaboratively implement the application using the CAE. After the evaluation session, we conducted oral interviews with the participants and they filled out a questionnaire about their experience using the CAE (cf. Figs. 5 and 6). The goals of this study were to assess the role of NRT collaboration for the development process and the agility of our approach. Further, we wanted to investigate whether our approach improves the integration of non-technical community members into the design and development of Web applications.

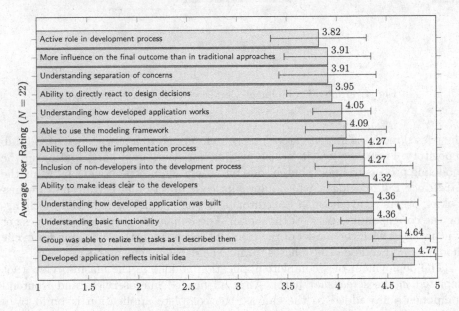

Fig. 5. Survey results of non-technical members

Results. In general, we received high ratings from non-technical members in terms of methodology, and developers felt they were able to implement the requirements formulated by the non-technical members. Most non-technical members felt integrated well into the NRT development process and the oral interviews revealed that they could follow the development process well. Although the question if non-technical members took an active role in the development process received the lowest score, the result is still pretty high, i.e. 3.82 out of 5. From the developer survey, we received the highest ratings for questions regarding the concept of CAE and its usability. Collaborative aspects were also rated rather high by both groups. The oral interviews revealed that most developers felt both the need for requirement analysis improvements regarding the inclusion of non-technical stakeholders as well as that the CAE can be used for this purpose.

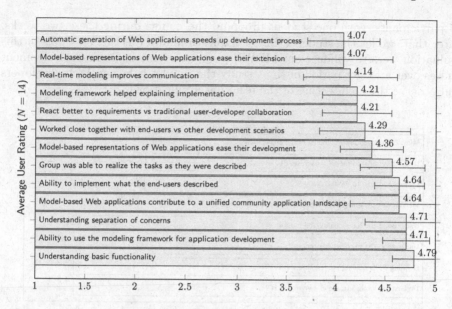

Fig. 6. Survey results of developers

Concerning proposals for improvement, an important mention in both groups was the augmentation of the collaborative usage with recommendations and increased awareness of others' actions. Ongoing research on the collaborative modeling process of SyncMeta currently focuses on modeling guidance and user nudging, which we hope to integrate into the CAE soon. A particularly often requested feature was the introduction of a second abstraction tier for the frontend component view, which could hide too technical aspects from non-technical members, concentrating more on the "visible" elements, putting the functionality into a second component view, which would then be used by the developers only. The evaluation showed the usefulness of the CAE to integrate non-technical members better into the development process. Developers saw the benefit of CAE's MDWE approach to contribute to a unified community application landscape. All in all, results indicate that designing a microservice architecture through MDWE takes a right step into raising the quality of modern community Web application engineering processes.

6.2 Evaluation in a Lab Course

We also evaluated our approach in a lab course of undergraduate computer science students. The students had basic programming knowledge, in particular in Java (4.6 of 5) from their first programming lectures, but our pre-survey indicated that none of them were really familiar with Web development (1.67 of 5) or microservice architectures (1.73 of 5). During a two week period, the students were asked to model and deploy the basic framework of their lab course prototype, a Web application for the gamification of Web services. We had

15 participants, with one student dropping the course during these two weeks. After that, we let the students fill out a questionnaire (cf. Fig. 7). Goals of this evaluation were to validate our MDWE process, its modeling and development phases over a longer period of time, study the impact it has on Web developers and observe the architecture of the resulting applications.

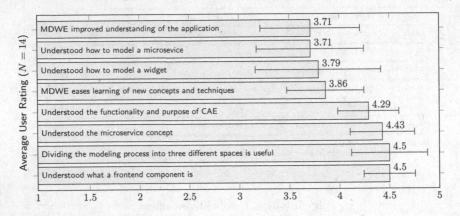

Fig. 7. Survey of lab course participants

Results. Besides the evaluation of the usefulness in general, in this user study we were especially interested in the question, how the CAE can help developers not yet familiar with the present development environment. Our questionnaire thus focused, besides some questions similar to our first evaluation regarding the general understanding and usage of the CAE, on the learning effects the CAE concept can apply to developers that have to integrate into a new development process. Our results indicate a high learning effect in terms of understanding the underlying Web development concepts of microservices (4.43 vs. 1.73) and frontend components/widgets (4.5 vs. 2.6). Also the concept and purpose of the CAE were understood by the majority of the students (4.29). We received rather high ratings in terms of MDWE easing the learning of new concepts and techniques (3.86) and MDWE improving the understanding of the resulting/generated application (3.71).

Interpretation. These first results of a realistic usage setting show promising applications of the CAE as a tool to teach developers of different domains the development of Web applications with a distributed microservice architecture. Our evaluation group had little to none experience with Web development and our pre-survey also showed that none of the students had ever worked in a team on a larger software project. This indicates that our results might be transferable to other communities of non-expert developers. The idea of using MDWE as a starting point for learning to develop Web applications was received well and our students showed high motivation of interacting with our infrastructure.

Study Limitations. Our evaluation was hampered by some technical problems that dimmed the results of our study. These mainly concerned the model synchronization and their persistence in the NRT collaborative setting, finally also impacting the deployment of the generated applications in a common lab course las2peer network. The problems were mainly due to the use of an experimental prototype which was never tested in an environment with more than a handful of people using it at the same time. Occurring boundary conditions and network latency problems lead to a cycle of fixes, version incompatibilities and newly introduced problems which in the restricted time period – even though they finally lead to major improvements of our framework – clouded the participant's impressions of CAE usability. As a result, the automatic deployment was a bit tedious, although eventually possible.

7   Related Work

First work in the domain of Web application modeling comes from the late 90s, with the Object Oriented Hypermedia Design Method (OOHDM) [21] being a well know early attempt to structure the development of Web applications by providing a detailed conceptual modeling approach, split up into four different steps, the conceptual design, the navigation design, the abstract interface design and finally the implementation. Currently, two actively developed concepts in the MDWE domain are *UML-based Web Engineering (UWE)* and the model-driven application development platform WebRatio with its underlying *Web Modeling Language (WebML)* as domain specific modeling language. The *UWE* modeling language [12] was developed as an extension to UML, a so-called UML profile. Following the separation of concerns approach, it splits up the modeling process into three parts, which are conceptual, navigational and presentation modeling. For both the navigational and presentational modeling phase, the UML profile includes UML stereotypes. These stereotypes are based on existing modeling elements and extend their semantic. UWE uses UML's tagged values to represent stored (current) user information in a modeling element. The UML constraint extension mechanism provides the possibility to specify new semantics linguistically for a model element. This can then be used for automated model checking. The current UWE tool support is called MagicUWE, realized as a plug-in of the CASE tool MagicDraw. *WebML* [4] was developed in 2000 as a "notation for specifying complex Web sites at the conceptual level". Like most Web modeling languages, WebML also follows the separation of concerns idea by using an orthogonal approach, splitting up the modeling task into a structural model that describes the sites content, a hypertext model that includes the composition model of the content and a navigation model that describes the topology of the links between different pages. The presentation model forms the third perspective of modeling. The initial specification of the WebML language did not foresee a metamodel, but a rather "grammar-like textual definition for specifying a structure for XML documents" [19]. The metamodel for WebML was developed five years later by the authors of [19]. Although initially created in an academic context for a small case modeling tool called "Toriisoft", WebML is now used by WebRatio, a commercial model-driven application development platform that supports the generation of full featured Web applications, using Eclipse as modeling environment and Groovy for code generation. In 2013, the WebRatio company extended WebML, which lead to the Interaction Flow Modeling Language (IFML)[2], a language that was adopted as a standard by the Object Management Group (OMG) [2].

Existing research in the domain of mashing up Web applications from existing components lays its focus on integrating heterogeneous application components into a mashup. MashArt [6] was one of the first approaches to also enable what the authors called "advanced Web users" into the process of mashing up existing components with the help of their editor. MAIDL [5] is a mashup generator for mobile Web applications, enabling fast prototyping and automatic adjustments of the resulting mashup code for both mobile devices and stationary computers. The authors evaluated their concept also with "novice mashup composers" and showed the usefulness of their concept for integrating otherwise not involved person groups into mashing up existing Web application components.

Previous research on MDWE focuses on support for professional developers in designing monolithic Web applications. Mashups concentrate on reusing existing components to integrate data from heterogeneous sources. In our work, we propose an agile process that concentrates on integrating all members in professional communities. By using MDWE techniques for creating microservice-based Web application architectures we achieve the necessary standardization to enable interconnectivity at a high degree in such systems.

8   Conclusions and Future Work

In this paper, we presented a NRT collaborative model-driven approach for microservice-based community Web applications. We implemented and evaluated the approach with CAE, a Web-based MDWE framework that, based on predefined templates, generates community Web applications. The evaluation results show that NRT collaborative modeling increases the culture of participation, where all members of a CoP build and extend their community applications together, ultimately supporting both the quality of the developed applications, as well as the evolution of the CoP through NRT collaboration. The results promise that a formalized way of developing microservice-based architectures with well-defined communication structures can advance Web application engineering and contribute to agile practices and rapid prototyping. Moreover, MDWE ensures that certain standards are met and provides means to reuse existing (pre-modeled) application components, may they be backend microservices or frontend components. The entire code involved in all components forming the CAE is open source and available on GitHub[3], making it easily accessible by online communities that want to boost internal development.

---

[2] http://www.omg.org/spec/IFML/1.0/.

[3] https://github.com/search?q=org%3Arwth-acis+CAE.

As we now have achieved a stable and more mature release of the framework after the conducted studies, in future we plan to further evaluate the framework in real-wold communities and improve its usability. This involves more specialized views on frontend components, where non-technical members can benefit from live preview of the current frontend functions and look and feel and developers can better concentrate on architecture and functionality. Also, we plan to introduce steering and guidance during the modeling process as a first step to ease participation within communities. This would present a good input for CoP members in terms of what to model next and how to model collaboratively. Furthermore, we want to encourage the active participation with the introduction of gamification into the framework, a field rather new to MDWE. Another area worth investigating in the future is the support for code-to-model transformations, which would also be a relevant feature for communities with existing applications.

References

1. Anderson, C.: The Long Tail: Why the Future of Business is Selling Less of More. Hyperion, New York (2006)
2. Brambilla, M., Fraternali, P.: Large-scale model-driven engineering of web user interaction: the WebML and WebRatio experience. Sci. Comput. Program. **89**, 71–87 (2014)
3. Ceri, S., Daniel, F., Matera, M., Facca, F.M.: Model-driven development of context-aware web applications. ACM Trans. Internet Technol. **7**(1), 1–32 (2007)
4. Ceri, S., Fraternali, P., Bongio, A.: Web Modeling Language (WebML): a modeling language for designing Web sites. Comput. Netw. **33**(1), 137–157 (2000)
5. Chaisatien, P., Prutsachainimmit, K., Tokuda, T.: Mobile mashup generator system for cooperative applications of different mobile devices. In: Auer, S., Díaz, O., Papadopoulos, G.A. (eds.) ICWE 2011. LNCS, vol. 6757, pp. 182–197. Springer, Heidelberg (2011). doi:10.1007/978-3-642-22233-7_13
6. Daniel, F., Casati, F., Benatallah, B., Shan, M.-C.: Hosted universal composition: models, languages and infrastructure in mashArt. In: Laender, A.H.F., Castano, S., Dayal, U., Casati, F., Oliveira, J.P.M. (eds.) ER 2009. LNCS, vol. 5829, pp. 428–443. Springer, Heidelberg (2009). doi:10.1007/978-3-642-04840-1_32
7. de Lange, P., Nicolaescu, P., Derntl, M., Jarke, M., Klamma, R.: Community application editor: collaborative near real-time modeling and composition of microservice-based web applications. In: Modellierung 2016 Workshop Proceedings, pp. 123–127 (2016)
8. Fatolahi, A., Somé, S., Lethbridge, T.: A meta-model for model-driven web development. Int. J. Soft. Inf. **6**(2), 125–162 (2012)
9. Fowler, M., Highsmith, J.: The agile manifesto. Soft. Dev. **9**(8), 28–35 (2001)
10. Gomez, J., Cachero, C., Pastor, O.: Conceptual modeling of device-independent web applications. IEEE Multimedia **8**(2), 26–39 (2001)
11. Klamma, R., Renzel, D., De Lange, P., Janßen, H.: las2peer - A Primer, No. 2016-020 in ACIS Working Group Series (AWGS). ResearchGate. doi:10.13140/RG.2.2.31456.48645
12. Koch, N., Kraus, A.: The expressive power of UML-based Web engineering. In: Second International Workshop on Web-oriented Software Technology, vol. 16, pp. 105–119 (2002)

13. Milicevic, A., Jackson, D., Gligoric, M., Marinov, D.: Model-based, event-driven programming paradigm for interactive web applications. In: Proceedings of the 2013 ACM International Symposium on New Ideas, New Paradigms and Reflections on Programming and Software, pp. 17–36 (2013)

14. Newman, S.: Building Microservices: Designing Fine-Grained Systems. O'Reilly, Sebastopol (2015)

15. Nicolaescu, P., Jahns, K., Derntl, M., Klamma, R.: Near real-time peer-to-peer shared editing on extensible data types. In: GROUP 2016. ACM (2016)

16. Nicolaescu, P., Klamma, R.: A Methodology and tool support for widget-based web application development. In: Cimiano, P., Frasincar, F., Houben, G.-J., Schwabe, D. (eds.) ICWE 2015. LNCS, vol. 9114, pp. 515–532. Springer, Cham (2015). doi:10. 1007/978-3-319-19890-3_33

17. Nicolaescu, P., Rosenstengel, M., Derntl, M., Klamma, R., Jarke, M.: View-based near real-time collaborative modeling for information systems engineering. In: Nurcan, S., Soffer, P., Bajec, M., Eder, J. (eds.) CAiSE 2016. LNCS, vol. 9694, pp. 3–17. Springer, Cham (2016). doi:10.1007/978-3-319-39696-5_1

18. Pastor, O., España, S., Panach, J.I., Aquino, N.: Model-driven development. Informatik-Spektrum 31(5), 394–407 (2008)

19. Schauerhuber, A., Wimmer, M., Kapsammer, E.: Bridging existing web modeling languages to model-driven engineering: a metamodel for WebML. In: Workshop: Proceedings of the Sixth International Conference on Web Engineering (2006)

20. Schlungbaum, E.: Individual user interfaces and model-based user interface software tools. In: Proceedings of the 2nd International Conference on Intelligent User Interfaces, pp. 229–232 (1997)

21. Schwabe, D., Rossi, G.: An object oriented approach to web-based applications design. TAPOS 4(4), 207–225 (1998)

22. Teichroew, D., Hershey, E.: PSL/PSA: a computer-aided technique for structured documentation and analysis of information processing systems. IEEE Trans. Software Eng. 3(1), 41–48 (1977)

23. Wenger, E.: Communities of Practice: Learning, Meaning, and Identity. Learning in doing. Cambridge University Press, Cambridge (1998)

24. Wilson, S., Daniel, F., Jugel, U., Soi, S.: Orchestrated user interface mashups using W3C widgets. In: Proceedings of the 11th International Conference on Current Trends in Web Engineering, pp. 49–61 (2011)

Making Interface Customizations Work: Lessons from a Successful Tailoring Community

Jeff Dyck, David Pinelle, and Carl Gutwin[✉]

Department of Computer Science, University of Saskatchewan, Saskatoon, Canada
{jeff.dyck,david.pinelle,carl.gutwin}@usask.ca

Abstract. The online game EverQuest – at one point the world's most popular MMORPG – represented a remarkably successful example of community-wide involvement in interface customization. A large majority of EverQuest users employed substantially modified UIs. We analysed EverQuest and its user community to identify the principles that led to the success of this widespread tailoring culture. We found several factors. Some have been discussed previously: that modifications require little effort, can be tested with minimal risk, and can be easily traded with others. We also found some factors that have not been reported before: scale effects resulting from the size of the user community; the use of collaborative filtering to identify better customizations; and the benefits of having support for community interactions built into the application. We believe that these principles can be applied more widely, to engender cultures of tailoring with other types of software.

Keywords: Interface customization · Tailoring · Tailoring culture · Interface design · Community · Collaborative filtering

1 Introduction

Research into customization and tailoring has been a part of HCI for almost two decades, and this work has identified a number of principles and factors that enable interface tailoring and make it effective (e.g. [3, 5, 7]). However, although there have been tailoring successes in some situations, there has never been a case where a commercial application with non-technical users has developed a widespread and sophisticated culture of customization.

This situation changed with the recent introduction of a new interface architecture for the online game EverQuest [10]. In one year, EverQuest has become a singular example of a commercial application that has a large and widespread tailoring culture: where the majority of players use a customized interface, where customizations are many and sophisticated, and where customizations are routinely shared with others. The evolution of this tailoring culture presents an opportunity to see what really works – to see the factors that figure strongly in a real-world case of widespread customization.

This paper reports our analysis of these issues. We first review earlier work on tailoring and customization, and summarize the principles that have been proposed as important for successful customization. We then report our findings: we outline the

© Springer International Publishing AG 2017
C. Gutwin et al. (Eds.): CRIWG 2017, LNCS 10391, pp. 229–243, 2017.
DOI: 10.1007/978-3-319-63874-4_17

customization capabilities in EverQuest, look at EverQuest tailoring from the end-user's perspective, and discuss how tailoring works at the community level.

Our study shows some success factors that have been identified in previous research, and some that are novel. Four critical principles from earlier research are:

- a system architecture that promotes customization;
- the ease with which modifications can be made;
- the ability to share customizations; and
- the ability to try modifications with minimal risk.

We also found three new factors:

- a large community means that a only small fraction of users need to be technically adventurous;
- community filtering provides a mechanism for identifying good modifications;
- support for community interaction is built into the application itself, providing opportunities to engage in discussions about tailoring and modification.

These principles (both the old and the new) could be applied to other commercial applications. The example of EverQuest shows that it is possible to engender successful tailoring cultures in large-scale commercial applications; at the end of the paper we discuss possibilities and barriers to achieving this situation for other kinds of software.

2   Previous Work on Interface Customization

Research into customization and tailoring is based on the idea applications cannot be designed for all of the situations where they will be used (e.g. [5, 11]). Giving users the ability to alter the application to better suit their work context can ease this problem. Previous research has looked at types of customizations and types of users, the barriers that prevent people from customizing successfully, and the value of involving the user community in the tailoring effort.

2.1   Types of Customization and Types of Users

There are a number of ways to modify a tailorable system, each with different effects on the application and each with different technical requirements. Parameters and options are settable variables that provide users with an easy way to modify the system's appearance and functionality at run-time (e.g. [12]). Integration involves adding or linking together pre-defined components or commands: for example, installing a plug-in or using a macro recorder (e.g. [5]). Extension is needed in situations where components themselves must be changed or where new ones must be created. This type of tailoring is both the most powerful and the most difficult, as it requires programming ability [5].

Different types of users undertake different types of customization. Three types are workers – the majority of users, with little technical interest in the system; tinkerers – "a worker who enjoys exploring the system, but may not fully understand it" [7, p. 176]; and programmers – people who understand the system and have training or experience with computing and coding. The majority of users are workers without technical knowledge implies that the more complex types of customization (integration and extension) will only be carried out by a few people – tinkerers and programmers.

2.2 Triggers and Barriers to Customization

Two main reasons for customizing are to improve efficiency for a particular task [3], and to change the appearance of the system [6] (although there are others, such as to learn about the system [3]). Separate from the reasons for customizing are the triggers that push people into undertaking the activity. Three common triggers [3] are: that external events cause a user to reflect on their work organization; that people notice that others have a modification that solves a particular problem; and that software upgrades cause changes to existing setups.

Despite the potential benefits of customizing, a tradeoff is noted by several researchers between the benefits and costs of creating and using modifications [3, 7, 11]. Three factors preventing people from customizing software systems are knowledge, effort, and risk.

- Not knowing what can be customized, or how changes can be made, is a barrier for workers who are uninterested in system capabilities that are not related to their primary tasks.
- Customization takes time, both to create the actual modification and to deploy the modification in the environment. Amount of effort was found by several researchers to be the largest reason that people do not undertake a customization that could benefit them.
- Customization involves risks – primarily, risk of causing problems to the existing setup. Risks are particular barriers in systems with interdependencies between different settings and components (e.g. login scripts in Unix) [3].

These barriers prevent software from being adapted to local work and task contexts. Several researchers have noted, however, that barriers can be overcome by letting someone else customize for you – by participating in a user community where customizations are shared.

2.3 The Importance of Community in Tailoring

Although customizations affect an individual's interaction with the system, customization clearly happens in a social context [2, 4]. There are several ways that the user community enables and assists tailoring.

First, being able to use others' modifications reduces customization barriers. If another person has already created a modification that solves a problem, then the costs for the next person are greatly reduced. Borrowing customizations is a common occurrence: in one study [4], all of the users had borrowed some or all of their X-Windows customization files from another person.

Second a community is of particular value to those without extensive customization skills. The large number of workers without technical knowledge can use modifications produced by a smaller number of tinkerers and programmers. New roles also arise: for example, translators [4, 7] are people who understand worker's task contexts and customization needs, but who also have the technical skills to create customizations.

In summary, there are a number of principles that have been proposed as contributors to successful tailoring:

- support tailoring in the software architecture [8]
- reduce effort required to create modifications [3]
- reduce the risk of trying a modification [3]
- enable sharing of modifications [4, 7]
- make it possible to determine the quality of modifications [4]
- enable discussion of modifications and tailoring [7]
- support different roles in the user community [2, 11].

However, these principles have not been widely seen in large-scale commercial application. We next consider the issues of tailoring by looking at the question from the other direction – by analysing a popular application that already has an active user community and a strong tailoring culture.

3   Customization in EverQuest

EverQuest was, in the early 2000s, the world's most populated massively multiplayer online role playing game (MMORPG). In 2003 it had a monthly subscriber base of over 650,000 users, of which as many as 115,000 could be found playing online concurrently [10]. In the game, people play a variety of different types of characters and engage in a variety of tasks, both individually and in groups (typically 2 to 50 members). The average age of EverQuest players is 26, they are mostly male, and they are primarily students or working in technology-related areas. The average weekly play time of an EverQuest player can be as high as 22 hours per week [14].

The EverQuest UI uses the mouse and keyboard for movement, and to control the view of the 3D world. Transparent windows lie overtop the main view and contain a variety of toolbars and buttons, as well as chat and information windows. The chat input area also serves as a command line interface for entering text commands (see Figs. 2 and 3).

The most important criteria for judging interfaces in EverQuest are the efficiency of communication and the speed and accuracy of command execution. Communication in EverQuest is critical to success – both to maintain strong relationships with others and when in battle to coordinate actions among group members. Almost all communication takes place in chat windows, which requires that there are fast methods for generating communication and simple means for sorting and filtering incoming information from other players or the system itself. There are hundreds of distinct commands in EverQuest. Command execution has to be fast, as the game takes place in real-time, and it must be precise, since executing the wrong command can result in disaster for the entire group.

EverQuest presents a wide variety of roles and tasks, each combination presenting different requirements for communication and command. The roles played by an individual are highly dependent on task, group, and strategy. For example, in a group that is killing a monster, a druid may play the roles of tracker, snarer, damage dealer, evacuator, buffer (beneficial spell caster), healer, or several others, depending on what type of monster is engaged and the other individuals in the group. There are also many other types of tasks aside from killing monsters, with different strategies for accomplishing each, and each requiring a different set of commands and a different communication strategy. This diversity makes the communication and command execution goals impossible to achieve with a single UI.

In Spring of 2002, a completely new user interface architecture was released for EverQuest, designed to meet the customization requirements of the game. This new interface has promoted large scale and widespread customization activity among EverQuest users.

3.1 Methodology

After the release of the new user interface, we followed the evolution of user customization in the game. Our study included two main activities: analysis of the mechanics of the interface that support customization, and observation of discussions of customization on message boards and in-game.

The mechanics of the user interface that support customization were analyzed by inspection. We looked at the system architecture supporting customization, what could be customized while playing, as well as what changes could be made directly with the UI data files. We then examined the actions and the degree of expertise that were required for a user to create or use each of these customizations.

We monitored EverQuest discussions of customization over a one-year period. Information regarding customization was gathered from within and outside the game. In-game, we used a chat logger to record discussions in a general meeting place, and also the conversations between members of a specific guild. Outside of the game, we watched message boards and web sites. By the end of the study, we were monitoring 22 individual web sites with message boards that focused on the EverQuest UI, which contained tens of thousands of messages about customization. These threads were examined by searching for keywords that were used in discussions about customization, as well as by perusing the text.

We also studied the user customizations themselves by downloading examples and installing them. We looked at what types of modifications were made, and judged their effectiveness for the tasks and roles they seemed to be aimed at.

In the next sections, we present a summary of each of these activities, and then discuss why customization has been so successful with EverQuest.

3.2 Customization Capabilities in EverQuest

EverQuest provides several mechanisms for tailoring the user interface. Some customizations can be done in-game, while other more advanced customizations require modifications to the user interface data files.

In-game customizations include organizing the layout and transparency levels of windows, building custom toolbars and buttons, building command and communication macros, and organizing and filtering chat and text information from the game. These types of operations are performed on a regular basis by most users. The operations are highly optimized to be fast and easy to perform.

The interface data is stored as a plain text XML structure and as image files. Individual UI designs are stored in separate directories and different UIs can be loaded in game with the '/load uiname' command. The UI data structure is well documented by the developer and the game ships with a UI developer's manual that describes the UI data structure. Versatile UI modifications can be made by editing the XML and image files directly.

The UI data structure has promoted both end-user customization and trading of components and entire UIs. Users can learn how to make interface modifications to XML files relatively easily. Since the data files for each UI are stored in a separate directory, trading a customized UI is as easy as zipping up a directory, emailing it or posting it somewhere for download, and unzipping it into the correct location on the other user's file system. Trying out the new UI is done with one text command, and switching back to a previous one is similar. Any errors in the UI files result in the default versions of the incorrect components to be installed as well as a clear plain English description of what was wrong. If any of the default user interface files provided by the developer are modified, they are replaced automatically with freshly downloaded copies the next time the game is started. This keeps risk low for both developers and end users who want to try out new UI components.

The XML UI data files provide simple hooks into data sources to enable action triggers. This makes it possible to build new custom UI widgets that change the way that commands are executed and how information is displayed to the user using only XML and images.

3.3 Customization Support in the Community

The EverQuest community is the foundation of the entire game – people cannot play unless they are online, and cannot get far unless they work with others. The community enables customization by creating awareness of the possibilities and benefits of customization, support for other customizers, and user feedback.

The community is made up of many smaller more specialized groups that operate both inside the game using specialized chat channels as well as outside of the game on message boards and web sites. For example, there are third party web sites dedicated to EverQuest guilds, to character classes such as Wizards, and to specific trade skills such as smithing. The presence of these subcommunities has led to specialized discussions and trading of interfaces that are best suited for guild interests, roles of character classes, and tasks at hand.

3.4 Overview of One Year of Customizing

The new UI was deployed in Spring of 2002. It was initially released as a public beta, and anyone could try it out by executing a text command, and switch back to the old interface whenever they wanted to.

The community played two important roles when it was first released: creating and providing tech support. As soon as the new UI was released, there was a buzz in the community that created awareness and enthusiasm, inviting others to try it out. Technical support for the new interface was provided in-game by the critical mass of concurrent users.

Early customization resulted mostly in new looks to interface components. Some were only aesthetic, such as a Darth Vader inventory window or a full interface built on a PDA theme. Others enhanced the graphical appearance with elaborate images that better suited the lore of the game and character classes. Users heard about UI modifications mostly through in game chat and on message boards, and people distributed customizations through email and by posting them to personal web sites. Users tested these appearance-only improvements, and since performance is critical in EverQuest, the ones that did not improve the playability of the game were mostly discarded by the community.

A community of customizers emerged quickly. New forums appeared on message boards aimed at supporting customizers, distribution of customizations, and getting feedback from users. After a few months, a new third party web site was deployed at EQInterface.com with the sole purpose of hosting the UI customization needs of Ever-Quest community. Users could upload their custom interface components, discuss any aspect of customization on message boards, and get feedback about their designs. Users could view other people's customizations organized by category, download the ones they liked, and view and participate in discussions about the submitted designs.

Graphic artists began contributing and exchanging ideas and designs, while performance-oriented users contributed designs that were more geared toward optimizing for roles and tasks. Over time, users began mixing and matching pieces of different customizations, and also adding improvements. Users were doing iterative design, leading to more attractive and more effective interfaces. Designs were also getting more specialized for specific roles and tasks.

One year after the new UI functions were released, hundreds of user designed interface components were available to mix and match. Message boards were full of advice on which user interfaces are best for which tasks and roles, as well as information about how to customize. Most advanced EverQuest players use interface components designed by other users, not by the game developer, and the use of user-developed components is continuing to gain momentum and popularity as they become more refined and as users become more aware of the possibilities.

4   Why Customization Works in EverQuest

Over one year, a vibrant tailoring culture developed within the EverQuest user community. This section describes the factors that have contributed to this success and presents some of our findings.

Awareness through community
The community focus of EverQuest makes people who are even the most casual players aware of the customizability options that are available. Discussions about UIs are

commonly seen in game chat as well as on message boards, which create awareness of possible solutions, and things that are 'neat' or useful. This is identified by Mackay as one of the major triggers that leads to customization [3]. This also helps to break the lack of knowledge barrier [7] by providing information about what can be customized.

Customization is easy

Customizing the UI is easy for users to learn and fast to perform in EverQuest compared to other applications. Some customization tasks are trivial and are accessible in game to even the most basic. For example, building a new macro requires only five operations, and macros can be easily dragged and dropped onto other button palettes (see Fig. 1). These types of simple but powerful user customizations are performed by almost all EverQuest users on a regular basis.

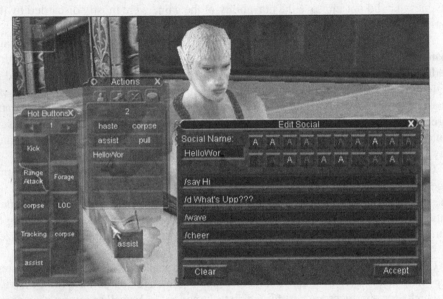

Fig. 1. Everquest's macro builder (right), palettes of customized components (left), and a component stuck to the mouse pointer being dragged to a new location.

To perform more advanced customization, the XML data structures and stored graphics must be modified. Each different UI is stored in its own directory, so users can have many – ones they use on a regular basis, some that are experimental or works in progress, and others that are used on rare occasions for performing specialized tasks like making armor.

Modifying XML requires only a text editor. Filenames mimic the structure of the UI, making it easy to tell which portion of the interface is represented by each of the files. Making a new interface only requires creating a new directory. If any files are not present, the game simply substitutes the default ones, so there is no need for redundancy if some defaults are desired.

To make or swap a new component, a new file with the correct name is added to the new interface directory. A simple approach is to copy another interface component that is close to what is desired, and make small changes until the desired component is achieved. Each of the data fields (e.g., numerical health remaining), their graphical representations (e.g., health bar), and action triggers (e.g., buttons) can be inserted into any component. The XML file controls where subcomponents are positioned, their sizes, and the layout of any custom graphics used in the component. This allows tremendous control over the composition of the interface without any knowledge of programming and with minimal study and effort.

Testing new components is simple – just load the new UI and try it out in-game. It typically takes 5–15 s to load a new UI. If there is an error in the file format, the game responds with a plain English problem description and substitutes components from the default set for the ones containing errors.

Tradable designs

Complete interfaces, as well as their individual components can be exchanged among users by simply putting XML and image files in the right spot on another user's computer. This can be done through any file trading means. Adding a new interface or component to a user's collection is usually as simple as downloading files and unpacking them in the correct spot. Some modifications, however, require a file to be renamed by the user or a portion of a file to be cut and pasted into another file. Even the most complex customizations are still easily tradable.

Trading still takes place by many ad hoc means, but most users are now using EQInterface.com, a web site dedicated to the exchange of interface components. New components can by uploaded to the site, where they are categorized by type of component, evaluated by the site editors, and checked for viruses in files. There are descriptions and images available for each component, which allows people to get an idea of the nature of the customization without needing to try it. Testing a component usually only requires downloading it, unpacking it, and loading the new or modified interface with a single command in game.

One important aspect of tradability is that it allows people to build on the work of others rather than start from scratch. Many of the best interface components available now are not original work, but rather modified work of others. This is because trading allows other users to fix bugs, streamline, or enhance other designs and add them back into the community. The large amount of existing work also reduces effort, as it is often possible to modify an existing component rather than to start from scratch, further breaking the effort barrier.

Low risk

Risk from customization is minimal in EverQuest, which helps to avoid another barrier to customization [3]. The UI has been designed to be resilient to problems in the XML specification, and has been built to recover automatically from errors. The default user interface cannot be destroyed, since defaults are automatically downloaded and replaced each time the game starts. Any time a UI is loaded that contains errors, the default component or entire UI is loaded in its place. Since each UI is stored in a separate directory, changes can be made to one set of files without affecting another.

Loading a new interface is done through a single command – so if a user doesn't like the UI, or it contains a bug, or if they can't figure out how to do something using a new layout, they can quickly revert back to a familiar interface.

Full-time technical support is available from the in-game community if there are any problems encountered when developing or trying interfaces. The critical mass of players within the game usually means that there is someone available who knows the answer to even specialized problems or can give a tip on where to look to find the answer. Additionally, there are message boards dedicated to supporting UI customization that contain help information, and that allow users to post questions.

Security risks from trading and building customizations are low, as EverQuest customizations do not give access to any system resources, but rather just determine how the interface is structured and displayed.

User evaluation

People can learn about which user customizations are the best for their particular situation from other users. People often discuss their UIs in-game through chat and provide recommendations and critiques. Additionally, many forums on message boards are dedicated to discussing UIs, many of which are geared toward specialized roles and tasks. At present, EQInterface alone contains about 15,000 posts discussing user-built UIs, of which about 1,400 posts were dedicated to discussing which UIs are best suited to which classes and roles. Posts on message boards are a rich source of information when shopping for a new UI, as they contain many suggestions and recommendations about what is best suited to supporting specialized needs.

Large workforce

EverQuest has over 650,000 monthly subscribers, with an average weekly play time of up to 22 h. Although a small percentage of users actually develops new interface components, there is still a large workforce of users continuously building and improving components (the programmers and tinkerers [7]). Evidence to support this comes from the many UI components available for download on the web. EQInterface alone contains about 350 complete interfaces and 900 individual components that have been uploaded by users over a nine month period. There are many more scattered around other websites, and more still circulating through email and other ad hoc means. UI developers have posted more than 7000 messages on EQInterface message boards in their developer discussions. It is clear that the workforce of users developing customizations is substantial, and that it has good support for continued development.

The workforce also includes the thousands of users who are testing these customized interfaces through real world use and providing feedback to developers (the workers [7]), as well as the people providing technical support to users (the translators [4]) and to developers, both in-game and on message boards.

Building a custom interface

The widespread success of customization in EverQuest comes from the combination of all of the above factors. We asked people in-game and read messages in discussions about how people got their customized UIs. The most typical process used was to hear about something that is effective or cool, browse some UIs on the web, try a few out, choose one or a couple that seem appropriate, and then customize them further if necessary.

To experience the modification process, we built an interface for the Enchanter class. We started by browsing through Enchanter-oriented UI discussions to see what UIs other Enchanters were using and to see what they looked for in a UI. We found that the most important things that Enchanters require include a wide field of view to facilitate rapid targeting, timers to know when spells will expire, clearer visualizations of spells to reduce errors, and a reduced set of controls for the Enchanter pet, as the pet controls are uncommonly used. We browsed screenshots of interfaces used by other Enchanters then downloaded a few complete sets that looked promising. We selected a complete UI that was closest to meeting our requirements, then started tailoring it in-game to see how much closer we could get by adjusting layout and transparency. The UI we chose did not have timers, so we followed a link we found on a discussion board to obtain a customized set of timers that were built to suit a suggested Enchanter configuration. Next, some of the individual components were replaced by ones that seemed more appropriate that we found on EQInterface.com. Last, we customized some of the components by modifying XML to remove some wasted space and maximize the field of view. The whole process took about two hours. The default UI and our custom UI can be seen in Figs. 2 and 3.

Fig. 2. The default EverQuest UI is not particularly optimized to the specialized needs of the Enchanter class.

Fig. 3. Our customized Enchanter UI mostly uses components developed by other users.

We then posted our interface on a guild message board for other Enchanters to try. We used it in-game and made several small modifications based on our own experiences and the feedback from other users. People using our interface seemed very satisfied with it and have been adding their own customizations to it and exchanging them with other users as well.

5   Discussion

Given the success of customization in EverQuest, it is reasonable to wonder why things have not worked out this way with other types of commercial software. In this section, we look at the case of a canonical office productivity application – Microsoft Word – and consider whether any of the factors described above are missing from that context. We finish with a discussion of what it would take to reproduce the success of EverQuest in other commercial software.

5.1   Comparing with MS Word

At first glance, Word has many of the attributes that appear to be necessary for a tailoring culture. First, Word is a general-purpose system that is used for a variety of more specialized tasks and roles. These different work contexts could certainly benefit from tailoring: for example, legal secretaries might want considerably different layouts, toolbars, and functionality compared to technical writers, or novelists. Second, Word is highly customizable: options, screen layout, toolbar organization, custom toolbars, macros, and templates can all be set or built (albeit usually with more effort than is needed in EverQuest). Third, Word has a huge user community, some of whom are both technically skilled and interested in sharing their expertise with the world. For example a Google search on "Microsoft Word" and "customization" results in more than 28,000 pages.

So what is missing? Why is customization in Word not as common or extensive as it is in EverQuest? Considering the principles identified above, it appears that the problems lie in how customizations are shared among the community.

The first problem is that customizations are not easily packaged. Word stores different types of modifications in different places: templates in a directory, macros inside documents or templates, options in the registry, and custom toolbars in a special file. This means that when someone does put together a highly effective interface, it is difficult to put the various pieces together such that the UI could be transported to someone else's system.

Customizations are also difficult and risky to install. Any potential user of a set of modifications will have considerable difficulty putting all of the pieces in their correct places. Since there is no easy way to back up the current Word setup, there is considerable risk in trying out any customization that might overwrite default behaviour. Even worse, Word macros can contain viruses, which essentially rules out any electronic transfer of macro files.

These problems mean that any sharing of Word modifications – although it does occur – must be done in a very laborious fashion. For example, a useful macro for pasting text into Word without retaining formatting is described on a 'tips and tricks' website [13]. To add this modification, a user must read a six page, 1330-word article, and repeat all of the steps carried out by the original builder of the macro, which takes about 15 min. This stands in sharp contrast to the procedure in Ever-Quest, which would require saving and renaming a file and executing a one-word command.

We believe that these relatively simple technical problems prevent the evolution of a culture of tailoring for Word. Because sharing modifications is difficult, and potentially dangerous, many of the other aspects of tailoring in EverQuest have not happened – such as iterative testing and revision of modifications by others, mixing and matching of modified components, clearinghouses for modifications, or discussions of tailoring.

5.2 Generalizing to Other Applications

The problems seen in Word suggest that a number of different pieces all need to be in place to support the transmission of customizations from tailor through to end user. We believe that tradability and sharing are the keys to the growth of a tailoring culture – and this is a change from what was identified in earlier research on customization. For example, simplicity in packaging and installing modifications appears to be more important than the ease of creating modifications in the first place, which was earlier identified as a serious barrier to customization. It appears that if the user community is large enough, there will always be people who are willing to build the customizations for others to use, even if building those modifications is difficult.

Some aspects of sharing already exist in most user communities – as can be seen in the web pages and discussion groups that exist for many commercial applications. However, some of the critical elements that allow trading of customizations are controlled by the software company. In EverQuest for example, improvements to packaging and installing were realized with the cooperation of the software company itself. The degree to which tailoring will succeed is certainly affected by the amount of interest shown by the builder of the system, although we are currently investigating whether some of these issues can be addressed with add-on tools that handle customization problems without the involvement of the software company.

6   Conclusion

Our study of user customization in EverQuest has revealed what led to the emergence of a large scale tailoring culture. Making components easy to trade and low risk to try were found to be of prime importance. A critical mass of community oriented users is also necessary for creating awareness of what is possible and to supply a large user-based workforce of component builders, testers, and technical support personnel. We believe that the approaches that led to success in EverQuest provide insight on how to enable tailoring cultures in other mainstream applications.

References

1. Grudin, J., Barnard, P.: When does an abbreviation become a word? and related questions. In: Proceedings of ACM CHI 1985, pp. 121–125 (1985)
2. Gantt, M., Nardi, B.: Gardeners and gurus: patterns of cooperation among CAD users. In: Proceedings of ACM CHI 1992, pp. 107–117 (1992)
3. Mackay, W.: Triggers and barriers to customizing software. In: Proceedings of ACM CHI 1991, pp. 153–160 (1991)
4. Mackay, W.: Patterns of sharing customizable software. In: Proceedings of ACM CSCW 1990, pp. 209–221 (1990)
5. Morch, A.: Three levels of end-user tailoring: customization, integration, and extension. In: Kyng, M., Mathiassen, L. (eds.) Computers and Design in Context, pp. 51–76. MIT Press, Cambridge (1997)
6. Page, S., Johnsgard, R., Albert, U., Allen, C.: User customization of a word processor. In: Proceedings of ACM CHI 1996, pp. 340–346 (1996)
7. MacLean, A., Carter, K., Lovstrand, L., Moran, T.: User-tailorable systems: pressing the issues with buttons. In: Proceedings of ACM CHI 1990, pp. 175–182 (1990)
8. Malone, T., Lai, K., Fry, C.: Experiments with oval: a radically tailorable tool for cooperative work. In: Proceedings of ACM CSCW 1992, pp. 289–297 (1992)
9. Resnick, P., Iacovou, N., Suchak, M., Bergstrom, P., Reidl, J.: GroupLens: an open architecture for collaborative filtering of Netnews. In: Proceedings of ACM CSCW 1994, pp. 175–186 (1994)
10. Sony Entertainment: EverQuest Web Site (2003). www.everquest.com. Accessed Sept 2003

11. Trigg, R., Bodker, S.: From implementation to design: tailoring and the emergence of systematization in CSCW. In: Proceedings of ACM CSCW 1994, pp. 45–54 (1994)
12. Trigg, R., Moran, T., Halasz, F.: Adaptability and tailorability in NoteCards. In: Proceedings of IFIP INTERACT 1987, pp. 723–728 (1987)
13. Tyson, H.: Paste Special Unformatted Text at Your Fingertips (2003). pubs.logicalexpressions.com/Pub0009/LPMArticle.asp?ID=128. Accessed Sept 2003
14. Yee, N.: Terra Incognita Web Site (2003). www.nickyee.com. Accessed Sept 2003

Analysis of Multidisciplinary Collaboration in Primary Healthcare: The Chilean Case

Cecilia Saint-Pierre[✉], Valeria Herskovic, and Marcos Sepúlveda

Department of Computer Science, Pontificia Universidad Católica de Chile,
Santiago, Chile
{csaintpierre,vherskovic}@uc.cl, marcos@ing.puc.cl

Abstract. Around 10% of the population suffers from diabetes, and this percentage is expected to rise. Healthcare guidelines propose a multidisciplinary, collaborative approach for treatment. However, there is little data to understand whether healthcare professionals are actually collaborating and how this collaboration takes place. We analyzed 4 years of data from 3 healthcare centers in Chile, corresponding to 2,838 patients. Patients were classified according to the composition of the healthcare team into four categories: highly multidisciplinary teams, specialized teams, physician-nurse centered teams, and non-collaborative treatment. Our results show that team prevalence is related to patient and healthcare center characteristics.

Keywords: Collaboration · Multidisciplinary · Primary care · Diabetes

1 Introduction

Globally, around 415 million people suffer from diabetes and this number is expected to rise beyond 642 million by 2040 [1]. In Chile, the percentage of diabetes patients for 2015 was estimated to be between 10 and 12% [1, 2]. Only 36% of patients with diabetes in Chile maintain good metabolic control (defined as HbA1c < 7%) [3]. Previous research posits that good diabetes outcomes require well-integrated multidisciplinary care [4]. The Chilean Ministry of Health guidelines also establish a multidisciplinary approach, based on a family health model, with periodic checkups [3]. In primary care, diabetes treatment teams usually consist of a physician/general practitioner (GP), diabetes nurses, dietitians, and in some cases, counsellors, psychologists, and pharmacists [5]. Medical specialists are included based on patient needs, e.g. endocrinologists, ophthalmologists, cardiologists, nephrologists, diabetic foot specialists [6], and in cases with mental health comorbidities, psychiatric consultants [7].

Collaborative, multidisciplinary primary healthcare teams may be classified into four types: (i) *Physician-nurse-pharmacist triad*, working with other primary care professionals in patients with several comorbidities and multiple medicines, (ii) *Highly multidisciplinary teams*, composed of a doctor-nurse duo that works with other medical and complementary disciplines, e.g. medical coordinator, podiatrist, midwife, diabetes educator, or counselor, (iii) *Specialized teams*, where a GP - specialist physician duo treat, with support of one or more primary care disciplines, patients that require specialist assistance for less common comorbidities, and (iv) *Physician-Nurse centered*

© Springer International Publishing AG 2017
C. Gutwin et al. (Eds.): CRIWG 2017, LNCS 10391, pp. 244–251, 2017.
DOI: 10.1007/978-3-319-63874-4_18

teams, in which care is provided by small teams based on a doctor-nurse duo, with participation from primary care disciplines for treatment of cases with few complications or comorbidities [8]. The aim of this paper is to analyze whether these teams can be found through data analysis, to analyze their characteristics, and to discover whether primary healthcare professionals in Chile are carrying out collaboration. This paper is organized as follows. First, we discuss related work. Then, we present methods, the results of the comparative analysis and a discussion section. Finally, we close with our conclusions and possible avenues of future work.

2 Related Work

Previous studies present collaboration as an effective treatment strategy for diabetes [9], with several team structures and collaborative practices [7, 10], but there are few comparisons between different team structures for similar settings in the literature.

On the analysis of team structure, some articles refer to specific roles, such as care coordinator or leader [9, 10], and to specific disciplines within a team, such as nurses as team leaders [11], or the incorporation of pharmacists [12]. A qualitative study defined a compositional typology for healthcare teams, specifying four types of teams based on stability/variability of roles and personnel in the team [13]. A literature review focused on nurses organized team structure in five types of interprofessional care models: Interprofessional team, Nurse-led, Case management, Patient navigation and Shared care [11]. Another review analyzed 51 interventions and grouped multidisciplinary collaboration by structure, process and outcomes [14]. By structure, they considered whether there was a primary care physician in the team or not, the number of disciplines, the patient population and the sectors included. Although the authors in this case describe team composition, they do not classify cases in terms of different compositions.

The review on which we base the present study included 109 papers describing collaborative treatments in primary care [8]. This study described collaboration in terms of team structure and proposed four collaboration categories (physician-nurse-pharmacist triad, highly multidisciplinary, specialized, and physician-nurse centered teams).

3 Methods

We obtained data from three primary healthcare centers, operated by the University the researchers belong to. We obtained an anonymized database log, containing 15 years of data (2002–2016), corresponding to 13,501 patients under cardiovascular disease treatment. We selected patients with Type 2 Diabetes Mellitus (DM2) diagnosis, an electronic medical record between May 2012 and November 2016, at least two measurements of HbA1c, and at least one appointment at the healthcare center (so they were not occasional patients). This left us with a population of 2,838 patients.

Patients were classified according to the disciplines involved in their treatment. First, we set out to find the four types of primary healthcare teams described in [8]. Since in the analyzed centers there were no pharmacists, the physician-nurse-pharmacist triad was not present in our data. However, the other types of teams were found: highly multi-disciplinary (849 patients), specialized (319 patients), physician-nurse centered (1581 patients), and we also found a fourth non-collaborative type (which naturally had not been discussed in [8]), with only one discipline during the time window (89 patients).

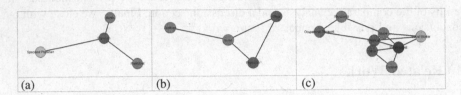

Fig. 1. Example collaborative structure of a (a) specialized team, (b) physician-nurse centered team, and (c) multidisciplinary team

Classification of the patients into each category was done by evaluating team composition as follows. Cases with only one professional were classified as non-collaborative. Specialized teams were cases where there was a family physician and a specialist, and in total, no more than 4 disciplines (Fig. 1a). Cases with up to 4 disciplines with no specialist, and cases with 5 disciplines and no specialists or complementary disciplines were classified as physician-nurse centered (Fig. 1b). Finally, cases with 5 disciplines that did not belong to the previous categories, and those with 6 or more disciplines were classified as highly multidisciplinary (Fig. 1c). The disciplines in the data were: family physician, nurse, social worker, dietician, occupational therapist, physiologist, psychologist, specialist, and other complementary disciplines.

Table 1. Percentage of the cases where the discipline is present for each team type

Team type	Family physician	Nurse	Social Worker	Dietician	Occupational therapist	Physiologist	Psychologist	Specialist physician	Other	Disciplines (mean)
Highly multidisciplinary	100%	100%	41%	88%	3%	42%	23%	64%	92%	5, 5
Specialized	100%	89%	5%	37%	0%	3%	1%	100%	33%	3, 7
Physician-nurse centered	100%	92%	9%	55%	0%	8%	3%	0%	48%	3, 1
Non-collaborative	87%	10%	0%	1%	0%	0%	0%	0%	2%	1, 0
Total	99%	92%	18%	61%	1%	17%	9%	30%	58%	3, 9

The number of disciplines present in each case was, on average, 3.9. Averages by team type varied according to their definition, from 5.5 in highly multidisciplinary teams, to 1 in the non-collaborative cases. Percentage of patients in which each discipline was present for each team type is presented in Table 1.

We tested independence for categorical variables with Pearson's Chi-squared test, and in case the null hypothesis was rejected, a test of proportions to establish the significance of the differences. In cases of numerical variables, we used the Shapiro–Wilk test to test whether population is normally distributed. When it was not, we used the Kruskal-Wallis test and we used ANOVA otherwise.

4 Results

4.1 Demographic Analysis

The team types treat different proportions of men and women. Gender and team type are dependent variables (p-value $\ll$ 0.01) and the different proportions are statistically significant (p-value $\ll$ 0.01). Table 2 displays the number, percentage, and normalized percentages (if there were an equal number of men and women) per team type. Highly multidisciplinary teams treat 37% of women and only 19% of men, while physician-nurse centered teams more often treat men than women. Non-collaborative treatment, although infrequent, is more likely for men (5%) than women (2%). Average age for the entire population was 62.2, with no statistically significant differences among team types (p-value = 0.071).

Table 2. Gender vs. team type

Team type	F (n -%)	M (n -%)	Normalized F (%)	Normalized M (%)	Total
Highly multidisciplinary	620 (37%)	229 (19%)	65.8%	34.2%	100%
Specialized	145 (9%)	174 (15%)	37.4%	62.6%	100%
Physician-nurse centered	857 (52%)	724 (61%)	45.8%	54.2%	100%
Non-collaborative	35 (2%)	54 (5%)	31.3%	68.7%	100%
Total	1657 (100%)	1181 (100%)	58%	42%	100%

4.2 Analysis by Healthcare Center

We compared how the 4 types of teams are present in each of the 3 centers. There is a clear dependence between healthcare center and team types (p-value $\ll$ 0.01), with statistically significant differences for the types of collaboration within each center (p-value $\ll$ 0.01), except for the non-collaborative cases that are similar for all centers.

As shown in Fig. 2, the biggest difference is in Center 1, in which physician-nurse centered teams are present in only 32% of cases, compared to 66% and 67% in the other centers. On the other hand, in this same center, highly multidisciplinary teams treat 46% of the patients, versus 20 and 25% in the other cases.

4.3 Years Living with DM2

On average, the patients in the dataset have been living with DM2 for 6.3 years (SD = 3.6). Patients that are treated non-collaboratively have been living with DM2 for fewer years, while patients who have longer disease spans require more specialized care (Table 3) All differences are statistically significant (p-value $\ll$ 0.01).

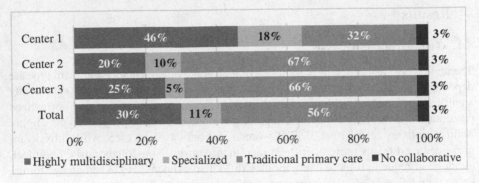

Fig. 2. Presence of collaboration types in each healthcare center.

Table 3. Years living with DM2, from diagnosis until the end of time window

Team type	Years living with DM2 (mean/σ)
Highly multidisciplinary	6, 7 (3, 5)
Specialized	6, 9 (3, 6)
Physician-nurse centered	6, 1 (3, 6)
No collaborative	4, 4 (3, 8)
Total	6, 3 (3, 6)

4.4 Severity and Comorbidity

Diabetes severity was assessed by assigning a score (0 to 2) on presence and severity of 7 categories of complications: cardiovascular, nephropathy, retinopathy, peripheral vascular disease, stroke, neuropathy and metabolic disorder [15]. For comorbidity, we used the Charlson index, which considers those comorbidities that increase mortality risk [16]. The index assigns a score (0 or 1) to the presence of pathologies grouped into 6 categories: cancer, gastrointestinal, skeletal muscle, pulmonary, mental and substance abuse. The averages of both indices are presented in Table 4. As we are working with data from primary care patients, the indices take low values. Highly disciplinary teams treat patients with greater complexity, while specialized and physician-nurse centered groups treat patients with an average comorbidity.

Table 4. Average of comorbidity index and severity index in patients by type of collaboration

Team type	Charlson comorbidity index (mean)	Diabetes complication severity index (mean)
Highly multidisciplinary	1.5	1.2
Specialized	1.1	1.1
Physician-nurse centered	1.1	0.7
Non-collaborative	0.8	0.4
Total	1.2	0.9

4.5   Number of Appointments

We define the *core team* as a subset of the team, considering only the three main disciplines present in DM2 treatment in Chilean healthcare centers: family physician, nurse and nutritionist. The follow-up protocol establishes that patients should have visits with these three professionals, regardless of their state of health. Table presents the number of patient visits per year for the core team and the whole team. Both variables presented statistically significant differences (p-value $\ll$ 0.01) (Table 5).

Table 5. Number of patient visits with the core team/whole team according to team type

Team type	Core team visits/year (mean)	Whole team visits/year (mean)
Highly multidisciplinary	10.9	14.8
Specialized	7.2	8.2
Physician-nurse centered	6.2	7.3
No collaborative	2.4	2.4
Total	7.6	9.5

The analysis shows that in patients treated by highly multidisciplinary teams, the number of visits per year is significantly higher in both cases. Given that specialized teams consider the participation of a secondary care specialist in 100% of cases, that extra attention is associated with this treatment characteristic.

Table 6. Average of physician visits and number of different physicians/year

Team Type	Physician visits/year	Number of different physicians/year
Highly multidisciplinary	6.9	2.7
Specialized	4.5	2.2
Physician-nurse centered	3.7	1.8
No collaborative	2.2	1.4
Total	4.7	2.1

More than 99% of patients have physician visits, regardless of team type; however, the number of visits per year is different (Table 6). The number of physicians is correlated with the number of physician visits (r = 0.73), but causality is not clear.

5   Discussion

Analysis using data from healthcare centers found that the collaborative team types described theoretically in [8] are actually found in practice. We found that in some cases, treatments were not collaborative at all, against diabetes clinical guidelines.

Treatment team size and composition is partially determined by the needs of the patients [17], which explains to a large extent the differences among teams. However, as is well known, other factors (e.g. team cohesion, culture, history) impact collaboration, so we found that, even with a similar population of patients, different healthcare centers employed different collaboration styles. Patient characteristics also may affect team collaboration. For example, diabetes-related comorbidities such as obesity are more frequent in women than men [18], which may explain that more women are treated by highly interdisciplinary teams, since they require additional treatment. Also, the lower participation of women in the workforce [19] may explain a higher availability to participate in more complex treatment, with a higher number of healthcare appointments. The number of visits in highly multidisciplinary teams is significantly more than in the other groups. Again, this corroborates that highly multidisciplinary teams not only have more disciplines, but also that they possibly treat patients of higher complexity, that require more hours of dedication.

The number of visits provided by professionals is similar in all groups. This can be explained by the high turnover of professionals in the centers. In the other groups, physician participation in the total care is also around 60%, with exception of the non-cooperative group who is 94%. The latter is reasonable because for diabetic patients dealing with just one professional, it is most likely to be with the physician.

6 Conclusion

This paper presented an analysis of collaboration styles in primary healthcare, for the treatment of diabetes mellitus type 2. We used 4 years of data from 3 healthcare centers, finding empirical evidence of the types of teams that have been described qualitatively in the literature. We also found particular characteristics of each team, describing e.g. the gender, comorbidity and severity, and how they are related to each team type. Future work will evaluate how collaboration affects patient outcomes, as well as recruiting patients and healthcare professionals to conduct qualitative analysis of how teams work and how patients interact with these teams.

Acknowledgements. This paper was partially funded by CONICYT-PCHA/Doctorado Nacional/2016-21161705 and CONICYT-FONDECYT/1150365 (Chile). We would like to thank Áncora UC Primary healthcare centers for their help with this research.

References

1. International Diabetes Federation: IDF Diabetes Atlas, 7th edn. (2015). doi:10.1289/image. ehp.v119.i03
2. Ministerio de Salud de Chile: Encuesta Nacional de Salud. Chile 2009–2010 (2013). http:// web.minsal.cl/portal/url/item/bcb03d7bc28b64dfe040010165012d23.pdf. Accessed June 2017
3. Subsecretaria de Redes Asistenciales, Guía clínica: Diabetes mellitus tipo 2, Ministerio de Salud de Chile (2010)

4. Maneze, D., Dennis, S., Chen, H.Y., Taggart, J., Vagholkar, S., Bunker, J., Liaw, S.T.: Multidisciplinary care: experience of patients with complex needs. Aust. J. Prim. Health. **20**, 20–26 (2014). doi:10.1071/PY12072
5. Wigert, H., Wikström, E.: Organizing person-centred care in paediatric diabetes: multidisciplinary teams, long-term relationships and adequate documentation. BMC Res. Notes **7**, 72 (2014). doi:10.1186/1756-0500-7-72
6. Campmans-Kuijpers, M.J., Baan, C.A., Lemmens, L.C., Rutten, G.E.: Change in quality management in diabetes care groups and outpatient clinics after feedback and tailored support. Diabetes Care **38**, 285–292 (2015). doi:10.2337/dc14-1860
7. Chwastiak, L.A., Jackson, S.L., Russo, J., DeKeyser, P., Kiefer, M., Belyeu, B., Mertens, K., Chew, L., Lin, E.: A collaborative care team to integrate behavioral health care and treatment of poorly-controlled type 2 diabetes in an urban safety net primary care clinic. Gen. Hosp. Psychiatry **44**, 10–15 (2017). doi:10.1016/j.genhosppsych.2016.10.005
8. Saint-Pierre, C., Herskovic, V., Sepúlveda, M.: Multidisciplinary Collaboration in Primary Care: a Systematic Review, Under Review (2017)
9. Ackroyd, S.A., Wexler, D.J.: Effectiveness of diabetes interventions in the patient-centered medical home. Curr. Diab. Rep. **14**, 1–16 (2014). doi:10.1007/s11892-013-0471-z
10. Lynch, C.S., Wajnberg, A., Jervis, R., Basso-Lipani, M., Bernstein, S., Colgan, C., Soriano, T., Federman, A.D., Kripalani, S.: Implementation science workshop: a novel multidisciplinary primary care program to improve care and outcomes for super-utilizers. J. Gen. Intern. Med. **31**, 797–802 (2016). doi:10.1007/s11606-016-3598-1
11. Virani, T.: Interprofessional Collaborative Teams. Canadian Health Services Research Foundation (2012)
12. Cohen, L.B., Taveira, T.H., Khatana, S.A.M., Dooley, A.G., Pirraglia, P.A., Wu, W.-C.: Pharmacist-led shared medical appointments for multiple cardiovascular risk reduction in patients with type 2 diabetes. Diabetes Educ. **37**, 801–812 (2011). doi:10.1177/0145721711423980
13. Andreatta, P.B.: A typology for health care teams. Health Care Manage. Rev. **35**, 345–354 (2010). doi:10.1097/HMR.0b013e3181e9fceb
14. Schepman, S., Hansen, J., de Putter, I.D., Batenburg, R.S., de Bakker, D.H.: The common characteristics and outcomes of multidisciplinary collaboration in primary health care: a systematic literature review. Int. J. Integr. Care. **15**(2) (2015). doi:10.5334/ijic.1359
15. Glasheen, W.P., Renda, A., Dong, Y.: Diabetes Complications Severity Index (DCSI)— update and ICD-10 translation. J. Diabetes Complications (2017). doi:10.1016/j.jdiacomp.2017.02.018
16. Sundararajan, V., Henderson, T., Perry, C., Muggivan, A., Quan, H., Ghali, W.A.: New ICD-10 version of the Charlson comorbidity index predicted in-hospital mortality. J. Clin. Epidemiol. **57**, 1288–1294 (2004). doi:10.1016/j.jclinepi.2004.03.012
17. Sevin, C., Moore, G., Shepherd, J., Jacobs, T., Hupke, C.: Transforming care teams to provide the best possible patient-centered, collaborative care. J. Ambul. Care Manage. **32**, 24–31 (2009). doi:10.1097/01.JAC.0000343121.07844.e0
18. Sandína, M., Espeltb, A., Escolar-Pujolarc, A., Arriolad, L., Larrañaga, I.: Desigualdades de género y diabetes mellitus tipo 2: la importancia de la diferencia. Avanc. En Diab. **30**, 1 (2011)
19. Instituto Nacional de Estadísticas, Enfoque Estadístico, Género y Empleo (2016).http://historico.ine.cl/genero/files/estadisticas/pdf/documentos/enfoque-estadistico-genero-y-empleo.pdf. Accessed June 2017

Exploring Collaboration in the Realm of Virtual Museums

Nelson Baloian[1]([✉]), Wolfram Luther[2], Daniel Biella[2], Nare Karapetyan[3],
José A. Pino[1], Tobias Schreck[4], Andres Ferrada[1], and Nancy Hitschfeld[1]

[1] Department of Computer Science, Universidad de Chile, Santiago, Chile
{nbaloian,jpino,nancy}@dcc.uchile.cl
[2] University of Duisburg-Essen, Duisburg, Germany
{wolfram.luther,daniel.biella}@uni-due.de
[3] American University of Armenia, Yerevan, Armenia
nkarapetyan@aua.am
[4] Graz University of Technology, Graz, Austria
tobias.schreck@cgv.tugraz.at

Abstract. Virtual museums have been very popular since the early days of the
World Wide Web and many scientific works have been published on this topic.
Although the rich variety of possibilities for supporting collaboration among the
users of virtual museums, today very few implementations offer support for such
kind of activities. This paper aims at settling the value of collaboration in virtual
museums by means of depicting and classifying collaborative organization and
co-curation activities in establishing, designing, planning, realizing, operating,
deploying and visiting a virtual exhibition applying action research. As a use case,
we present ongoing work to realize a virtual museum devoted to Armenian cross
stones (Khachkars).

Keywords: Virtual museums · Taxonomy of collaborative activities

1 Introduction

A virtual museum VM is a software artifact that presents a reconstruction of physical
museums or parts of them; it displays digital reconstructions or born digital art in an
exhibition, room and museum setting. Hazan et al. [4] define a VM as "a communication
product accessible by a public, focused on tangible or intangible heritage. It uses various
forms of interactivity and immersion, for the purpose of education, research, enjoyment,
and enhancement of visitor experience. VMs may be typically but not exclusively
denoted as electronic when they could be called online museums, hyper museum, digital
museum, cyber museums or Web museums".

The realization of a VM goes on in several stages: Establishing, designing,
constructing, running, and operating a VM within its lifespan. Different skills are needed
from people working on these various stages; even for one stage, several persons may
be related to it. Main roles are curators, software engineers, instructors, architects,
experts, sponsors/authorities, and visitors; the latter ones may be museum enthusiasts,
special user groups, tourists, students, etc.

© Springer International Publishing AG 2017
C. Gutwin et al. (Eds.): CRIWG 2017, LNCS 10391, pp. 252–259, 2017.
DOI: 10.1007/978-3-319-63874-4_19

Collaboration in virtual museums has not been explored as much as it should, despite the various interesting possibilities which were highlighted in [1] already in the year 2001. Therefore, in this work, we would like to focus on collaboration possibilities involving stakeholders with different roles in the process of creation, administration and visiting a virtual museum.

2 Collaboration in a Virtual Museum

We focus on interdisciplinary collaboration; no contribution to collaboration inside groups is intended. The stakeholders concerned in the collaborative co-curation process encompass the coordination of group building, task allocation, motivation of team members, communication in the context of collaborative evaluation and testing, knowledge generation and problem solving via information processing in the creating and visiting process of virtual exhibitions.

Group members are often distributed across a wide area; they constitute a multidisciplinary, multi-professional team. Individuals have various motivations and goals when working together. Co-curation within the generation process is paired with collaboration during a visit to an exhibition. Sacher et al. [7] explain: "The generated data from collaboration can range from visitor's annotations or comments regarding specific exhibits up to complete exhibit models and room (re-)designs created in a virtual environment. … Collaboration (in virtual environments) is implemented as users being co-located in the VM, which enables information exchange and awareness of user actions via face-to-face communication." Recently, a new metadata standard and new modeling language for virtual museums, the VM and Cultural Object Exchange Format (ViMCOX) has been developed in order to provide a semantic structure for exhibits and complete museums [8]. It combines community contributions to administrative and descriptive metadata with technical and use metadata provided by the institution operating the museum. This partition implies the following classification:

- Level 1: Organizational collaboration
- Level 2: Descriptive process-related collaboration, i.e. co-curation

Level 1: Communication about the nature of the problem (classification, identifying and describing the problem solving approach, depicting the process workflow: hierarchical description and generative metadata-based process modeling, call for crowdsourcing). Coordination: team composition (team description & parameter selection, e.g., team size and structure, task distribution, crowd participation, motivation, remuneration), evaluation planning, etc. [5].

Level 2: Co-curation activities: Exhibition space design (designing VM, expositions – spatial, metaphoric design, software tools, metadata acquisition, tour planning, interaction design), information processing (created, used, modified), communication/interaction (various forms of communication and interaction between group members as well as persons and items during the whole collaborative co-curation process – formal description, mode, technical parameters like frequency, quantity, reliability, intent [10]).

The collaborative work of promoters, curators, and intended users mainly concerns communication and coordination on level one including motivation, aim, need, team building and further administrative tasks. Sacher [8] suggests the use of a conception matrix linking issues, curators and other groups like team building & experts; room design, installation & architects, software engineers; themes & sponsors; presentation goals & museums' enthusiasts; administrative tasks & experts. Activities are in detail:

- Thematic classification, content conception, motivation, need.
- Team building.
- Reviewing old exhibitions.
- General design consideration – participatory design.
- Artwork selection and maintenance throughout its lifecycle (incl. metadata).
- Gathering of spatial constraints.
- Administrative tasks: financing, regulations, rights, insurances.
- Monitoring the museum narrative, conflict management and tool support.

2.1 Designing and Planning the Virtual Museum

In level two as defined above, the major challenges in the collaborative work process faced by curators and software engineers are collaborative problem solving and information processing. This includes the creation of sketches, drawings, mind maps, storyboards, plans and models with respect to the following issues:

- **creation of exhibition space designs** and **digitization/selection of exhibit:** it involves the crafting or selecting of room models, buildings and outdoor areas as well as their connectors,
- **import** of metadata instances, **collection** and **positioning** of artifacts, interactive/ animated exhibits, content and information,
- **floor planning and tasks layout, metaphorical design:** ground plan, lighting, wall layout, guiding visitors, i.e. navigation aids. Spatial parameters and architecture can influence content and form of the digitized content, thus re-scaling may be necessary,
- **presentation, publication and dissemination:** virtual exhibition/museum (local/ web), selection of widgets and input/output peripherals, HUD (minimap), monitor, projector, keyboard, touch, gamepad or other VR devices. Preview on-the-fly utilizing various navigation modes and avatar sizes, exhibition catalog, archiving construction plan, archiving user behavior.

To support metadata-based content construction, in our application example of a Khachkar museum we have to build a XML-formatted list of Khachkars with the following metadata: Name/item, century, master, style, ornaments at the bottom, back side, text, motif, size, purpose for erection, first location/monastery, actual location, function, surrounding, stone parameters, source, etc.

Among the many tools for collaborative software development there is *gitlab* [9], which integrates a complete workflow from writing down an idea, issue tracking, commenting, planning, code managing, documentation to testing, reviewing, deployment and feedback management. Tools like issue trackers, wikis, distributed software repositories with version control, continuous software integration servers, and deployment engines have already existed before but gitlab makes all of these accessible in a single web-based platform.

Gitlab's features are not limited to software development but can also be used for the configuration management. The built-in user management allows the assignment of curators and software developers to the roles they need to plan, design, code, and evaluate a VM in a distributed and collaborative environment.

2.2 Constructing the Virtual Museum

This stage concerns the following tasks for software engineers, curators, the crowd, museum enthusiasts and experts in the context of co-curation in galleries, libraries, archives and museums (GLAM) with the aim of using the inspiration/expertise of non-professional curators to create exhibitions:

- Digital 2D/3D model creation: Digitization and reconstruction of Armenian Khachkars mainly done by students and anonymous collaborators in a crowdsourcing modality, collection of metadata, artwork description and classification respecting the ViMCOX standard with the aid of experts.
- Design of artwork settings: Placement in appropriate surroundings with respect to typical arrangements.
- Web-based interface for checking and transferring artworks, metadata and rights.
- Various presentation modes using WIMP or post WIMP interaction devices.
- Attendant evaluation and requirement validation during the whole workflow.

2.3 Operating the Virtual Museum

This stage encompasses contributions by various user groups, engaged visitors, instructors, and the use of reconstruction software and collaborative tools: Tour selection, construction and publication, metadata-based artwork linking, knowledge creation (affecting creator, époque, original-replica discussion, style, material, dedication, inscription etc.), interactive artifact (de)construction, storytelling, collaborative scenarios with shared workspaces.

- **Commenting, improving and publishing** (e-guest book opportunity, evaluating visitor's annotations or comments regarding specific exhibits, exhibit models manipulation or completion, considering room (re-)designs elaborated in a virtual environment, publishing individual tours and preferential artwork [2].
- **Navigation and interaction** (proposing, tours, points of interest, interacting with artifacts, changing their geometry, scaling, translation, rotation or changing the internal structure).
- **Institutional collaboration** utilizing standardized metadata from other museums or experts as well as social media integration.
- **Technological progress** in VM generation, new presentation forms, museum instances operated by multiple users and attendant evaluation should contribute to a virtual museum lifecycle in the long term.

3 A Collaborative Virtual Khachkar Museum

As stated in the first section, we began this long-term research with an action research approach. For this purpose we have already developed an application which implements virtual 3D environment in which curators can set up Khachkars exhibitions in a collaborative way and visitors can explore them interacting in various ways with the curators and other visitors. The application was developed using the Unity framework, originally intended for developing 3D collaborative games. It was chosen given its versatility to include various types of 3D models, the way it allows users to navigate and interact with the created environments (including multi-user features) and the fact that the created application can be exported to web format.

Before developing the actual application we had to build a library of Khachkars which would be available for curators in order to create their expositions. For the first stage of the work we selected about 80 stones according to this criterion: they must be easily reached, there is some interesting data available about them, and they should be of various styles, ages and regions. We used mainly two different methods: the first one was a lightweight approach, in which photographs are taken from the front, back, two lateral sides and from above. Then a graphic model is created "by hand". The second is taking a set of photographs covering a 360 degrees view and reconstructing the 3D view using online services like MeshLab.

In order to add a stone to the application's library, metadata should be provided according to the description in Sect. 2.1. There is also the possibility to add text to explain some particular characteristic of the stone. All this information will be used by the application and shown to curators and visitors by request. A ground perspective of this work is that the addition of new Khachkars to the library remains open to additions during the museum's lifecycle using a crowdsourcing modality.

A new exposition is created by entering the name and a short description about what is intended to show with it. Then a main menu lets curators choose the scenario where the exposition will be deployed. Currently there are five options: a countryside, which has two variants, with or without a church on the background, a wall with niches where the stones can be put, an alley and on a rocky mountainside. These are the most typical settings in which Khachkars can be found in the real world (Fig. 1).

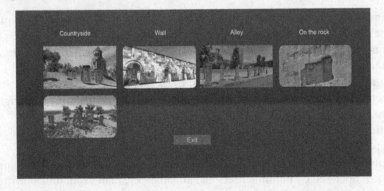

Fig. 1. Access to Khachkar formations and arrangements

Then, a collaborative workspace is accessed in which the chosen scenario is shown without any stone. At the left hand side there appears a scrollable menu with all the available stones which have been previously digitized and included in the Khachkars library of the application (Fig. 2).

Fig. 2. Curators' collaborative environment

Curators can place a stone in the chosen scenario by dragging it from the icons menu and dropping it on the chosen scenario. They can also re-arrange the original setting by rotating and moving the stones. Various awareness elements have been incorporated into this workspace to support the collaborative work among co-curators. One of them is the set of icons representing each one of them, which is surrounded by a frame of a particular distinctive color. When one curator is working with a particular stone on the scenario (e.g., by moving it) this is highlighted with the color associated to the curator's icon.

The most basic interaction for visitors to the exposition is by clicking on each stone and seeing its metadata. A more elaborated interaction with the application is the implementation of suggested "viewpoints" which can be used indistinctively by visitors and curators. Navigation in 3D environments can sometimes be difficult, especially for beginners, and they may miss some interesting characteristics of the exhibition. In order to help visitors not to miss a certain important view of the exposition curators can include points of view in it, by saving a certain location and view orientation in the scene. These points of view will be shown as avatars in the form of human silhouettes when a person visits the exhibit (Fig. 3).

Clicking on an avatar, the visitor's view will be "teleported" to that location. Each "viewpoint" has a blog associated in which the author can explain the reason for visiting it and visitors can leave comments and feedbacks.

Fig. 3. A scene with viewpoints shown as human silhouettes

Based on experiences in former projects [6, 7], we will make an evaluation concerning establishment, design, and system realization. This evaluation will take into account the viewpoints of all relevant stakeholders [11].

4 Conclusions

Collaboration is fundamental to ensure quality and limit costs in building and operating virtual museums. This paper proposes a two-tier classification of collaborative group activities framing the creation process and use of virtual exhibitions. It highlights a new interdisciplinary project devoted to the realization of a virtual Khachkar museum. The paper also presents a preliminary development of a virtual museum which implements most of the activities mentioned in this classification. This implementation will allow us to conduct further research about the way stakeholders of a virtual museum would benefit from cooperating inside the environment by introducing this tool in the community. For this purpose, we have already made the relevant contacts with experts in the area of Armenian ancient architecture and art, including Khachkars, and we have their commitment to support the testing. Further work should examine intergroup and intra-group collaboration, the automatized co-curation and GLAM as special form of crowdsourcing, create a worldwide motivating and remuneration concept, and address the question of how we could measure and rate collaboration with respect to the various quoted forms [3].

References

1. Barbieri, T., Paolini, P.: Cooperation metaphors for virtual museums. In: Museums and the Web 2001, pp. 115–126. Archives & Museum Informatics, Pittsburgh (2001)

2. Biella, D., Pilz, T., Sacher, D., Weyers, B., Luther, W., Baloian, N., Schreck, T.: Crowdsourcing and co-curation in virtual museums: a practice-driven approach. J. Univers. Comput. Sci. **22**(10), 1277–1297 (2016)
3. Chounta, I.-A., Avouris, N.: Towards a time series approach for the classification and evaluation of collaborative activities. Comput. Inform. **34**, 588–614 (2015)
4. Hazan et al.: (2014). http://www.v-must.net/virtual-museums/what-virtual-museum
5. Ostergaard, K.J., Summers, J.D.: Development of a systematic classification and taxonomy of collaborative design activities. J. Eng. Des. **20**(1), 57–81 (2009)
6. Sacher, D., et al.: The Virtual Leopold Fleischhacker Museum (2013). http://mw2013.museums andtheweb.com/paper/the-virtual-leopold-fleischhacker-museum/
7. Sacher, D., Weyers, B., Kuhlen, T.W., Luther, W.: An integrative tool chain for collaborative virtual museums in immersive virtual environments. In: Baloian, N., Zorian, Y., Taslakian, P., Shoukouryan, S. (eds.) CRIWG 2015. LNCS, vol. 9334, pp. 86–94. Springer, Cham (2015). doi:10.1007/978-3-319-22747-4_7
8. Sacher, D.: A generative approach to virtual museums using a new metadata format: a curators', visitors' and software engineers' perspective. Ph.D. dissertation, University of Duisburg-Essen (2017)
9. The Platform for Modern Developers. https://about.gitlab.com/
10. Herskovic, V., Ochoa, S., Pino, J.A., Neyem, A.: The iceberg effect: behind the user interface of mobile collaborative systems. J. Univers. Comput. Sci. **17**(2), 183–201 (2011)
11. Antunes, P., Herskovic, V., Ochoa, S., Pino, J.A.: Structuring dimensions for collaborative systems evaluation. ACM Comput. Surv. **44**(2) (2012). Paper 8

Author Index

Printed in the United States
By Bookmasters